Strategic Human
Capital Management

'Human, not financial, capital must be the starting point and ongoing foundation of a successful strategy.'

Christopher A. Bartlett and Sumantra Ghoshal
MIT Sloan Management Review
Winter 2002

Strategic Human Capital Management

Creating Value through People

Jon Ingham

ELSEVIER

AMSTERDAM • BOSTON • HEIDELBERG • LONDON NEW YORK • OXFORD
PARIS • SAN DIEGO • SAN FRANCISCO • SINGAPORE • SYDNEY • TOKYO
Butterworth-Heinemann is an imprint of Elsevier

Butterworth-Heinemann is an imprint of Elsevier
Linacre House, Jordan Hill, Oxford OX2 8DP, UK
30 Corporate Drive, Suite 400, Burlington, MA 01803, USA

First edition 2007

British Library Cataloguing in Publication Data
A catalogue record for this book is available from the British Library

Library of Congress Cataloguing in Publication Data
A catalogue record for this book is available from the Library of Congress

ISBN-13: 978-0-7506-8134-6
ISBN-10: 0-7506-8134-9

For information on all Butterworth-Heinemann publications
visit our web site at http://books.elsevier.com

Printed and bound in the Netherlands

07 08 09 10 11   10 9 8 7 6 5 4 3 2 1

Contents

Foreword

Tim Miller
Director, People, Property and
Assurance, Standard Chartered Bank

At Standard Chartered Bank, we've long recognized the importance of human capital management (HCM). Before sharing our philosophy, first a few words about who we are; why HCM is so important to us and why we welcome this book.

Standard Chartered is a long-established international bank, listed on both the London and Hong Kong Stock Exchanges and currently in the top 20 FTSE 100 companies. With 44 000 people, we're naturally a diverse organization, representing 89 nationalities in 54 countries in the Asia Pacific Region, South Asia, the Middle East, Africa, the United Kingdom and the Americas. Our core businesses are wholesale and retail banking. The wholesale bank provides services to multinational, regional and domestic corporate and institutional clients in trade finance, cash management, custody, lending, foreign exchange, interest rate management and debt capital markets. Our retail banking business provides credit cards, personal loans, mortgages, deposit-taking activity and wealth management services to individuals and medium-sized to small businesses. We've performed well over the last three years, doubling our revenue. Our goal is to continue this momentum, both through organic growth and selective acquisitions in our key growth markets. Market expectations of us are high and we're operating in an increasingly competitive and unpredictable environment. During this time, we've focused heavily on building a performance culture through building employee engagement.

So why is human capital management and measurement important to us? Partly this stems from the need to anticipate and respond to the changing world in which we operate. It's also to do with our fundamental belief that to take human resource management to the next level, we need to better understand our people predictors of future business performance and how we're building our people capabilities.

The world is changing quickly. Customer profiles are changing, so too are their needs and expectations. Growth of the middle classes in India and China and increasing female economic participation are obvious examples. Demographic trends indicate we're going to face tougher competition for talent in our key markets. All this means that we've got to be better than ever at attracting and retaining the best talent that reflects our customer profiles and builds our people capabilities. This is one argument for making sure we configure our people HR processes and policies to ensure we meet these challenges.

However, our role in HR goes way beyond a simple 'best fit' approach of aligning people strategy to business goals. We need to build people capabilities and a workplace climate that gives us the competitive edge in responding to market changes and evolving business strategies. This is critical in an unpredictable world. Who'd ever have predicted 9/11, the 2003 SARs endemic or the 2004 tsunami? And yet all these had an impact on our business, calling for new and different types of responses.

Standard Chartered Bank's approach to human capital management is different to many organizations. We adopt a 'strengths-based' philosophy. In practice, this means we help employees to understand their individual talents using numerous tools, and then focus on leveraging these talents at work so they can be the best they can be. What do I mean by talents? Put simply, these are recurring patterns of thought, feelings and behaviours that distinguish each of us. These are normally hardwired in us in our mid-teens after which we can't do that much to change them. This strengths-based approach is woven into everything we do, with three fundamental principles guiding our approach to human capital management:

- Focus on talent for the job at all levels, by building tools and processes that identify, reward and retain high performing employees.
- Help individual employees know and focus on their strengths and, where necessary, manage their limitations.
- The development of exceptional managers and leaders who can identify and develop talent and build employee engagement.

We believe in positioning people for success by putting them in roles which naturally use their talents – play to their strengths as we call it – and then provide them with the knowledge and skills to be successful. Take salespeople for example. We know from our talent research that the very best salespeople are highly competitive and establish rapport quickly. You can't train people to be competitive – they either naturally want to beat their rivals to the point of being very poor losers, or they don't. You can't train them to be competitive. You can give them the basic product knowledge and sales skills through training, such as how to overcome objections or knowing when to close the deal. But without the right talents they're never going to be more than mediocre performers. What company wants mediocre salespeople? And yet, many companies take a remedial approach to training. They identify what a person's poor at, spend all their time trying to remedy the weakness, say through training, and pay scant regard to whether the weakness lies in an area of talent, knowledge or skill. They may end up getting the employees to be an OK performer, but they'll be demoralized in the process. They'll certainly never be world class. So, you need to know what talents your top quartile performers have and select more people like them.

Does this mean we ignore weaknesses? Absolutely not. We help employees identify their non-strengths, but the focus is on helping people build support systems to manage round them, partly through building complementary and diverse teams. A great example is one of our FX markets salespeople. A sales genius, but poor at planning and administration. Sounds familiar? He added more value to the company through selling and this is what he was paid to do. But his manager didn't get the talent equation. He still judged him on his administration, his Achilles heel. So our sales guy just made sure that he had a team member who could sort out the detail for him. He continued to deliver exceptional results, while dealing painlessly with the admin.

Employee engagement also sits at the heart of our strengths-based approach. We've been using Gallup's Q12 to measure and improve employee engagement across all our markets since 2000. It gives us powerful insights into our culture and how well our managers are managing. Within a single country, with the same national culture, the same economic conditions, and the same HR policies, there are wide variations in engagement of our employees. This is mainly down to the manager, the way they manage their teams. This picture somewhat debunks the school of thought that there is one best bundle of HR practices, or a silver bullet for high performance.

Knowing that managers have the biggest impact on engagement wasn't enough for us. We wanted to know *how* they do it and get inside the 'black box' of performance. So we studied our very best managers, those who create highly engaged teams and deliver business results. We found that great management is about ensuring each person has clarity about their deliverables, using the person's unique strengths to position them for success, and providing positive reinforcement for doing the right things through praise and recognition. Our best managers are also great storytellers. They create meaning for their people and a connection between what they do and the bigger organizational goals simply by telling stories that bring it alive in vivid language. For example, a branch manager in Ghana will talk about growing the business in terms of farming analogies. We've woven our findings into our management development programmes, how we communicate within the Bank, and we're starting to translate this into how we select managers.

Our strengths-based approach has had a bigger organizational and emotional impact than we'd even first anticipated. Managers across cultures and markets now have a common language where they talk about their strengths in the same way. It's also helped managers to manage their teams more effectively – many managers know the dominant talents of their team members through the tools we use. This means they can adapt their management style to each person to really get the best out of them. We call this individualization. Ever been managed by someone who treats you the same as your colleague sitting next to you, when you're fundamentally different people, with fundamentally different styles, needs and motivations? It's pretty frustrating. And it limits your potential. Our leadership development approach is based on a rigorous assessment of individual talents and development planning based on their strengths. The feedback is that it's had a huge impact on performance – while also being liberating compared to our old remedial approaches.

But the best part about our strengths-based approach is that it gives us greater capability than if we'd purely focused on strategic fit. Hiring for talent gives us a bigger gene pool to play in. This is critical in those growing markets where competition for people is tough. China's a great example. Many companies are expanding rapidly in China. We're no exception. But people with banking skills are in short supply. We're hiring people with the right talents and values for our roles – and just training them to give them the right skills and knowledge. Sounds obvious but few companies do it.

All this is woven together by a strong set of organizational values, what I call the DNA or glue of the company. Our HR and Brand people worked together on building a distinct brand, through developing a brand promise to our customers based on their needs and wants, but also by building the brand from within – focusing on the values behaviours that are at the core of our brand. Our values are all-pervasive now. They provide a strong sense of who we are and what we stand for.

So we've got a clear approach to people management. But we also need to know how well we're building the right sort of people capabilities to deliver. This is where rigorous and robust human capital measurement comes in.

There is a lot of talk about balanced scorecards, much of which makes a great deal of sense. Most companies are in good shape when it comes to reporting financials, customer satisfaction and loyalty, and measuring process efficiency. But the final quadrant of the balanced scorecard – people metrics – tends to be pretty poor. Human capital measurement is all about our ability to measure how well we're doing on the people measures that matter, both to help us understand how we've been doing but also to help predict how we'll be doing going forward on key business enablers.

So the first question is what should we be measuring? Sounds simple, but in reality it's quite complex. My advice is to be clear about the difference between HR efficiency metrics, such as the ratio of HR to employees, volume of recruitment and so forth, and human capital measures. Companies have to avoid the temptation of reporting on what's easy to measure as data for data's sake is unhelpful. Some companies who purport to do it well haven't yet got beyond 'gee whiz' metrics such as average training days per employee. What on earth does the number of training days tell you about how well you're building capability? It tells you nothing about the quality of training, or more importantly the impact on the bottom line. As bad are statistics that are so aggregated as to be little more than useless. You need to focus on what will add value to the business. And it has to be driven by strategy.

Our HCM philosophy is simple. We take an integrated approach to human capital management and measurement to ensure we measure and then develop the effectiveness of our processes in building strategic capability and the return on investment of key activities, such as engagement and training. So how do we do it? Our starting point is the strategic goals for each of our businesses. We then work out what people levers will help achieve these, and frame a series of questions that probe how well we're doing in pulling these levers. Our key questions are around how we are building resources to deliver future growth, both from a quality and quantity perspective. For example:

- Is our level of resourcing in line with future growth needs?
- Are we *growing* the talent pipeline through quality selection and development?
- Are we *accelerating* development of our best people so as to increase the succession pool of senior leaders?
- Are we retaining our best people?
- Are we rewarding disproportionately our best performers and high potential staff?

Our metrics are designed to provide deep insights into business questions like these. However, in practice, it's tough to deliver well. The second question is how to report people measures in a helpful and meaningful way and that have credibility with the business. It's difficult to get off first base if you haven't the system capability to do this. We're in a fortunate position to have established one global HR information system a few years ago where all our people data is held. This acts as the HCM engine for us.

One of the big prizes is that we now have common scorecards for our different business units and markets, with consistent measures calculated in a standard way, giving us the ability to compare across the business. It's like having a standard P&L but focused on people. It gives us confidence that we're all looking at the same thing.

The other element of our approach to HCM is measuring the business impact of what we do. Take employee engagement. Through our modelling we know that business units with high levels of engagement outperform others on a range of measures, including revenue growth, profit margin, employee retention and customer satisfaction. This is so much part of our DNA now that managers accept the business argument for engagement. We can tell you too about the revenue impact of our sales training – and we know we have a quick payback for the investment.

So what are the benefits of better HCM measurement? To start, it's given us granular insights into how well we're managing our people capability. It acts as an early warning signal for us about things we need to put right before they become major challenges. It gives HR the ability to challenge the business constructively in a way we haven't been able to do before. It also helps us make better decisions, for example, about how quickly we should be moving our talent around.

There's also the external reporting debate, a highly public one in the UK at present, especially given the history of the Operating and Financial Review (OFR). How and what do we report externally around people is a complex issue which involves regulators and governments alike. We also believe in greater transparency with our external stakeholders and helping analysts understand what people measures they should be looking for in assessing the value of companies, beyond the usual rather narrow question of top-team succession. For this reason, we're continuing to evolve what we report externally, whether through our Annual Report and Review or our Corporate Responsibility Report. Some companies are still squeamish about doing so, using the argument of commercial sensitivity to do nothing. However, this is a smokescreen; HCM reporting doesn't necessarily mean other companies can easily replicate what you're doing in managing people. It usually means they haven't got their act together on their metrics or what they're doing in HCM.

Given the growing interest in HCM I welcome this book. A lot of companies talk about it but few have yet to share their approach or how to do it in practice. The book will contribute enormously to raising the bar on the standards around HCM.

Preface

Unleashing the Chain Reaction

I initially became interested in human capital management (HCM) after having come across T.O. Davenport's book, *Human Capital* (1999) while working as an HR Director for Ernst & Young. Davenport explains that the 'employees are our biggest asset' metaphor is outdated and misguided. Instead, employees are more like investors of their own human capital. Organizations do not own this human capital but can rent it from their employees. Because of this, human capital is highly precarious and is in constant danger of being lost when an employee walks out of the door.

When I joined Penna Change Consulting (previously Crane Davies and subsequently, Penna Board Partnership) as Head of HR Consulting in 2001, I started to think more deeply about this area. I also worked with several clients to help them maximize the human capital that their people were investing. In 2002, Penna published its first report on HCM, explaining that:

> HCM leverages your most valuable asset – your people – to improve business performance and grow competitive advantage. Focusing you on the issues that attract, motivate and inspire the best talent, HCM mobilizes every aspect of your operations to achieve a single goal: sustained business success.
>
> (Finn, 2002)

Although this was still early days in our thinking, we had managed to capture two very important points:

HCM is about Leveraging Value from People

Human resource management (HRM) treats people as an organizational resource. The term 'human resource' implies an available supply that can be drawn on and used up to support or help in a particular task. And resources appear as costs in traditional accounting practices.

HCM recognizes that people are investors of their personal human capital and that this provides the main source of value for an organization. Of course, financial reporting standards will not allow us to account for human capital in the same way as financial capital, but with a nominal shift from the right-hand to the left-hand side of the balance sheet, the term 'human capital' at least implies the right level of importance. It describes an investment, not a cost. It indicates something that can appreciate if it is managed appropriately over time, rather than being utilized for short-term gain. It also recognizes that organizations do not have to own the capital to utilize it, but that it will only be made available for as long as investors (the people working for the organization) gain value in return for making their investment.

HCM is about Business Success and Competitive Advantage
HCM is about managing people in a way that leads to the optimal accumulation of human capital: for the individuals who are investing it; the organizations which are using it and also the financial investors who are funding it. In fact, HCM provides a way of reconciling the views of people in economic and in human terms. In this way, it supports the stance taken by Libby Sartain, previously Vice-President of People at Southwest Airlines and now at Yahoo!, that head and heart should not be considered mutually exclusive (Sartain and Finney, 2003).

HCM's role in creating value for investors is highlighted by Brian Becker and Mark Huselid, the co-authors of books on the HR and workforce scorecards:

> HR can have an important influence on the shareholder value ... To create this value, however, requires a fundamentally different perspective on HR; a perspective probably more accurately described as human capital management than as HRM. The concept of human capital management emphasizes the essential point that a firm's human resources and subsequently its HRM system can be more than a cost to be minimized.
>
> (Becker *et al.*, 1997)

Taking Measures of HCM

Shortly after Penna published its report on HCM, the UK government set up the Accounting for People taskforce to look at ways in which organizations could measure and report on the quality and effectiveness of their HCM practices. I still believe the review was a useful intervention as it highlighted the importance of people and put the value of people management firmly on the business agenda. However, as I explain further in Chapter 1, the review did not actually relate that closely to what I understand as HCM. Another HCM consultant, Paul Kearns (2004), has also explained that, in his view, the linking of HCM and the measurement and reporting of people management has really been quite accidental:

> It is really just coincidental that these developments have happened at a time when the term human capital has come to prominence. Hence, the people reporting requirements have now just become human capital reporting requirements.

I believe that this accidental connection, supported by the sales pushes of software vendors and benchmarking providers has led to a lot of poor thinking on HCM. For example, have a look at this comment from Leslie Weatherly (2003), HR Content Expert at the US Society for Human Resource Management (SHRM):

> Only by ensuring that HR metrics are recognized and valued on an equal footing with other business metrics routinely used by the CEO and management can the HR practice leader be assured an equitable position as a key member of the senior management team. These metrics must, of course, measure the value and return on investment in human capital to the organization.'

I believe that HCM does provide an opportunity for HR to take on a more strategic role, but improving recognition of metrics cannot be the only (or even a particularly important) way to do it. As David Longbottom (2005), previously HR Director at DSG International, explains:

> Playing the numbers game won't raise the profile or improve the performance of the HR profession; nor will it secure HR's place as a strategic business partner to the chief executive.

HCM as 'Managing the Measurement'

However, some of the linking of HCM with HRM measurement is a result of different, and I believe, wrong, rather than just poor thinking. Take this comment from Eric Flamholtz (2005), one of the founders of the field of human resource accounting, who proposes a version of HCM based on:

> The need to change the perspective of HRM from a behavioral field anchored in social and organizational psychology to a field rooted in measurement and analytical tools.

This is almost the complete opposite of the people-centred approach to HCM I described before. At its most extreme, this version of HCM is now being seen as a decision science (Boudreau and Ramstad, 2004) in which people management is focused on the financial worth of individual employees and the organization as a whole. Actions are only taken if it is predicted that the resulting increase in financial worth will provide an appropriate return on investment (ROI). This is an approach I describe as 'managing the measurement' because the financial measures become the main focus of decision-making. Some HR professionals believe that this approach will help them talk the language of Finance and that doing this will give HR more credibility in the business. However, it seems strange to me, particularly at a time when existing accounting methodologies are struggling to measure the tangible outputs of a business effectively, that HR should be trying to adopt these approaches and apply them in areas they were never even designed to cover.

HCM as 'Measuring the Management'

Of course, measurement is important. But I think the growing focus on measurement is based more on improvements in the supply of information than changes in demand. Better technology means that many businesses can generate lots of data and of course it is important that we respond to the new possibilities that more information gives us. But information only helps to the extent that it enables us to do something differently and the purpose of measurement is to support, not replace, the management of people. As the Penna report (Finn, 2002) explained:

> We believe organizations should measure success, and not people. Few businesses will benefit from extensive number crunching and searching futilely for a financially based evaluation system. Instead, decide the criteria for the success of your HCM programme – and monitor your progress in achieving them. What people issues feed through to the performance of your business? What are you going to do to address them?

The approach is about 'measuring the management', not 'managing the measurement'. This means that people remain the key focus of decision-making, with financial and other measures used as inputs. Of course we are still interested in the financial impact of our decisions, but not everything can be evaluated in financial terms.

If HR is going to be different in future, it is not because HR professionals have become experts in measurement, but because we are adding more value. Measurement is an important means to this end but it is not the difference that makes a difference between strategic impact and operational irrelevance.

Strategic HCM

I have called this book *Strategic Human Capital Management* to emphasize that I am focusing on a strategic and people-focused rather than a measurement-led agenda. The book describes the outputs of my recent thinking and consultancy work within my new consultancy roles as Executive Consultant at my own company, Strategic Dynamics, and as Director of Human Capital Consulting at Buck Consultants.

Part 1 focuses on the creation of value in HCM and looks at a number of different factors that seem to me to be important in creating this value and ensuring it leads on to business success.

Chapter 1 builds on the work of the UK's Accounting for People taskforce to highlight the need to balance data with knowledge. Chapter 2 introduces ideas from complex systems theory which underpin a lot of my thinking of HCM. Chapter 3 explains why best fit is an essential part of an approach to HCM and Chapter 4 extends this to thinking about intangible value and the way that organizations can create more value by ensuring best fit. Chapter 5 provides a strategic approach to talent management as an example of HCM. It concludes that one differentiating feature of HCM is that, at least in some ways and on some occasions, people management becomes the true driver of business performance. Chapter 6 moves the focus of the book towards measurement and develops a value matrix that can be used to track and improve HCM strategies and programmes.

The second part of the book describes the cycle of processes that are needed to develop, measure and implement an HCM strategy. Chapter 7 describes the HCM strategy development process and Chapter 8 looks at how measures can be identified to support HCM programmes. Chapter 9 describes approaches for collecting measurements and benchmarks and Chapter 10 focuses on how organizations can use their measures to improve what they are doing, rather than simply for telling them whether something has or has not been achieved. Chapter 11 returns to the issue of reporting on HCM and Chapter 12 considers the roles that are required to support the HCM processes that have been described.

References

Becker, E.B., Huselid, M.A., Pickus, P.S. and Spratt, M.F. (1997). 'HR as a source of shareholder value: research and recommendations', *Human Resource Management,* **36**(1), Spring, 39–47.

Boudreau, J.W. and Ramstad, P.M. (2004). '"Talentship": a decision science for HR', *Strategic HR Review,* **3**(2), January–February, 28–31.

Davenport, T.O. (1999). *Human Capital – What It Is and Why People Invest It.* Jossey-Bass Publishers.

Finn, R. (2002). *Unleashing the Chain Reaction: Using Human Capital Management to Tap the Power in Your People.* Penna Consulting.

Flamholtz, E.G. (2005). 'Human Resource Accounting, Human Capital Management and the Bottom-Line'. In *The Future of Human Resource Management: 64 Thought Leaders explore the critical HR issues of Today and Tomorrow* (Losey, M., Meisinger, S. and Ulrich, D. Eds). John Wiley & Sons, pp. 268–77.

Kearns, P. (2004). *One Stop Guide: Human Capital Management.* Personnel Today Management Resources.

Longbottom, D. (2005). 'Numbers game only adds to confusion'. *Personnel Today,* 22 November, 15.

Sartain, L. and Finney, M.I. (2003). *HR from the Heart: Inspiring Stories and Strategies for Building the People Side of Great Businesses.* American Management Association.

Weatherly, L. (2003). *Human Capital – The Elusive Asset: Measuring and Managing Human Capital: A Strategic Imperative for HR.* SHRM Research, Quarter 1.

Acknowledgements

I would first like to thank my current colleagues at Buck Consultants for their commitment to helping clients create value and for supporting me to apply the approaches described within this book. This includes Alan Gibbons, Tim Knight, Simon Byng, Graeme Hudson, Katie Leeman, Ruth MacGregor, Francine Watson, Nick Blackwell, Eleanor Cross and Mark Howarth.

Secondly, I would like to thank everyone who helped in developing the thinking for this book, particularly my former colleagues and associates at Penna Change Consulting/Penna Board Partnership (previously Crane Davies), including Robin Davies, Sue Wotruba, Roberta Gardner, Peter Horncastle, Jeremy Webster, Alasdair McKenzie, Sol Davidson, Trevor Lambert, Carole Bozkurt, Stephanie Wheeler, Katie Fell, Deborah Castle and Alison Dexter. I would like to pay special tribute to Richard Finn, who inspired my interest in this area and developed earlier versions of the models used within the book. Similarly, thanks to Geoff Pye for first proposing the HCM value chain and also for his earlier support as Head of HR, UK at Ernst & Young. And thanks to all my clients who helped in developing and testing the ideas presented in the book, particularly Margaret Savage, Frances Allcock, Tina Beeden and Oleh Godun at BT; Nigel Holt, Steve Lewitt and Claire Owen at the LSC and Cynthia McCague and Ben Legg at Coca-Cola HBC.

Thirdly, I would like to thank all those other individuals who provided their time and insights about their organizations, not all of which is included in the book. This includes Helen Ogden, BAA; Andrew Whitney, Bain; Nigel Paine, Peter Hallard, Ian Hayward and Josie Barton, BBC; Bob Stack, Cadbury Schweppes; Elizabeth Warren, Deutsche Bank; David Longbottom and Ben Bengoudam, DSG; Mohan Yogendron and Stevan Rolls, Ernst & Young; Karen Martin and Claire Hurley, Firstplus; Rob Lake and Jane Goodland, Henderson Global Investments; Julie Harding, HSBC; Annette Turner and Dave Gartenberg, Microsoft;

Norman Ross, Mark Doughty and Vanessa Loughlin, Motorola; Ian Gearing, National Grid; Alison Speak and Annette Frem, Orange; Leisa MacLellan and Jane Cotton, Oxfam; Greig Aitken, RBS; Andrew Thompson, Scottish Re; Peter Merrick, Siemens; Mark O'Connell, Skandia; Tim Miller, Debbie Whitaker and Drew Watson, Standard Chartered; Penny Davis, T-Mobile; Steve Langhorn, Whitbread and Helen Russell, Yahoo!

More thanks for providing additional information to Kate Charlton, Ashridge Business School; Phil Hanson; Mindy Wilson and Anne Godfrey, CBI; Peter Reilly, Institute for Employment Studies; Peter Howes and Keith Krut, InfoHRM; Ruth Spellman, Investors in People UK; Chris Nutt, FiSSInG; Steve Joyce and Gary Baker, Hackett Group; Steve O'Keefe and Sara Powell, Financial Services Skills Council and Laurie Bassi, McBassi.

Thanks also to Ailsa Marks, Olivia Warburton, Deena Burgess and the team at Elsevier, and Jonathan Partridge at XpertHR.

And finally, thanks to my wife, Sandra, for her ongoing support and encouragement, in life generally, not just with the book.

Part 1

Creating Value in HCM

1

Accounting for People

Reader: *'Why are you starting the book with Accounting for People, particularly if, given your points in the Preface, you don't think the taskforce really dealt with 'HCM'?'*

Author: 'I think I had to really. Accounting for People has played a key role in shaping the HCM agenda within the UK, and it deals with issues that are being discussed within other countries too. So I think, whether or not you are from the UK, that you may need a short recap or reminder of the work of the taskforce, in order to understand the context of some of the comments which are made later on. However, I certainly don't dwell on this, and avoid entering the whole debate on Accounting for People versus the Operating and Financial Review (OFR) versus the Business Review. Not that I don't have views on this, but I think that time has moved on.

The other reason for starting with Accounting for People is that it does open up an interesting discussion about the nature of value in HCM and the way this value can best be measured and described. Most of the chapter focuses on this...'

Strategic Human Capital Management

The Accounting for People Taskforce

The UK's Accounting for People taskforce was asked to recommend ways in which organizations could measure and report on the quality and effectiveness of their HCM practices and to identify the most helpful performance measures to include in HCM reports. One of the obvious opportunities for reporting was expected to be the updated Operating and Financial Review (OFR) that had been announced in the white paper *Modernizing Company Law* (Department of Trade and Industry, 2002). This white paper addressed the need to improve company reporting, recognizing that increasing complexity means that financial statements no longer provide the strategic information that investors need. The white paper stated that:

> The Government agrees that companies should provide more qualitative and forward-looking reporting ... It recognizes that companies are increasingly reliant on intangible assets such as: the skills and knowledge of their employees, their business relationships and their reputation. Information about future plans, opportunities, risks and strategies is just as important to users of financial reports as a historical view of performance.

Denise Kingsmill (2003a), who chaired the Accounting for People taskforce, described the problem she had set out to solve:

> If talented workers – which a company spends time and money employing and training – are not managed properly, they will leave. Often falling straight into the welcoming arms of the competition, with potentially devastating effects. Organizations then have to spend further time and money on recruiting replacements. As an investor, the chances are you will not be aware that this has happened. You won't have any means of judging the impact, good or bad, that the business's human capital management has had on performance.

The taskforce's definition of human capital was 'the relevant knowledge, skills, experience and learning capacity of the people available to the organization'. It defined the management of this human capital, HCM, as 'a strategic approach to people management that focuses on the issues that are critical to an organization's success'. It also emphasized that 'HCM is a performance, not a social, issue ... that treats

4

human capital as a positive – and active – asset to be developed, not a passive cost.'

I agree with all of this but am still not clear whether the taskforce ever really understood what they meant by it. Much of what the task-force produced did not seem particularly strategic. For example, at the launch of the taskforce's consultation process, Kingsmill described how the group would look at whether firms should be compelled to publicly justify their pay policy for the whole workforce, as well as top executives. Kingsmill asked:

> How can you have a productive, well-motivated workforce if they're not being fairly paid? You have to have a fair pay system which is as transparent as possible. (Stewart, 2003)

While an important topic, this is also clearly an issue of compliance or operational rather than strategic significance.

The taskforce also referred to the importance of measurement, stating that HCM, 'seeks systematically to analyse, measure and evaluate how people policies and practices contribute to value creation' (Kingsmill, 2003b). Once again, as long as systematic measurement takes a back seat to the strategic management of a people, I can easily agree with this.

The taskforce provided a number of sample 'HCM' reports but the lack of a clear definition of HCM resulted in a very diverse selection of samples. Some of these demonstrated a fairly traditional, operational approach to the management of people. Other sample reports, particularly the RAC's, focused on the measurement rather than the management of people. Unilever's report described a more strategic approach to people management and RBS's emphasized the need for both a strategic approach and the measurement of that approach.

I think the taskforce's half-hearted emphasis on 'a strategic approach to people management', together with a fairly strong focus on measurement, and the mixed group of sample have reports have contributed towards some people perceiving HCM as a measurement-focused approach to HRM. However, as well as wanting to see reporting of standard measures that would allow comparisons to be made across organizations, the taskforce did recognize the need to give companies the discretion to focus on their own strategy and to determine their own model of HCM. The difficulty was in balancing these two needs. Kingsmill summarized the issue well at the start of the taskforce's consultation period, saying, 'We don't want prescription and box-ticking, but we don't want a lot of clichéd rubbish either' (Stewart, 2003).

Kingsmill's taskforce recommended that all UK organizations producing voluntary or mandatory OFRs (where the latter have now been replaced with business reviews) should include within them information on HCM or explain why this is not material. HCM reports should have a strategic focus and be based upon the aspects of people management that a company's Board believes are key to its performance. However, although Kingsmill argued that, short term at least, it would be impossible for common standards to be set, the taskforce did state that reporting should be based on sound and objective data.

Value Reporting

In fact, the paradoxical need for both strategic and standardized reporting had already been addressed elsewhere. The global professional services firm, PricewaterhouseCoopers (PwC), owners of benchmarking firm Saratoga, has emphasized the need to balance the reporting of hard, standardized and financial metrics with more discretionary and strategic information. Calling for a 'value reporting revolution', the firm has reported on research finding that only 19 per cent of investors and 27 per cent of analysts 'found financial reports very useful in communicating the true value of companies' (Eccles *et al.*, 2001).

One particularly interesting piece of PwC's research was conducted in collaboration with Schroders Asset Management. A control group of analysts at Schroders was given an annual report for the Danish company Coloplast that was regarded as an example of good practice in non-financial reporting. A second group was given an edited version of the report which omitted all the contextual information and non-financial data. Compared to the control group, the second group came up with generally higher earnings estimates for the company, but across a very broad range. Whereas 60 per cent of the control group issued a 'buy' recommendation, 80 per cent of the second group strongly recommended selling the company's shares (Thomas, 2003).

PwC recommends, that more information about intangibles be communicated to investors by including broader financial and non-financial key performance measures in reports. To explain this need, PwC provides a three-tier model of corporate transparency (Figure 1.1), emphasizing that reporting needs to address all three tiers (DiPiazza and Eccles, 2002).

PwC's triangle does need updating for our purposes. The firm calls the bottom tier in their model Globally Generally Accepted Accounting Principles, or Global GAAP. In fact, the firm's desire to have a globally agreed set of accounting principles is rapidly becoming a reality as international financial reporting standards gain momentum worldwide. However, changing the focus of this level to people management rather than accounting makes it look a lot more daunting. There is a long way to go to before we have a common set of generic standards for people management data.

The next tier in PwC's model consists of standards that are 'industry-specific, consistently applied, and developed by the industries themselves' and the top tier includes guidelines for 'company-specific information such as strategy, plans, risk management practices, compensation policies, corporate governance, and performance measures unique to the company' (DiPiazza and Eccles, 2002).

Although I think PwC's insights on reporting are largely correct, I believe an even more important point lies behind them. This is about how the nature of information changes at each level in the triangle and the value this provides to understanding. So I suggest

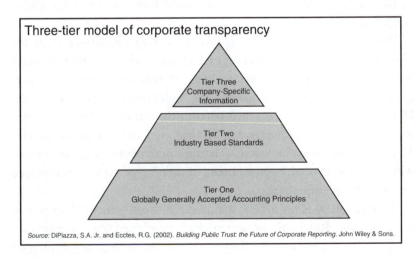

Figure 1.1 Three-tier model of corporate transparency

updating the model for HCM to emphasize this hierarchy of information and renaming the three levels as data, information and knowledge. As T.H. Davenport and Prusak (1998) stress in their book, *Working Knowledge*, organizations need to understand the different requirements and benefits of these three levels:

> Data, information and knowledge are not interchangeable concepts. Organizational success and failure can often depend on knowing which of them you need, which you have, and what you can and can't do with each. Understanding what those three things are and how you get from one to another is essential to doing knowledge work successfully.

Data

Data is the most basic level of information and is used in what I call metrics: factual, objective, quantitative and especially financial measurements and statistics that provide reliability and comparability over time. Metrics can help gain the attention of CEOs and CFOs who are traditionally more interested in issues that have numbers attached to them, believing that 'if you can measure it [meaning objectively and quantitatively], you can manage it'. However, metrics alone are not going to enable the comparability across organizations that analysts and investors require in order to make buy or sell decisions. This requires the use of standards or key performance indicators (KPIs) that are based on commonly accepted terms and definitions. Clearly some sets of measures already exist and these could form the basis for global GAAP-like standards.

One example is the *Sustainability Reporting Guidelines* from the Global Reporting Initiative (GRI) which are used in many Corporate Responsibility reports. These standards are now into their third generation and are used by more the 600 companies worldwide. Organizations can choose which parts of the standards to use depending on their size, sector and other factors. The standards contain 12 core performance indicators relating to employment issues, one of which is a measure of 'average hours of training per year per employee by category of employee'.

However, there is no similar standard specifically focused on people management. Referring to approaches developed by Mercer (see Chapter 2), Watson Wyatt (Chapter 3) and Penna (that are developed within this book), employment relations journalist Stephen Overell (2004) describes his view that it should be possible to develop a core set of standards:

> It is true that there are many diverse approaches to HCM. A quick survey of Watson Wyatt's Human Capital Index (which purports to link HR practices to financial performance), Penna Consulting's 'strategic measures' (things like employee motivation levels and leadership abilities), and Mercer Human Resource Consulting's 'internal labour market analysis' (a bid to track patterns in employee behaviour statistically) is enough to prove the point. But that is not to say you can't have common standards around which a debate can mature.

I largely agree with this perspective and was quoted by Richard Donkin in the *Financial Times* suggesting that Saratoga's benchmarks would be the obvious base for this development:

> In the meantime, he believes companies are in a position to reach some consensus on standard external measures. An industry standard, he says, may eventually settle on sets of existing measures, such as those pioneered by EP-First and Saratoga Institute, the human capital arm of PricewaterhouseCoopers that runs an index of more than 100 performance indicators across the HR field. (Donkin, 2004)

Despite this potential opportunity, Accounting for People realized that it would not be possible to pick on one of the competing sets of standards and felt that there was not enough demand to specify a new set of standards during the period of their review. They therefore proposed that the way forward was through an 'evolutionary approach' in which the momentum created by the taskforce would encourage more reporting and an increasing opportunity to specify standards. With the encouragement of Donkin, who is also the author of a report on HCM (Donkin, 2005), the owners of the UK's existing standards on best practice in people management, Investors in People UK (IIP UK), have set up a Human Capital Standards Group. This group includes representatives from organizations that have conducted recent research in this area: the Work Foundation; the Institute for Employment Studies (IES) and the Chartered Management Institute (CMI), as well as Saratoga. I am also involved in the group on behalf of my consultancy, Strategic Dynamics.

I talked to IIP UK's Chief Executive, Ruth Spellman, about the role of this group:

> I think this work fits with our role very well. Investors in People can explain things that get quite complicated in quite simple terms – it's our USP if you will. And it fits with our stakeholders' needs. The Department for Education and Skills wants to have better measures to understand the stock of human capital in the country and the Department of Trade and Industry (DTI) wants to know about how well this is being deployed in organizations.
>
> We're looking for the 10–12 measures that make up most of the difference between organizations' performance. The measures need to appeal to a broad range of stakeholders and they have got to have real predictive value or they'll be too easy to dismiss. This might be about the way they act together – so if you take a combination of three or four indicators they don't make a difference, if you have six or seven you're heading in the right direction and so on. I think effective performance has to be about a combination of things – it's not just about one indicator. You couldn't just look at recruitment and selection without considering the impact on diversity. We need to keep this holistic and look at the cross-overs rather than focus on the divisibles.
>
> We also want to look at more strategic measures in a later phase of the project as I think these will flow from the standard metrics. We know that business and HR plans need to march together. We know from working with the Investors in People standard that if organizations have self-standing HR plans that don't relate to the business, if their quality isn't high and the quality of the business plan is shoddy, then these organizations are not going to get much from their people – they're barking up the wrong tree. HR plans have got to be flexible and high quality. They've got to be both externally and internally driven. Often they're too internally focused so there's no account of labour market issues for example. We need to look at how we can enable organizations to plan better. We operate in a very turbulent environment these days – organizations need to be flexible in their planning and to be able to anticipate change and to innovate. And we know that organizations that do this well perform well. But I think providing some standard metrics with common definitions has got to be the biggest win. We've got to think about the smallest companies as well – to some of them this is like swimming in treacle – it should be a lot simpler.

The UK's Chartered Institute of Personnel and Development has also set up a Human Capital Champions Panel to encourage and disseminate best practice and will be producing regular material to track the development and use of data and measures to demonstrate the value and contribution of human capital. Similar work is also under way outside the UK, particularly through the HR Metrics Consortium in the USA. This is an independent non-profit organization supported by staffing.org which has been at the forefront of developing metrics in resourcing. However, the selection of the right list of metrics faces various difficulties which is the reason why no agreed standards have yet emerged. As Duncan Brown at the CIPD explains:

> There is a tremendous opportunity for us to demonstrate in the annual report how effective people management really does add value. But there is also a tremendous difficulty: just what do you put in there? Labour turnover rates? But these vary substantially by sector. Is a total growing workforce a good or a bad thing? What's the best measure of labour productivity? Would you risk using your employees' attitude survey data? And if you revealed your organization's commitment to staff development in the form of a major training spend, are the financial and investment communities likely to applaud you or see it as an opportunity for savings? (Brown and Baron, 2003)

We can take headcount as an example, as this is probably the most obvious and well-used metric, forming a base for Brown and Baron's example of labour turnover and providing the denominator in lots of different metrics like revenue per employee. First of all we need to get agreement on what we mean by headcount. Organizations gain access to human capital through a variety of sources in addition to their permanent employees. So we need to agree on a common way of treating part-time staff – do we report total heads or full-time equivalents (FTEs)? – and, more importantly, temporary staff, subcontractors, consultants, freelancers and outsourced providers. The difficulty in doing this is one reason why a lot of standard metrics use a measure of total people costs rather than numbers of employees for the denominator. Without this, metrics can be easily distorted. For example, revenue per employee can be doubled by outsourcing half the people and their work at the same cost, even though productivity has not changed.

Secondly, to ensure we can look at headcount in more detail and still compare like with like, we need some standardized ways of breaking down headcount by demographic groups, functions and business units. We also need some standard definitions for regretted and unregretted turnover. Ideally we would also want to provide more granularity, for example by cutting turnover data according to employee performance and potential, but because these categories are also defined differently by each organization this combined metric would be even more difficult to define in a standard way.

Even if and when standards are developed, there are two remaining problems at this level of reporting. Firstly, standards will always be limited in that they can only ever be, by definition, independent of a particular firm's strategy. Measures that do link to competitive advantage, for example, regretted turnover of particular high potential individuals, are much harder to define as a simple metric, even within a single company. It would be next to impossible to define something like this that could apply across organizations. Secondly, both metrics and standards need to be supported by contextual information to make them relevant and useful. For example, without understanding the context it is impossible to say whether any particular headcount or turnover is good or bad, or whether a particular level of turnover should be higher or lower. Without particular reasons to justify it, the most common response to a growing headcount is to want to cut it to improve productivity, but this could just as easily limit revenue growth and reduce profitability. Similarly, you would generally want to reduce employee turnover but this might limit improvements in diversity or moves to a new culture or business model.

Standards are never going to provide enough coverage on their own – they will also need to be supplemented by non-standard metrics and contextual information providing more substantive meaning. Without this, metrics are more liable to be used inappropriately. For example, Jeffrey Pfeffer at Stanford (1997) warns that:

> We know that for complex decisions, as Peter Drucker once stated, anyone over the age of 21 can find the facts to support his or her position. What facts and measures often do is to justify the position or claims of one particular person or interest group. Effective department leaders have well-developed skills in advocating measures that favor their units' interests and are skilled at massaging numbers to get them to support their units' deservingness and worth.... Although the numbers are never in reality precise, they do provide the illusion of precision, and in that sense, are powerful weapons in political battles. Because of the norm of rationality and the associated rhetoric, which associates the measures with knowledge (even if the measures are misleading or erroneous), those who are best able to develop the measures and methods that demonstrate the worth of their units or the soundness of their thinking are advantaged in most political contests.

An extreme example of this is the perspective put forward by an academic attending the *Personnel Today* HR Directors Club in June 2005 who said 'HR directors are frightened to make numbers up, but sales and marketing do it. As long as they are based on some sort of detail, it is fine. Work out what you believe and then find statistics that back you up' (*Personnel Today*, 2005).

Continuing the battle metaphor, Pfeffer (1997) notes that shrewd HR leaders have got better at using financial 'weapons' like economic value added and discounted cash flow to support their positions in a war with accountants but cautions:

> Equipping human resource managers with additional analytic tools and language is all to the good, as far as it goes. In the end, however, all one accomplishes is being a more skilled player at someone else's game. By so doing, one buys into the ultimate sensibility and reasonableness of the basic measures and ideas in the first place; this is often a mistake.... Being skilled at the wrong game is not a very promising strategy for either the company or the human resources function. It is unlikely that human resources will ever be able to win playing the number games against those with much more experience who also get to set the rules. Even if they do win, the victory may have extracted a large cost in terms of losing the distinct perspective and competence of human resources in the process of becoming like other staff functions ... If all human resources becomes is finance with a different set of measures and topic domains, then its future indeed is likely to be grim.

Pfeffer's warning emphasizes that HCM should not focus too much on the use of metrics, standards and quantitative analysis at the expense of other forms of measurement that might have more validity for the types of attributes being measured.

Information

Information is data that has been put into a context and is structured to enable interpretation and analysis. Information provides an insight into the relationships and connections between data. It provides answers to questions of 'who', 'what', 'where' and 'when'. It is typically presented using tables, graphs and three-colour traffic light gauges.

Most reporting of data is too aggregated to extract useful information for decision-making. Within large diversified organizations, this may hide a wide variety of issues that each need different metrics for reporting.

I talked about this with Peter Howes, Chairman of benchmarking consultancy InfoHRM (see Chapter 12):

> Aggregate benchmarks can be very dangerous. There's an implicit assumption that organizations are homogeneous whereas they're actually quite heterogeneous. The benchmarks can say there's no problem when there actually is. For example, you might have a voluntary turnover rate of 7 per cent. It looks like it's a good figure – a bit of turnover but not too much. But this can range from 1 per cent to 20 per cent. It means you've got problems everywhere but these are lost in the aggregation.

The information level of reporting recognizes that different metrics may be needed for different countries, particularly where there are major differences in culture and employment legislation. This is why in Shell's Environment and Society Report, the company states for the GRI measure of training hours that 'although employee training is very important in our company, this indicator is not reported since it is not meaningful at a global level'.

The industry level analysis that makes up the middle tier in PwC's model provides a form of information because it enables like-to-like comparison with similar organizations. This ensures that metrics and standards are used, applied and compared in meaningful ways. So, for example, reporting on their research that informed the CIPD's guide to *Evaluating Human Capital*, Elias and Scarborough (2004) commented on the different styles of HCM reporting they had found:

> It is possible to identify, first, a broad influence on practice relating to sector and/or forms of human capital. Thus, the high-tech firms in our sample were concerned with specialized skills and focused on the value of highly talented individuals. The retailers, on the other hand, developed measures that were applicable to the whole of their workforce and which were focused on the creation of customer value and loyalty.

Kingsmill frequently compared Rolls-Royce and Sainsbury's, emphasizing the differences between the high-tech and retail sectors. Due to the length of time it takes to design and manufacture an aerospace engine, Rolls-Royce needs its people to have a deep repository of knowledge about the business, its products and its culture which provides an intangible 'engineering memory'. So Rolls-Royce's key requirement is to retain their key people for at least 20 years. Sainsbury's do not have any similar expectations but need to ensure that all of their checkout operators are always cheerful and efficient in dealing with the retail chain's customers.

Using similar examples, the OFR DTI's Working Group (Department of Trade and Industry, 2004) showed how sectoral differences influence the measures that should be included in a report:

> The detail of employment policies and practices, and the associated metrics, will depend on the nature of the business. For example, a company in the business of delivering large, long-term, technically complex projects will regard low staff turnover in key areas of the business as extremely important. Customer handling skills, by contrast, may be essential to a much more limited extent. But high volume, high throughput retailing may regard staff turnover as of less significance, and customer handling skills as the key core competence for many of its staff.

Within each sector, it should also be possible to develop more intelligent measures which are particularly relevant in that sector. For example, retail might define a particular measure of turnover for front-line customer service staff that only makes sense within, and can be compared across, that sector.

There is a similar need within functional area too. For example, within financial services, different metrics, or at least different targets for the same metrics, will need to be set for a business-to-business sales team and a retail customer services call centre.

Knowledge

Knowledge is the collection and presentation of information in a form in which is it useful and meaningful. It provides an understanding of patterns within data and information and answers 'how' questions. Data supports the creation of information and when we have information, knowledge can emerge. But knowledge can also emerge from feelings and intuition.

Russell Ackoff (1989), previously a professor at Wharton, adds further categories of understanding and wisdom beyond these three levels. I include understanding, which provides answers to 'why' questions, within the knowledge level. Wisdom, which provides an understanding of principles, is then something that emerges from conversation and reflection on all three levels of information.

The knowledge level of reporting recognizes that every organization is different and therefore no one-size-fits-all system of reporting will work for all organizations. Brown and Baron (2003) explain the point, stating:

> Just as we know there is no universally successful formula for effective people management, so there is no single accounting formula or set of 'people numbers' that could be applied uniformly to all types of business. The whole point of an effective people strategy is to differentiate, to create competitive advantage.

This highly specific and strategic information generally needs to be reported through some sort of management commentary, such as the Management Discussion and Analysis used in the USA. This is a narrative commentary that allows a company to convey a much greater breadth and richness of information. One useful approach is for a company to tell a story about how it is investing its available resources; the activities that it considers to be important to its success; the outputs it hopes to achieve from these activities and what impact it believes these outputs will have on the business. Where possible, an organization should also explain how these factors act through chains of correlation and causation. However, an organization still needs to support its story through some type of evidence. As McKinsey (Koller, 2005) explains:

> Effective communications should link a compelling message with the value that management expects to create. This investment story should help investors understand what the company stands for, how it differs from other companies, and why its prospects are better than those of its competitors or even of companies in other industries. A compelling investment story has three key elements: aspirations, strategy, and evidence ... Evidence – which doesn't necessarily mean detailed disclosure but should include success stories – helps investors to assess whether the strategy can actually achieve the company's aspirations.

Knowledge is often heavily subjective and relies as much on impressions and feelings as it does on facts and figures. It is also often best shared through conversation rather than written reports, whether these are casual conversations around the coffee machine within organizations, or more formal briefings to institutional investors. These attributes are what led Henry Mintzberg (1994) at McGill University to observe that:

> While hard data may inform the intellect, it is largely soft data that generates wisdom. They may be difficult to 'analyze', but they are indispensable for 'synthesis' – the key to strategy making.

In a more recent interview, Mintzberg went further than this, challenging management's fixation on quantitative measurement, saying (Caulkin, 2003):

We've become prisoners of measurement: audits, league tables, targets. It just destroys creativity. Look, I'm not opposed to measuring things that can be measured – I'm opposed to letting those things drive everything else out … What would happen if we started from the premise that we can't measure what matters and go from there? Then, instead of measurement, we'd have to use something very scary; it's called judgment.

Warren Bennis (Bennis and O'Toole, 2005) at the University of Southern California supports Mintzberg's view. Criticizing what he sees as the faulty reliance on the scientific model in business schools, he has commented that:

When applied to business – essentially a human activity in which judgments are made with messy, incomplete and incoherent data – statistical and methodological wizardry can blind rather than illuminate … Most issues facing business leaders are, in the final analysis, questions of judgment… Strategic decisions, especially, are likely to go awry when based purely on quantitative factors.

It is the qualitative information around context and strategy and the linkages between different information that form the basis for making strategic judgements appropriately. This form of knowledge or wisdom cannot provide the same reliability of measurement as the data level, but can potentially improve validity if it succeeds in describing the issue of concern more effectively than by using numbers. In a *Harvard Business Review* article describing potential breakthrough ideas for 2005, Roger Martin contrasted the analysis of objective data providing consistent results with the need to embrace 'fuzzy' data, variability and inconsistency. Objective data provides reliability but does not necessarily mean that much and Martin compares it to a 'well-tuned car that runs full speed off a cliff'. 'Fuzzy' data provides validity and opens the door to meaning, innovation and growth:

Companies don't realize that when they make their systems more reliable, they render them less valid or meaningful. In other words, the processes produce consistent outcomes, but the results may be neither accurate nor desirable. That's because, to make their processes more reliable, companies have to reduce the number of variables and standardize measurements. To achieve high validity, however, systems must take into account a large number of variables and use subjective measurements. Adding squishy variables and using gut feel allows for outcomes that are more accurate, even though the processes may not be able to deliver accurate results consistently....For instance, CEOs should go out and talk in person to customers, even if the sample size isn't statistically significant, rather than sit in their offices and make decisions based on statistically significant market research. (Martin, 2005)

However, this need to use qualitative measures is not just based on the abstract views of American academics but is also the conclusion of the OFR Working Group whose guidance (Department of Trade and Industry, 2004) concluded:

The requirement in the Regulations to provide a description of resources, however, clearly raises matters of quality as well as quantity. In some instances, therefore, qualitative information may not only be the best that can be done in the absence of hard numbers, it may actually represent information that is crucial to an assessment of the potential for achieving the business strategies.

I think the Working Group raises a really important point. Narrative descriptions can be just a poor replacement for objective metrics that for whatever reason cannot be provided. So for example, Harvard professor Michael Beer (in Beer *et al.*, 1996) suggests that measures can be substituted by free text. Beer is right in saying that this saves an organization from using measures that are inaccurate, not credible or cannot be generated at a reasonable cost. However, this is about using narrative data because it is the best of a set of poor alternatives. From a knowledge perspective, narrative description is not a compromise solution, it is simply the best way of communicating this information.

Combining levels of reporting

Despite its limitations, we tend to focus on data rather than other types of information because it is the easiest type to manage. Author David Boyle (2000) explains that:

You can put information into figures, tables and graphs, but you can't necessarily do the same with knowledge. So most organizations and bureaucracies very much prefer the first kind. They call it 'data'. The other kind of knowledge, often simply the kind of informal know-how which people exchange over coffee or a cigarette – but equally important to the bottom line – often gets ignored because it can't be measured.

Doing this can cause problems. So, for example, author and philosopher Charles Handy (1995) refers to Robert McNamara's experience in leading the US Department of Defense during the Vietnam War. McNamara has said that hard analysis led to overweighting the value of quantitative as opposed to qualitative information and Handy quotes McNamara as explaining, in what has become known as the McNamara Fallacy, the train of thought that leads to this type of situation:

The first step is to measure whatever can be easily measured. This is OK as far as it goes. The second step is to disregard that which can't easily be measured or to give it an arbitrary quantitative value. This is artificial and misleading. The third step is to presume that what can't be measured easily really isn't important. This is blindness. The fourth step is to say that what can't easily be measured really doesn't exist. This is suicide.

The well-known analogy for McNamara's first step is the man searching for his lost car keys under the street lamp. When asked if he lost his keys nearby, he answers, 'No, but I can see better here. Doing this is not going to do any harm, but the man is not going to find his keys.

Boyle (2000) also writes about the way we attempt to measure things we know are not really measurable, the behaviour McNamara refers to in his second step:

Then they measure, measure, measure, knowing that what they measure is alive and will not keep still, and suspecting that maybe – however much they count – they will not capture the essence of the question they are asking. Things have to keep static if you're going to count them: that's probably why the first statisticians were known as 'statists'. But real life isn't still … If you make the attempt but measure the wrong thing, it isn't just wasted effort. It can destroy everything you've worked for. Like the school league tables that make teachers concentrate on getting borderline pupils through at the expense of their weaker classmates. Or the hospital waiting lists that fell because only quick simple problems were treated.

As Boyle explains, the consequences of this step are often to encourage dysfunctional behaviour as people try to achieve what is being measured, rather that what their organizations really want them to do.

An example of McNamara's third step is the reaction that some people have to intangibles which are the focus of Chapter 4. In this view, intangibles are too difficult to be measured and organizations should ignore them until they are converted into tangible value. For example, Kearns (2004) argues that creativity can only be measured when it has been converted to tangible output and can be given a financial value:

> Let's look at the idea of people being creative at work. Creativity sounds like it fits the definition of 'intangible' perfectly. You cannot touch it, it is difficult to analyse, and you cannot guarantee it will still be there tomorrow. Yet we all know that creativity – producing new ways of working and new products and services – is bound to be a source of value. Creativity is only worth something when it translated into value … we will only know we are being creative in the right way, when creativity results in more output … In other words, from an HCM perspective, all intangibles that are worth something become tangibles eventually … Moreover, once intangibles are translated into tangible, added value measures, they can be included in an HCM report that will convince those who need to be convinced.

The way of not descending down this path is to understand that data does need to be supplemented by knowledge, outputs by intangibles, hard metrics by subjective descriptions. However, reporting effectively should not be just a matter of choosing between data and knowledge or a middle path of industry-focused information. The need is to combine the different levels of measurement which make each one work effectively. It is by using this combination of levels that organizations can meet Kingsmill's objective of reporting that is both strategic and based on sound data.

Take something like an organization's commitment to staff development, suggested by Brown and Baron (2003) as an example of a particularly difficult measure to report on.

The most important information is knowledge about what the organization is trying to do – what is its business strategy and its people management strategy, what is the staff development designed to achieve? Measures at this level will provide a broad insight into what the company is trying to do and some individual or team case studies might help tell a story about how successfully the company is in doing it.

Sector-related information will help provide further understanding. So, as already noted for example, customer services training would potentially have a different impact in retail than in a high-tech environment. Therefore, this level of reporting might include a graphic comparing the amounts and outputs of customer service training in the company and its competitors or other retail chains.

Some more objective metrics will help make these measures clearer and more comparable. This might include figures on training spend, numbers of courses and numbers of employees trained. On their own, these figures would be meaningless and potentially dangerous. As Brown and Baron (2003) noted, a high training spend could be applauded as an effective investment or be seen as an opportunity for savings. An investor would only be able to decide on which by being given all three levels of information.

Training spend and knowledge of the business strategy would give investors the information they need to know whether a high training spend reflected a business-driven commitment to employees' development or an unfocused approach to development or even the result of poor recruitment practices.

Training spend and knowledge of the people management strategy would give them more contextual understanding of the organization's approach to development, for example whether a large proportion is on-the-job training, mentoring and coaching. This could incorrectly suggest a lower commitment to development than in companies using predominantly more formal training.

Balancing these levels is not just about combining data with narrative in the reports. Organizations need to change the way they use this sort of report. And so a natural consequence of the move towards intangibles is that organizations need to become as comfortable with qualitative as they are with quantitative information. Investors also need to respond to more qualitative information but an internal approach to strategic HCM reporting comes first – investors will get interested in this once they see the opportunities inherent in the information and knowledge that can be provided.

These difficulties do not detract from the potential benefits of having a common set of standards. But they do emphasize the problems, limitations and potential consequences of reporting on standards if this is not supported by new types of higher-value information.

Summary

Reader: *'What are the key points I need to take away from this?'*

Author: 'In the Preface I made the point that HCM should be focused more on creating value than on measuring the value that has been created. On management rather than measurement. Of course, measurement is still important and it actually forms a very large proportion of the book. But this is about using measurement to support the management of human capital, not as an end in itself.

The key point in this chapter is that if measurement is to provide useful information for management and reporting, if it's going to inform managers and investors, then we need to think about using information and particularly knowledge, rather than just data. The use of accountant's language; playing the numbers game; the use of data and financial metrics; return on investment: they're all useful to a point. But I think human capital and HCM takes us past this point. So we need to use our judgement and our wisdom in understanding and dealing with HCM.

I have used the difficulty experienced by Accounting for People in wanting both strategic and standardized reporting, and PwC's corporate transparency model, to illustrate these points. I've also suggested that we should update PwC's triangle, and call its three levels: data, information and knowledge. This will now form the basis for the key model in the book. In each chapter, we'll be taking a look at the three levels in this triangle from a slightly different point of view. My hope is that by the end of the book, we'll have covered enough perspectives to have developed a fairly clear understanding of what HCM is all about.'

References

Ackoff, R.L. (1989). 'From data to wisdom', *Journal of Applied Systems Analysis*, **16**, 3–9.

Beer, M., Eisenstat, R. and Biggadike, R. (1996). 'Developing an Organization Capable of Strategy Implementation and Reformulation'. In *Organizational Learning and Competitive Advantage* (Moinglon, B. and Edmonson, A., Eds.). Sage, pp. 165–184.

Bennis, W.G. and O'Toole J. (2005). 'How business schools lost their way', *Harvard Business Review*, June, 96–104.

Boyle, D. (2000). *The Tyranny of Numbers: Why Counting Can't Make Us Happy*. HarperCollins.

Brown, D. and Baron, A. (2003). 'A capital idea', *People Management*, 26 June, 42–5.

Caulkin, S. (2003). 'The scary world of Mr Mintzberg', *The Observer*, 26 January.

Davenport, T.H. and Prusak, L. (1998). *Working Knowledge: How Organizations Manage What They Know*. Harvard Business School Press.

Department of Trade and Industry (2002). *Modernizing Company Law White Paper*, Command Paper CM 5553-I. HMSO.

Department of Trade and Industry (2004). *The Operating and Financial Review: Practical Guidance for Directors*. HMSO.

DiPiazza, S.A. Jr. and Eccles, R.G. (2002). *Building Public Trust: the Future of Corporate Reporting*. John Wiley & Sons.

Donkin, R. (2004). 'The rise of people power', Sponsored Report: Understanding Human Capital Management, *Financial Times*, 28 April, 3.

Donkin, R. (2005). *Human Capital Management*. Croner.

Eccles, R., Herz, R., Keegan, M. and Philips, D. (2001). *Value Reporting Revolution*. John Wiley & Sons.

Elias, J. and Scarborough, H. (2004). 'Evaluating human capital: an exploratory study of management practice', *Human Resource Management Journal*, **14**(4), 21–40.

Handy, C. (1995). *The Empty Raincoat: Making Sense of the Future*. Random House.

Kearns, P. (2004). *One Stop Guide to Human Capital Management*. Personnel Today Management Resources.

Kingsmill, D. (2003a). 'Measure for measure people really are your greatest asset', *Personnel Today*, 27 May, 16.

Kingsmill, D. (2003b). *Accounting for People: Report of the Task Force on Human Capital Management*. Department of Trade and Industry.

Koller, T. (2005). 'Don't expect too much of your share price', *The McKinsey Quarterly*, 2005 special edition: Value and performance, 29–37.

Martin, R.L. (2005). 'Seek validity, not reliability', *Harvard Business Review*, February, 9–11.

Mintzberg, H. (1994). *The Rise and Fall of Strategic Planning*. Prentice Hall.

Overell, S. (2004). 'All counting for nothing', *Personnel Today*, 25 May, 10.

Personnel Today (2005). 'Human Capital Management Feedback', *Personnel Today*, 13 June, 3.

Pfeffer, J. (1997). 'Pitfalls on the road to measurement: the dangerous liaison of human resources with the ideas of accounting and finance', *Human Resources Management*, **36**(3), 357–365.

Stewart, H. (2003). 'Taskforce puts equality back on the agenda', *The Guardian*, 21 May.

Thomas, A. (2003). 'A tale of two reports', *European Business Forum*, **16**, Winter, 79–81.

2

People Management Strategy Dynamics

Introduction

Reader: *'So if HCM needs to be focused on creating value rather than on measuring the value, how does that value get created?'*

Author: 'We'll actually consider this later on, particularly in Chapters 3, 4 and 5. Before we do this, I want to spend some time considering what we believe about the current business environment, how organizations operate and how people contribute to organizations within this environment. Much of what is written about HCM suggests rather mechanistic thinking about these issues. For example, 'wouldn't it be wonderful if we could predict exactly how people would react to a planned merger'. Sorry, but it's just not going to happen; life's too complicated for this.

I think this level of thinking is a problem — as I don't believe that HCM can be both strategic and mechanistic. In my view, HCM needs to be more than just 'what' we do to manage people better, it also needs to focus on 'how' we do it and this 'how' needs to take account of the fact that the capital we are dealing with originates in people not in machines. This chapter will look at three different perspectives on business, organizations and people management which demonstrate different levels of thinking in this area.'

Reader: *'And these three perspectives are what, exactly?'*

Author: 'They're based on the fact that people do not participate directly in the real world. We create our own pictures, we construct our own versions of reality, based upon various generalizations and assumptions. We call these pictures mental models, mindsets, paradigms, schema, scripts (of events) or stereotypes (of people). They simplify and filter the huge amount of information that is constantly available to us and help us understand what's going on. They influence how we perceive and respond to actions in the world around us.

My proposition that people do not participate directly in the real world is an output from my mental models about people and their environment. I also have a meta mental model about this – a mental model about mental models. This suggests that there are at least three very different mental models describing how things work internally within organizations and how these organizations interact externally with factors in their environment. Which one of these three possibilities forms the main mental model that is shared by key people in an organization results in profound differences in the way that strategy is designed and implemented, including how people are managed.

The three models are causal chains, dynamic systems and complex processes. I don't think it matters too much whether you share this meta model but I hope you'll agree that there are some major, qualitative differences between the three levels, and that each of these provides a substantially different context for thinking about HCM ...'

Causal Chains

This mental model describes a stable, Newtonian environment consisting of single cause and effect relationships between mechanical parts behaving in a deterministic fashion. The relationships are straightforward and unidirectional – A will always lead to B. In organizational terms, the model describes a deliberate change from one state of equilibrium to another.

An example is the model of transformation developed by Lewin (1948) which involves unfreezing from one state, making a change and freezing again in a new position.

Competitive Strategy

This belief in basic causality underpins the classic strategy development process that was especially common in the stable and growing economy of the 1960s and early 1970s, but is also still in use today. In its purest form, the process involves a complicated series of sophisticated analytical activities that is typically owned by a corporate planning department. It begins with a long-term mission and vision that is generated by a powerful individual, usually the CEO. The external environment is analysed to determine potential opportunities and threats and an internal audit is conducted to identify the organization's strengths and weaknesses in relation to the mission and vision. Strategic options are evaluated to determine which one will best help the organization achieve its mission and a long-term plan is developed and cascaded down the organization. The approach assumes that the long-term future will resemble the present and that it can be predicted by extrapolating from the past. It also assumes that a company does not need to worry too much about the ongoing actions of its customers or competitors, or potential discontinuities in the environment.

Another example of thinking from this perspective is Michael Porter's competitive positioning (Porter, 1985). Porter, a professor at Harvard, emphasizes the need for strategic fit in which an organization adapts its resources to take advantage of opportunities provided by its environment. This involves selecting one of three generic strategies (differentiation, cost leadership or focus) and supporting this through a system of integrated and coherent activities. A tool called the value chain (see Chapter 4) helps ensure that these activities are aligned with external competitive positioning. Developing strategy involves making trade-offs – deciding not to do something so that the company can concentrate on what it is going to do. Porter assumes that once a unique market position has been identified, this position can be sustained over the long term (Porter suggests a horizon of a decade or more). He also assumes that once a strategy has been selected, it can be easily and effectively implemented.

Formal planning processes like these have been criticized for focusing excessively on quantifiable data leading to the neglect of important qualitative changes in the environment because this is more difficult to measure. For example, Robert Heller (1972) challenged the process stating that:

> What goes wrong is that sensible anticipation gets converted into foolish numbers: and their validity always hinges on very loose assumptions.

Other criticisms have related to over-formalizing and divorcing planning from line managers and the unqualified acceptance and misapplication of various analytical techniques that have substituted for critical thinking (Lenz and Lyles, 1985).

People Management within Causal Chains

There is little need to think about people management strategy when competitive advantage originates from outside the company and any competitive strategy can be easily implemented. As Peter Boxall at Auckland University and John Purcell from Bath University (2003) explain:

> Personnel management, as it was then called, did not feature at all when strategy analysis first emerged as a business, and especially business school, discipline in the 1960s and 70s. One could search the index of the plethora of strategy books for any reference to people, employees, workers or staff without success. The reason for this was that business strategy … was primarily about the relationships between the firm and its competitive environment. What happened inside the company was, as one leading analyst asserted, all to do with implementation, just as tactics are the implementation of battle strategies.

In this environment, people are simply part of the way that an organization responds to a particular opportunity and are typically considered to be 'costs on legs'. People management is based on behavioural psychology in which a certain stimulus will elicit a particular response. People are aligned with business strategy through formal cascades of objectives and are rewarded for the achievement of these objectives. Treating employees as costs means that they tend to be treated as any other costs – by cutting them.

Measuring People Management within Causal Chains

If we accept that cause and effect provides a valid model for understanding organizations then although measurement of people management is not necessarily going to be easy it should at least be fairly straightforward. However, if you believe, like me, that causality only applies to people management within certain narrow contexts then this form of measurement is going to be severely restricted in its use. In fact, it only really applies to the most tangible aspects of people management, for example to recruitment and retention and other activities affecting headcount and to the observable behaviour of people and their readily assessable (for example, technical) capability. Measurement tools that can be used within this area include a range of innovative statistical analysis tools developed by Mercer to map the flow of individuals through an organization, for example, Internal Labor Market Analysis® and Business Impact Modeling® (Nalbantian *et al.*, 2004). However, this level of thinking is a lot less appropriate when dealing with less tangible attributes like alignment with values or engagement (see discussion on intangibles in Chapter 4).

Measuring People Management within Causal Chains at T-Mobile. Another example of measuring people management in a context where cause and effect can be assumed is the experience of T-Mobile, Deutsche Telecom's mobile communications division, that won *Personnel Today's* prize for HCM measurement in 2003. T-Mobile UK employs 5800 people and, although it is now growing less quickly than in the past, still has significant, focused recruitment needs. For example, the company was planning to open another 200 new stores at the time the following conversation took place. Together with a high level of turnover within the sector, this means that the company needs to recruit between 2000 and 2500 people per year. To help them do this, T-Mobile has developed a staffing model identifying the results of its recruitment activities minus the impact of turnover. The company believes that the model has been instrumental in supporting the company's rapid growth. I talked about this with Penny Davis, Head of HR Operations:

> We live in a data-driven world and for HR to talk to the business at a partnership level, it needs the same level of understanding and sophistication in the way it uses its data as the rest of the business. My last MD was very data driven and when I met with him I only ever talked about data. We've been focusing on this for about five years. The first thing we did was look at attrition but you can't do this in isolation from the whole employee experience. So in the same way that we look at

customers, analysing our data in different ways to understand what it means, for example about what causes customers to churn, we looked at our employees.

Over the last five years we have brought statistical expertise into the team. With this additional expertise we developed an extremely robust model and did some very sophisticated analysis looking at employees' propensity to leave. Once you know something you have a choice about whether you're going to act on this. If you know that a certain life event is likely to make employees consider their working life, their team manager has an opportunity to intervene and re-engage. Or not, but they have a choice. Historically, the biggest events have been performance reviews or shift changes. From this you can predict leavers and we were able to develop a tool for predicting our headcount in 90 days' time and for the end of the year.

We did some work on attrition and absence and their total impact on the business – we looked at the numbers, we costed them and benchmarked them. We reviewed a lot of biographical details – things like where staff come from, what's their journey to work. It showed we had high attrition in some geographic areas so again we have a choice. Either we don't recruit there or we do something about people's travel arrangements. We looked at recruitment and retention – what sort of people stayed and left from a demographic point of view. We found that younger men were the shortest and widowed men the longest stayers. The data gives you a choice. We can make the work environment more suitable or say we know that this type of people is not a target group.

But the thing about data is that you can do fantastic stuff but the data is only as good as the action it drives. We do a data pack each month for the management committee in the UK. It's quite low level – sickness and attrition and so on – but it does drive action. We can ask, 'Where are your people? They're not coming to work; you'd better do something about it'. In my view, HR needs to become more data focused and more commercial in its use of data. And the system part is quite critical. Having SAP is great and means that we have a single source of data. You need to be able to manipulate the data and have the skills and techniques to use the sophisticated technology to push HR to a new level.

Dynamic Systems

The second mental model I referred to earlier is that of dynamic systems. These are formed where the relationships between interconnecting parts of a system are mutual and circular – A may cause B but B will also influence A. I think that most people would agree that this two-way interdependence between elements in the system better reflects real organizational relationships than do causal chains. However, the circular causality makes it very difficult to say what causes what or to predict the future. This is uncomfortable, which is why people tend to fall back on simple cause and effect chains.

In the simplest, cybernetic form of system, all feedback is negative or damping. Here, the current state of a system is compared against a set target and feedback acts in the opposite direction to the gap that has been detected, bringing the state of the system back into line with the target. A commonly quoted example of negative feedback is a regulator for a domestic heating system that compares a house's temperature against that set on a thermostat and takes appropriate action to control the heating of the house. If the temperature on the thermostat is turned up, the regulator turns the boiler on and pumps in heat to warm up the room. Once the new target temperature has been reached, the regulator turns off the heating. The control system therefore helps the system remain close to a state of equilibrium or move between different states of equilibrium as appropriate.

More complex patterns of movement between equilibrium states are formed when feedback is positive or amplifying and the relationships between elements are non-linear. This can mean that as a system diverges from an equilibrium state, positive feedback can act to support, reinforce and accelerate movement away from that state. An example is the S-shaped or sigmoid curve described by Charles Handy (1994). This curve describes the typical life cycle of products, companies, economies, jobs and people. The curve shows how progress starts slowly, picks up over time and increases more rapidly as positive feedback loops take effect. Eventually, however, the curve plateaus out and a new state of temporary equilibrium emerges as negative feedback takes control. Finally, this leads to decline and death. For products and for jobs at least, there will be a second curve. Handy explains that the increasing pace of change means that these new curves are proliferating and that their life cycles are being completed ever more quickly. This is leading to increasing dissonance and confusion. Handy believes the paradox of change is that the movement from one curve to the next needs to take place when there is the least apparent need for it. If people wait until they need to change, resources and energy will already have been depleted. At this point, they have momentum for change but little capability to achieve it.

Andy Grove (1999), co-founder of Intel, developed a similar concept he terms a Strategic Inflection Point. For Intel this meant that the more successful the company was in microprocessors the more difficult it would be to become something else. Grove encouraged his managers to think of the company as a strategic challenger rather than a strategic aligner and never to be comfortable with the status quo. His approach to strategy was based on 'buying options' – trusting those with 'knowledge power' to make the right decisions for the future even if this meant challenging the company's existing approach.

At a further level of complexity, positive feedback loops can cause tiny disturbances to escalate, leading to self-sustaining 'virtuous' and self-destructive 'vicious' cycles. A popular example of a vicious cycle is a price war where one competitor lowers prices to such an extent that other competitors feel forced to respond. This causes the original company to reduce prices still further to retain its differential. The whole market quickly accelerates towards non-sustainability where none of the competitors is charging enough to be profitable.

System complexity can be further increased by introducing loose couplings between factors, causing delays and changes in cause and effect relationships. In this situation, actions can have varying, unintended and surprising effects.

Resource-based Strategy
Ever since the first oil price shock of 1974, with its fuel shortages and inflation that few companies could have predicted, change and uncertainty have become increasingly prevalent. Managers have lost faith in long-term predictions and turned to shorter-term, more open, inclusive and flexible approaches to strategy development and implementation. Progress in this environment is largely by trial and error. For example, Quinn (1978) describes a process of logical incrementalism in which most strategic decisions are made outside of formal planning systems. Managers may know where they want the organization to go but they are flexible about how they get there, continuously scanning the environment and evolving strategy in response to external changes.

These approaches include the use of scenario planning to develop complex series of 'what ifs' in response to different possibilities. For example, after the first oil price shocks, Shell developed a series of scenarios that included one for permanently rising oil prices but also other scenarios that anticipated significant price decreases. When prices did fall from $27 to $10 a barrel in early 1986, Shell's lateral thinking and scenario planning meant it was better prepared for this new environment than its competitors (De Geus, 1988).

Another development has been a switch in the focus of attention from finding the best competitive positioning in the market to identifying and leveraging an organization's own resources and capabilities to provide competitive advantage. The internal environment has become more complex too but at least there is some opportunity to influence it. The result is an inside-out or resource-based strategy which focuses on the acquisition and use of a company's tangible and intangible resources. Developing this approach, Barney (1991) argued that bundling a company's resources together in unique and dynamic ways could provide a source of strategic advantage. Grant (1991) observed that in a volatile external environment, organizations have to look to internal capabilities for a stable sense of direction, otherwise they would constantly need to change course. He also distinguished between resources and capabilities where:

> The capabilities of a firm are what it can do as a result of teams of resources working together....Creating capabilities is not simply a matter of assembling a team of resources: capabilities involve complex patterns of co-ordination between people and other resources. (Grant, 1991)

Resource-based strategy is a more dynamic form of strategy development than competitive positioning even though both resources and competitive positions need to be developed over the same sort of length of time. In competitive strategy, once a company has selected its positioning there is not much it can do other than to deepen the alignment of its activity system and improve its operational effectiveness. In resource-based strategy, an organization's resources are reapplied in different ways to take advantage of opportunities as they occur.

For sustainable competitive advantage, resources need to be valuable to the company, improving its efficiency or effectiveness. Resources also need to be unique or at least rare so that they cannot easily be possessed by lots of other companies and to be 'sticky' or sustainable so that they last over a period of time. They must also be difficult or uneconomic for a competitor to imitate or acquire. This will be the case if they are based on an ambiguous and complex mix of elements resulting from path dependency or causal ambiguity. Path dependency means that the practices and networks of individuals have been developed over time. Causal ambiguity argues that although resources are easily understood at a superficial level, they actually depend on numerous, subtle interrelationships where cause and effect is not readily observed or easy to explain (Collis and Montgomery, 1995). Lastly, the resources must be difficult to substitute with other factors.

A well-known approach within resource-based strategy is that of core competencies, proposed by Gary Hamel at London Business School and C.K. Prahalad at Michigan. Core competencies describe what an organization is uniquely capable of doing and act as a source of competitive advantage:

> Core competencies are the collective learning in the organization, especially how to coordinate diverse production skills and integrate multiple streams of technologies ... it is also about the organization of work and the delivery of value. (Prahalad and Hamel, 1990)

Examples of core competencies include Sony's capabilities in miniaturization which allows it to make everything from the Walkman to video cameras to notebook computers. Hamel and Prahalad explain that the skills and capabilities required for miniaturization, for example a deep understanding of customer needs and technological possibilities, take many years to develop and hence are not readily available to competitors. This is an example of path dependency and provides the company with competitive advantage. Prahalad and Hamel (1990) also explain how core competencies are enabled by a positive feedback loop:

> Core competence does not diminish with use. Unlike physical assets, which do deteriorate over time, competencies are enhanced as they are applied and shared.

So the more core competencies are used, the deeper and the more valuable they become, meaning that they have greater potential for being used, and so on. Hamel and Prahalad (1989) emphasize that as well as being internally rather than externally focused, another difference between strategic fit and leveraging resources is the scale of their ambitions:

34

Both models recognize the problem of competing in a hostile environment with limited resources. But while the emphasis in the first is on trimming ambitions to match available resources, the emphasis in the second is on leveraging resources to reach seemingly unattainable goals.

The two professors further explain that resource leveraging:

> Seeks to get the most out of the resource one has – to get a much bigger bang for the buck. Resource leverage is essentially energizing while downsizing is essentially demoralizing. (Hamel and Prahalad, 1993)

Resource leverage is supported by what Hamel and Prahalad call a strategic intent – a challenging and stretching shared vision of the future. Strategic intent implies a misalignment between current resources and aspirations meaning that new core competencies need to be acquired. Hamel and Prahalad recommend meeting this gap through alliances, licensing, mergers and acquisitions. However, we are more interested in internal means to develop capabilities.

People Management within Dynamic Systems

People strategy is an important part of a resource-based approach. People are treated as assets or resources and are the key leverage points in a system. Treating employees as assets means that employees are at least elevated to the status of valuable resources like buildings and machinery rather than just as costs to be cut. The approach taken to managing people depends on the complexity of the system.

Hard HRM

Hard HRM is an approach to people management that applies well in a cybernetic system where the prime objective is control. Hard HRM focuses on the rational management of people like any other 'factor of production' in order to benefit the organization. Emotions play a very minor part in the approach and to the extent they are recognized, are there to be controlled and reduced.

In McGregor's (1960) terms, this is Theory X. Employment is seen to be a promise to obey commands but ensuring obedience still needs tight managerial control. Planning, budgeting, performance management and performance-related pay are all based on negative feedback.

The role of the manager is to control, impose order, make accurate predictions of resistance to change and manage this resistance.

Hard HRM is a strongly quantitative approach and is the thinking behind most of the measurement based case studies referred to in the Accounting for People report. It is underpinned by cognitive psychology which sees people as essentially rationale and logical. Having said this, hard HRM also recognizes that people do not process information like computers, relying purely on cause and effect, but perceive a distorted view of the world and make systemically biased judgements and decisions. This puts further limitations on the usefulness of data.

Cognitive Psychology and Bias in Hard HRM. We use a range of short cuts to support decision-making. These include heuristics or rules of thumb that we use rather than relying on purely logical means of judging probabilities. Our judgements can also be influenced by the way that things are described, so, for example, we will typically regard a more explicit description of an event as having greater subjective probability than precisely the same event described in less explicit terms. These factors emphasize the need for decisions on people management to be based on more than just data or purely intuitive judgements. Instead, decisions should be based on knowledge and learning about the linkages between people management activities, the way these activities affect the development of human capital and the way this capital impacts on business and financial results.

Loss aversion means that we are much more sensitive to possible losses than to potential gains. This can lead organizations to focus on cost leadership rather than on differentiation, or on a resource-based approach. It can also result in under-commitment of resources to achieve potentially significant but unproven results. For example, if companies review training metrics without any contextual information about the additional capability that will be created, then there is a danger that they will simply want to reduce training costs. We need to get better at managing the subjective and intangible aspects of a business in order to develop our confidence in making these investments.

People's judgements are generally affected by overconfidence in their abilities. We also construct versions of the world in which we feel we are in control even though we are not. In organizations, these biases mean that people tend to underestimate the challenges involved in implementing change and make overly positive forecasts for their success. Although this could be taken to mean that companies over-invest in their people as they believe they can achieve more than they can, I think it actually means that they tend to underestimate the challenges in achieving business results and to under-invest in people management as an enabler towards achieving these results. We still need to get better at planning how we are going to get people on board when we are introducing change.

People are averse to ambiguity so we tend to seek out facts and opinions that support our own beliefs and ignore conflicting information. We selectively recall facts and experiences that reinforce our views and assumptions. We construct our own reality based upon information that agrees with our existing views. This provides a positive feedback loop in which our mental models inform what we pay attention to and this influences the development of our mental models. In organizations this confirmation bias can mean that people will quickly accept evidence which supports our views. In contrast, evidence that contradicts our views will either be ignored or rigorously evaluated in the hope that we will find some flaw we can use to reject it. So a CEO who asks to see a return on investment (ROI) on people management may simply not believe that the return is there, and is looking for an excuse to cut costs. HR would do better to improve the value of their solutions rather than worry about finding more data to support a case for an appropriate level of return – a case that it is never going to be possible to prove.

All of the above biases will be further influenced either consciously or unconsciously by the need to be able to justify a decision after having taken it. This is a reason for the herding instinct where people do not want to make a mistake but certainly do not want to be the only ones to make it. For example, writing in SHRM's *HR Magazine*, Robert Grossman (2005) explains why few investment analysts are prepared to look at new forms of company valuation:

> 'Burned by the dot-com bubble and debacles surrounding Enron, MCI and others, they are less likely to pursue new theories or perspectives ... They're sticking with the safety zone, engagement in what Boris Gryosberg, assistant professor at Harvard Business School, describes as 'maintenance research', following the same quantitative formulas and analytic techniques as their peers.

These are potentially serious findings and do have an impact in practice as well as under research conditions. Take the number of decisions to proceed with mergers and other major change programmes when research shows success rates for these sorts of programmes are well under 50 per cent. Yes, outcomes are always uncertain so the decision to proceed with a particular programme will always be a judgement based upon a range of rational and other factors. But predicting the weather takes place in the same level of uncertainty and, although weather forecasts may be wrong about whether the sun will shine tomorrow, they do not predict twice as many sunny days as they should.

In summary, people are not purely rational economic decision makers. A mechanistic model of information processing has serious shortcomings when thinking about people just as it does when considering organizations. It should not be assumed that just by having robust data it will mean that people will take rational decisions. Cognitive psychology suggests that there is at least some reason for believing that more qualitative information will result in more informed and better grounded decisions.

Decision-making needs to be part of a process of learning and supporting this process may provide a much bigger win for HR than improving the quality of its data. This accounts for the findings of Dave Ulrich and Wayne Brockbank (2005), Directors of the Centre for Strategic HR Leadership at the University of Michigan in their 2002 Human Resource Competency Study that 'strategic decision-making' accounts for as much as 7 per cent of HR's overall influence on business performance (it accounts for 17 per cent of the 'strategic contribution' competency that in total accounts for 43 per cent of HR's overall impact).

Cognitive psychology also helps to understand the issues involved in hard HRM, for example, the use of variable reward as a motivator. Since people tend to overestimate their own performance, they are likely to see variable payments as unsatisfactory and these may then act as a demotivator rather than in the way they were designed.

Soft HRM

Soft HRM recognizes that the addition of positive feedback to the model means that the organization cannot be controlled at an equilibrium state. This approach therefore attempts to replace control by commitment. It is based on McGregor's Theory Y, Maslow's (1954) focus on self-actualization and Herzberg's (1959) motivators (acting as a counterpoint to hygiene factors like pay). These models are based on humanistic psychology which recognizes that cognitive processing and rational analysis may often be replaced by emotional decision-making based on intuition and gut instinct. For example, neuroscientist Antonio Damsio (2006) explains that what we may think is a rational and data-based decision is often an emotional one where we have constructed a rational argument to explain our decision. In addition, this emotional decision-making can often result in better choices than more rational and intellectual decision-making.

Responding to this understanding, soft HRM emphasizes the importance of engaging people at an emotional rather than a purely rational level. This includes focusing on communication, motivation and leadership to engage people's hearts and minds. The need for inspiring visions like Hamel and Prahalad's strategic intent also originates from this. Soft HRM also requires traditional intellect to be supported by emotional intelligence and, as Lynda Gratton from London Business School comments, for facts to be balanced by feelings:

> I believe passionately that the reality in organizations falls well short of the rhetoric that 'people are our most important asset'. Until we face up to this gap, until we can stare reality in the face and until we can care as much about feelings as about finance, we are doomed to create organizations that break the soul and spirit of those who are members – and that reduce, rather than build, human potential. (Pickard, 2000)

Gratton's points emphasize the need for soft HRM focused on the 'human' in human resources, which requires the sort of high commitment and high involvement practices discussed in Chapter 3.

The Learning Organization. A particular example of soft HRM that is relevant to dynamic systems is provided in Peter Senge's writing about learning organizations in his book, *The Fifth Discipline* (1990). Noting the impact of negative and positive feedback through the action of balancing and reinforcing loops, Senge identifies five disciplines for building learning capabilities in organizations: personal mastery, mental models, shared vision, team learning and systems thinking.

Personal mastery involves a special level of proficiency based upon lifetime learning. It enables people to 'consistently realize the results that matter most deeply to them'.

39

I have already introduced the role of mental models in simplifying and filtering what we perceive and in providing an efficient way of processing information. However, in new situations these shortcuts can constrain us by obscuring threats and opportunities. The problem is that mental models act largely unconsciously so are unlikely to be questioned and are difficult to change. Senge suggests that people need to be able to surface their mental models, keeping them fluid and, where necessary, modifying them, or abandoning them and replacing them with something more appropriate.

Building a shared vision is about building and sharing mental models in a way that leads to high engagement rather than just compliance.

Team learning is created through dialogue between team members and enables a team as a whole to make discoveries that individuals working on their own could not have made. It needs to include both single and double loop learning (Argyris and Schön, 1978). Single loop learning is based upon a process of review and consideration, acting as a negative feedback loop. Learning from the consequences of previous actions may mean altering the feedback response. Double loop learning involves an additional positive feedback loop to surface mental models and question whether they are appropriate. Learning means that, where necessary, mental models are replaced with new models that will be more useful. Consider this example of learning about measurement in HCM. First loop learning sets up systems to measure and correlate people management and business performance better. Second loop learning might ask, 'what would it be like if we could manage what we can't measure?'

Systems thinking involves an individual or team becoming aware of the negative and positive feedback loops that inform how the whole system functions rather than just their own role in the system. It also helps to recognize leverage points where the system is highly sensitive to change. This should give people insight into the potential consequences of their actions and so avoid instability in the system.

The late Sumantra Ghoshal, formerly at Harvard, and Christopher Bartlett at London Business School link increasing complexity, resource-based strategy and the learning organization:

> One implication of this change has been a gradual fading of corporate management's quarter-century-long love affair with strategic planning. Two closely related forces have dimmed the previous enchantment. On the one hand, the rapid pace of change in the business environment

has undermined the relevance of long-range plans that often were little more than projections of the past. And this, in turn, has forced managers to refocus their attention from a preoccupation with defining defensible product-market positions to a newly awakened interest in how to develop the organizational capability to sense and respond rapidly and flexibly to change. As a consequence, managers worldwide have begun to focus less on the task of forecasting and planning for the future and more on the challenge of being highly sensitive to emerging changes. Their broad objective is to create an organization that is constantly experimenting with appropriate responses, then is able to quickly diffuse the information and knowledge gained so it can be leveraged by the entire organization. The age of strategic planning is fast evolving into the era of organizational learning. (Ghoshal and Bartlett, 1998)

Measuring People Management within Dynamic Systems

In a complex environment, there are only two ways of predicting future performance. One is by looking outside the system to observe inputs and outputs over a large number of events and identifying statistical correlations between them (like the HCM measurement case studies in the Accounting for People report). The other way is to use computers to model the system as a whole. We will review both of these approaches.

Predicting People Management Performance at RBS and other Organizations. The RBS Group's approach to measurement is based on a human capital model which links a range of people management metrics with business performance indicators to inform decision-making (Figure 2.1).

On the left-hand side of the model is the data RBS pulls together from more than 30 disparate sources around the world, staff opinion and local pulse employee surveys, joiner and leaver surveys and, more unusually, turndown surveys. These latter surveys are completed by potential employees who fail to take up an RBS job offer and may tell RBS something about the way they are projecting themselves to potential candidates.

In the middle, the model identifies the elements of the Group's employee proposition that contribute towards employee engagement. The bank's data helps it understand the influence of these elements on why employees join, stay and leave, and how they influence employee engagement while they stay, at different points in an employee's career.

41

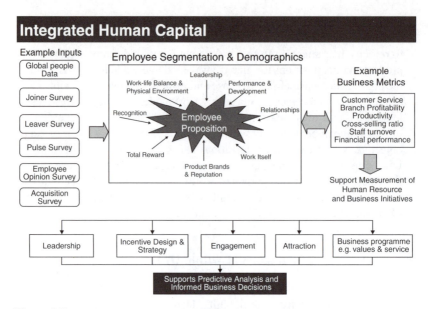

Figure 2.1 RBS Group's Human Capital Model

Engagement has been found to vary according to different factors across different groups of positions. For example, in some areas managerial staff are most affected by work–life balance factors and clerical staff by their relationships with customers supported by the quality of the brands. The Group can also review how engagement is affected by HR practices. For example, it has identified that engagement levels increase by up to 20 per cent for staff who take three or more of RBS's flexible benefit options.

On the right-hand side of the model are the business indicators that are used to track the impact of employee behaviours and engagement. This allows the group to see how engagement impacts on business results, calculating the value of people issues in financial terms. For example, the group has found that just a 0.1 per cent reduction in absence would provide an annual saving of £2 million. As another example, the average cost of turnover has been calculated to result in a break-even period of ten months before recruitment costs are recouped and a new employee starts to add net value to the organization.

Case studies demonstrating similar experience to that of RBS have also been published for Sears (see Chapter 4); Standard Chartered (see Chapter 6); B&Q, a chain of home improvement retail stores;

Nationwide, Britain's largest mutual building society (thrift) and Whitbread, a group of leisure and hospitality businesses. David Maister also presents an extensive case study of experience at what is thought to be Omnicom in his book, *Practice What You Preach* (2001).

According to presentations made by former HR Director Mike Cutt in 2003, B&Q has calculated that if all stores could reach the same levels of employee engagement as their best performing ones, this would save £2.45 million in turnover costs, £3.15 million in absence costs, and £10.16 million in shrinkage. Additional sales would provide £76 million and the resulting additional profit would be £24 million. Based upon these findings proving the value of people management and development, managers' bonuses have been linked in part to the engagement of their staff; the training budget has been increased by 60 per cent and a new reward scheme (a B&Q home renovation) has been introduced for exemplary employees.

Nationwide has put employee retention at the centre of its HCM model, called Genome, which is explained in the 'better society' section of the society's website. Nationwide's focus on the drivers of retention, retention itself and its links to customer satisfaction provides an interesting contrast to RBS's focus on engagement and one that aligns with Nationwide's business strategy of developing long-term relationships with the society's customers.

Whitbread's HCM analysis was conducted in response to a desire to find one single measure for people management that HR could contribute to a corporate scorecard. This was designed to monitor a common set of measures covering investors, guests and people in each of Whitbread's units, brands and at group level. After analysing the group's dataset, it became clear that although no single measure universally predicted superior business outcomes in all of its businesses, team turnover represented the most common driver. This is now one of two people measures (alongside health and safety) incorporated in its scorecard.

Although I think these case studies are all examples of HCM, this is not just because these organizations use measurement so well (and I do not believe organizations necessarily need to do anything like this amount or have this sophisticated level of measurement to do HCM). These case studies are examples of HCM because the companies have used measurement in a way that supports their business strategies and in environments where a deep focus on measurement makes sense.

43

The case studies generally describe large businesses and many have a number of brands and business units and operations in different countries. So a high degree of sophistication and specialization in head office makes good economic sense. Apart from Maister's example, all the organizations mentioned are retail-oriented businesses providing a particularly clear line of sight between people, customer and financial results. In addition, RBS, Standard Chartered and Nationwide are retail finance businesses where accounting language gives HR extra immediate credibility. I talked about this with Steve O'Keeffe, Director of Operations, and Sara Powell, Head of Accreditation and Business Development at the Financial Services Skills Council (FSSC). O'Keeffe explained that there are other reasons why HCM measurement may work well in financial services:

> As a heavily regulated sector we are good at collecting data because we need to be – especially in retail-focused firms with regulated roles. There's a vast amount of KPI data that firms need to keep – appointments, sales, the quality of their fact finds, the quality of their advice, the balance and mix of services and so on. For non-compliance with the rules, there are heavy fines that can be imposed by the FSA. Financial services firms are broadly comfortable with costs and benefits so HCM benchmarking fits – they understand the idea that training needs to provide a return on investment.

Retail finance companies also consist of relatively similar bank branches and call centres which means that they are highly amenable to internal benchmarking. They tend to be relatively stable – a call centre's operations do not change much from day to day. This means that correlations and causations identified on a historic basis have a high degree of predictive value for the future.

Smaller, less single bottom line, more complicated and more complex organizations are probably not going to find this measurement focused approach as beneficial. So a typical finding of an HCM measurement-approach is that somebody needs to work in an organization for at least a year before their cost of recruitment is paid off. However, for many businesses, by the time they have calculated how much it has cost them to recruit somebody life has moved on; they are not recruiting that type of person anymore. And even if they know that it takes a year to recoup this expense, so what? Unless they are recruiting hundreds of people into a role, this statistic is not going to change how or who they recruit, and it should not make any difference to the importance of retaining talented people for as long as they can. So I suspect few organizations are ever going to find that this extensive focus on measurement provides them with more value than it subtracts through management time and costs of technology.

I think these case studies demonstrate that the appropriate use of data is always important and can even form a basis for competitive advantage. But I also think this is about competing on analytics, not on human capital. As T.H. Davenport (2006) has noted, 'Some companies have built their very businesses on their ability to collect, analyze and act on data. This is a perfectly fine way to compete, but it is a different field, and a different book. Competing on human capital involves a different set of techniques and does not need an extensive focus on analytics to support it. These other ways of developing competitiveness will be reviewed later, particularly in Chapters 3, 4 and 5.

Computer Modeling System Dynamics. Kim Warren (2000), who lectures in Strategy Dynamics at London Business School explains the value of computer modelling relationships in a dynamic system:

> Unless these dynamics of accumulation, depletion and feedback are captured, there is no possibility of explaining historic performance, and no means of anticipating the time-path of future prospects. (The mathematics of integration is the only means of accomplishing this task.)

Warren (2002) proposes that tracking the changing availability of tangible and intangible resources over time and modelling the impact of positive and negative feedback between the interdependent resources enables organizations to answer three critical questions:

- Why is performance following its current path?
- Where is it going if we carry on as we are?
- How can we design a robust strategy to radically improve performance into the future?

Warren and Kourdi (2003) believe that answering these questions provides a basis for managers to control this dynamic time-path of performance:

> Building on this solid foundation will clarify the links between organizational groups and the business levers they control. Armed with

this understanding, you will be able to understand how people-oriented initiatives will develop through time, track and adjust those initiatives to keep them on course, and trace their impact on your goals.

For example, Warren and Kourdi (2003) provide an example of using computer models to understand why major technology firms such as Lucent, Nortel and Ericsson had to announce a second and larger round of redundancies just months after they had announced an earlier round in response to the disastrous downturn in the sector in early 2001:

> This situation arose because of the unrealistic expectation that the rapid expansion of the late 1990s would continue. With business growth often exceeding 20 percent per year, staffing requirements in sales, customer support and other functions had rocketed. On top of this growing need, firms had to cope with high rates of staff turnover as a vicious war for talent tempted staff to move from firm to firm. Annual attrition rates of 25 to 40 percent were common. Taken together, the growth requirements and turnover meant that departments could be hiring as many new staff each year as the number they started with! Although it was never realistic to assume that this boom would continue for ever, many firms were nevertheless taken by surprise when business turned down during 2000. It took a few months to realize just how severe the collapse in business activity was going to be, by which time staff numbers had grown well beyond what we needed.
>
> Naturally, hiring rates were slashed, and redundancies were worked out in order to bring staffing back to the lower levels required. In estimating the layoffs that would be needed, companies allowed for natural attrition. Unfortunately, many assumed that the previous high staff turnover rates would continue. In the event, the rapid drop in job security led many staff to stay, so that turnover dropped sharply, often to as little as 5 to 8 percent per annum. That's why companies had to revise their estimates and go through a second round of layoffs.

This example describes a similar analysis to that conducted by T-Mobile although the scenario plays in the opposite direction (downsizing rather than recruitment). But the most important difference is that in Warren's example, calculating attrition rates needs to take account of the way that downsizing causes negative feedback that limits the reductions. In contrast, T-Mobile's recruitment estimates did not need to take account of any changes in the company's ability to retain people (other than by maintaining a proportional link between turnover and total headcount). This makes Warren's scenario more a rather simple demonstration of dynamic systems than an example of causal chains.

Warren's approach also copes with much more complicated systems than this example and can incorporate differences in resource attributes, rivalry for resources, intangible resources and the building of organizational capabilities. Clearly, it also has most use as a predictive rather than an interpretative tool, but its usefulness is limited to systems where cause and effect relations may be subtle and hidden, yet still exist.

Complex Processes

While systems can describe a certain level of complexity, their focus on cause and effect chains limits the level of uncertainty that can be described. Donald Sull (2005) at London Business School comments that:

> Visibility in volatile markets is sharply limited because so many different variables are in play. Uncertainty would be manageable if only one thing changed while the rest remained fixed, but of course business is rarely so simple. In volatile markets, many variables are individually uncertain, and they interact with one another to create unexpected outcomes.

Because of this, a more appropriate mental model than either causal chains or dynamic systems may be this one built through analogy with complex adaptive systems in natural science. In some of these systems, even relatively simple positive and negative feedback loops acting autonomously can produce behaviour so complex that differences between cause and effect become unclear and the links between them disappear. This is not yet about a state of chaos where there is no pattern or order but a level before this, the edge of chaos.

This is a paradoxical state which is neither stable nor unstable, neither random nor repetitive. It is a zone of creativity and new opportunities in which various directions of change are possible and change may take place very rapidly and spontaneously. It can also be easily disturbed at certain leverage points at which very tiny fluctuations can have dramatic consequences, for example, the well-known example that the flapping of a butterfly's wings over China can affect the weather patterns in the UK.

When in this state, living systems show the capacity to self-organize into new, unpredictable and emergent patterns that are often greater than the sum of parts. This means that analysing the constituent parts of the whole system no longer provides useful information. Understanding the whole system needs synthesis rather than analysis, knowledge rather than data.

Hence one of Senge's (1990) rules of systems thinking, 'cutting an elephant in half doesn't get you two smaller elephants; it gets you a mess'.

The edge of chaos contrasts with a state of equilibrium which in a living system is a precursor for death and extinction. However, there is no guarantee of development and the system is just as likely to self-destruct as to evolve and self-organize into more complex and sophisticated forms.

Applying this capacity for self-organization and emergent complexity to organizations often helps people make more sense of their actual experience of working in them. For example, Ralph Stacey (2000), Director of the Complexity and Management Centre at the University of Hertfordshire comments:

> My experience is that, despite the rational analysis, the forecasts, the visions, strategic intents, team building and so on, organizational outcomes are very frequently surprising and unexpected ... The response is then to put more effort into gathering and analysing information to overcome ignorance....Or new motivating and controlling systems are installed to prevent poor implementation and bad behaviour. When the surprise is a large one, these responses are usually accompanied by the removal of the individuals who are conspicuously associated with the surprise from the organization. However, none of these responses puts a stop to it all happening again.

Organizational paradoxes that need to be accommodated at the same time include rapid change and continuity, data and knowledge, best practice and best fit (see Chapter 3). Managers have to work with these paradoxes, searching for solutions that balance 'both/and' rather than 'either/or'. For example, Ulrich and Lake (1990) state:

> Managing the paradoxes inherent in any business transition means focusing not on conflicts and polarities (for example, 'Let's move the organization *from* one state *to* another state') but on formulating responses that meet simultaneous, disparate demands and resolving the conflicts among them (for example, 'Let's make sure the organization accomplishes simultaneously its financial, strategic, and employee goals').

Emergent Strategy

In this environment of economic turbulence, partial ignorance and internal complexity, strategy itself is emergent, being created from chance events and cultural and political processes as well as by formal and deliberate planning. For example, Henry Mintzberg (1994) has observed that while strategy is often thought of as a plan in which we 'think in order to act', it can also be regarded as a realized pattern of consistent although unintended behaviour. From this viewpoint, the development of strategy is non-deterministic and evolutionary, recognizing that we sometimes need to 'act in order to think'. This type of strategy development cannot be top-down as no one individual, including the CEO, is able to see the whole picture. It is an uncomfortable position for a CEO and other leaders to be in because they are never going to be in possession of all the facts or in complete control as there are too many variables to manage.

Linda Holbeche (2001), previously at Roffey and now at the Work Foundation, believes both emergent and planned strategies are required:

> Organizations need both planned approaches which are sufficiently flexible and adaptable that they can cope with changing circumstances and the seemingly haphazard proliferation of activities in which employees are developing new ideas. The challenge is to get the best out of both approaches, perhaps by co-ordinating apparently disparate initiatives and helping people to see where linkages may occur.

The need to manage diametrically opposing and self-contradictory approaches to strategy development emphasizes the paradoxical qualities of complexity. Another important paradox is that although the future is inherently unknowable managers cannot stop thinking about and planning for the future. Indeed the fast pace of change and transformational nature of complexity means it is imperative to aim at fundamental not just incremental change. Businesses need to attempt to create their own future, not just adapt to externally induced change. However, it is only really possible to predict developments over the short term and detailed long-term planning is impossible. Because of this, Sull (2005) recommends keeping the long-term vision fuzzy to provide a general direction but the short-term priorities absolutely clear. It also means that plans need to be reviewed very regularly to check whether they remain realistic and the external environment needs to be scanned and monitored to help identify potential opportunities and threats. It may even be possible to develop capabilities in identifying trends and anticipating changes.

Richard Pascale, co-author of *Surfing the Edge of Chaos*, (2001) provides an interesting example of an emergent approach to strategy development, reinterpreting Honda's entry into the US motorcycle industry that had been used as an example of strategic intent by Hamel and

Prahalad (1989). Pascale (1996) explained that Honda's intended strategy of selling 250cc and 350cc bikes was nearly a disaster but that a successful strategy of selling smaller machines emerged when the 50cc Japanese bikes that Honda executives were using to ride around Los Angeles started to attract attention.

Most importantly, the organization needs to understand that changes to the plan will happen and be agile enough to take advantage of opportunities as they emerge. Supporting this, Brockbank (1997) argues that Hamel and Prahalad's core competencies limit a firm to a short-term perspective and that instead of core technical competencies, organizations need to think about core cultural competencies:

> The key core competence, however, is not what a firm does based on what is known, but is, rather, a firm having a culture which encourages flexibility, change, learning, creativity and adaptability to customers.

People as Investors of Human Capital

The difference between dynamic systems and complex processes is not just about a quantitative increase in the amount of complexity but a qualitative change in its nature. A complexity perspective recognizes that the capital in HCM comes from people: individuals with their own perspectives, desires, thoughts and feelings. Even if people have objectives that are aligned with the business strategy and with each other, they interpret these objectives and make choices about achieving them in their own, and potentially irrational, ways. Individual differences between people are amplified in the non-linear interaction between them and this produces new and unexpected forms of behaviour. This type of complexity increases with the numbers of people involved, their diversity and their level of interconnection with other people.

Also, thinking about knowledge workers in particular, people's skills, activities and outputs are all largely intangible. So it is very often the people performing particular roles who have the greatest knowledge about the activities they are performing and can generate the best ideas about improving them. As Gratton (2004) explains, people can choose whether to make this additional and discretionary effort:

> In the Democratic Enterprise the basis of ownership of an individual's personal human capital shifts from an asset to be managed by the company, to that of an investor, where individuals build, deploy and

invest their own personal human capital. The analogy here is with the way in which personal financial capital is invested and deployed. The differences between the notions of asset and investor are profound. They highlight differences in ownership, but also in the feelings individuals have about themselves, their self-determination, their self-awareness and their capacity to make choices based on this self-awareness. As asset has no freedom to act; it is simply a resource to be assigned and re-assigned. But an investor has both the autonomy to choose and the freedom to act.

Leslie Weatherly (2003) explains that:

Human capital can be developed and cultivated, but it can also decide to leave the organization, become sick, disheartened, and even influence others to behave in a way that may not be to the advantage of an employer, thus usurping or siphoning off resources intended for use elsewhere in the organization. In other words, the performance of an organization's human capital is not always predictable and/or within the control of the employer. So, the measurement and the management of human capital becomes part art and part science.

These factors mean that it is not totally appropriate to consider people to be parts of an overall system and for this reason Stacey (2000) suggests thinking in terms of 'processes of interaction' rather than systems.

People Management within Complex Processes
At this level, strategic capability, or the ability to be strategic, becomes more important than the actual strategy at any point in time. Developing strategic capability is largely about increasing interaction between people. Complex responses are going to happen anyway so the choice is either to try to pretend that they do not exist and think in terms of cause and effect, or go with and influence what is actually happening. The opportunity here is to stimulate complexity internally in order to be well placed to meet and create change in the external environment.

The relevant paradigm from psychology is social psychology and in particular, social constructionism. This recognizes that, increasingly, the most important resources within organizations are intangible, things like relationships with customers, knowledge and human capital. All explanations of these intangibles are socially constructed – they cannot be a straightforward account of reality since, by definition, intangibles do not physically exist. These constructions are formed and shared through social interaction, particularly through conversations. This means that the most important resources in an organization are constructed through conversation between the people in the organization. Changing the way these concepts are constructed changes the context in which people can act and interact and therefore opens up new possibilities for emergent strategy to develop.

Social Psychology and Bias in Complex Processes

I have already described people's biased perception of objects and this applies to social objects too. Research into social cognition has shown that our mental models can lead us to exaggerate the similarities within categories of people (role, demographic, personality and so on) and the differences between these categories. So, because of this stereotyping, we might make important judgements about someone's ability because of his or her category membership before we know anything about that particular individual's actual ability.

In addition, fundamental attribution error means we tend to favour internal rather than external reasons for other people's behaviour, but the actor/observer effect means this tendency reverses when explaining our own actions – instead, we tend to favour external causes. Psychologists have also identified a self-serving bias in which people have a tendency to attribute their successes to internal causes and their failures to external causes. So if someone else fails to achieve their targets we are likely to assume they are a poor performer, or at least that he or she had not made sufficient effort to ensure they deliver. But if I was in the same situation, I would be more likely to explain my own behaviour in terms of external causes that made it more difficult for me to complete the activity as planned.

Once again, these issues emphasize the need for data to be supplemented by knowledge in order to provide meaning and enable insight and understanding.

These unconscious distortions may be further compounded by unconscious or conscious deceptions where there are conflicts of interest between the people making the decision and the organization's overall goals. This can result in people communicating deliberately misleading information. A recent article in *The McKinsey Quarterly*

(Lovallo and Sibony, 2006) identifies the following conditions that frequently create these principal-agency problems:

- 'Misaligned time horizons, i.e. focusing solely on time horizon for one's current position.'
- Misaligned risk aversion profiles, i.e. real or perceived career risks in projects with moderate corporate risks.'

These deceptions can further discourage organizations from making long-term investments in people.

- 'Champion bias, i.e. accepting evaluation of proposal more willingly when proponent is trusted associate.'
- Sunflower management, i.e. collective consensus around senior person's presumed opinion.'

The fact that a high proportion of CEOs were previously Finance Directors (FDs) is likely to be part of the reason why financial language remains so prized. In addition, CEOs are likely to trust their FDs more than their HR Directors (HRDs). These factors will take time to change even though it is becoming increasingly clear that people management and therefore HR have a potentially more important role than Finance in the emerging sigmoid curve.

Of course, just like the biases discussed under cognitive psychology earlier on, these issues are important in other areas of business management as well. But these issues may be particularly relevant within a strategic approach to HCM which, as we will review in Chapter 4, depends so much on judgements about intangibles. Because of this, information is always uncertain and incomplete and people cannot therefore always be sure themselves on what grounds they are making a decision. For example, Stacey (2000) notes the difficulty in placing money values on all the costs and benefits of particular strategic action options, particularly when dealing with intangibles, is that:

> The analysis therefore involves many subjective judgements upon which there is likely to be disagreement that cannot be resolved by rational argument. In the end the decision has to be made by political processes or persuasion and conversion, or even force. The analysis is there to aid this process by making the factors that need to be taken into account explicit and by creating the appearance of rationality. This appearance of rationality can be instrumental in persuading people to accept a

particular choice and it legitimizes the decision, in effect giving it a seal of 'scientific' approval even though such rationality was not actually used to make the choice.

Conversations as Strategy in Complex Processes

Within social constructionism, our most important management tool is our conversation and in particular the conversations we have which are created by small, self-organizing groups of people coming together to share issues and ask important questions. Ideas and strategy emerge from these groups and will develop if other people become excited by them. So people partake in strategy development through their participation in conversation rather than through a formal planning process. Because of this, Gratton (2000) suggests measuring the success of strategy development through energy developed in the process rather than the end result:

> This whole endeavour will live or die simply on the depth and richness of the strategic dialogue it generates. The process itself has no other real function. Unless people from across the organization begin to debate the future of the company, unless they are invigorated and excited and are prepared to take action, this becomes another piece of managerial bureaucracy which will atrophy as soon as management attention lapses.

Senior managers can use conversations to develop strategic capability and direction in four ways. Firstly, they can pay attention to the way they are participating within both formal and shadow conversations and the sort of future they are creating through this participation. The quality of conversation dictates the quality of strategy so it is important that people do not get stuck in habitual patterns leading to repetitive conversations. For example, rather than simply considering return on investment (ROI) and whether it has or has not been achieved, more productive conversation would be produced by encouraging debate around people management and the way it drives organizational performance and leads on to financial outcomes.

Secondly, managers can purposefully intervene in other conversations that are taking place to encourage and sponsor those interactions they believe could result in emergent strategies and encourage their development. This is what Mintzberg (1994) is referring to when he notes that strategies 'grow initially like weeds, they are not cultivated like tomatoes in a hot house' and explains that managers should be 'finders not designers of strategies'.

Thirdly, managers can also ensure that the organization environment supports high quality conversations. This is about developing a dialogue-oriented culture in which conversations can start up spontaneously and where people focus on asking questions and listening rather than providing answers. So, for example, identifying a type of creative dialogue that is inspiration and sense-making and that is created by both analytical rationality and emotional authenticity, Gratton and Ghoshal (2002) recommend that to create the context for these conversations, organizations should:

- Institutionalize questioning and doubt
- Create time and space for conversations
- Legitimize big, broad questions
- Develop some new rules and forums

Fourthly, managers can influence the people who are employed or otherwise linked to an organization to influence the type of conversations that will be generated. Improving the diversity of the workforce increases complexity and the variability of conversations which can lead to a greater range of potential behaviours and more opportunities for creative responses.

Any individual or a small group located anywhere at any level within an organization can have a very large impact on the strategies and direction which emerge. So organizations need to take a very real interest in their people and the way they are engaged and interconnected with other people. Increasing selected turnover, internal career moves and personal development can challenge the organization's culture and stop it becoming stale, and can also increase the quantity and quality of interconnections in the organization.

These actions do not make implementation of any particular strategy easier but can move the organization into a higher quality dynamic. This point emphasizes that although Finance may be the language of strategy, HCM is the language of strategic dynamics.

Reinforcing the above points, Bartlett and Ghoshal (2002) explain how senior managers' roles change within this new approach to strategy development:

> Their main contribution has shifted from deciding the strategic content to framing the organizational context. That means creating a sense of

purpose that not only provides an integrating framework for bottom-up strategic initiatives, but also injects meaning into individual effort. It means articulating company values that not only align organizational effort with the overall enterprise objectives, but also define a community to which individuals want to belong. And it means developing organizational processes that not only get work done effectively, but also ensure the empowerment, development and commitment of all members of the organization. The philosophical shift requires executives to expand beyond strategy, structure and systems to a simultaneous focus on the company's purpose, process and people.

Measuring People Management within Complex Processes

One interesting consequence of this last discussion is that from a complex processes perspective the underpinning theory behind HCM originates from social not natural sciences, as is the case from a causal chain point of view. Social science is about developing understanding through rich and reflexive analysis. It is not about the development of universal, context-independent laws and it loses most of its value when it tries to provide this. For example, writing on this point, Bent Flyvbjerg (2001), professor at Aalborg University in Denmark, explains that:

> Social science never has been, and probably never will be able to develop the type of explanatory and predictive theory that is the ideal and hallmark of natural science.

This point explains why we need discursive and qualitative knowledge rather than just data when we seek to understand the complexities of how organization works and the patterns of behaviour generated by the system as a whole. This also means that rather than making predictions, we need to have conversations about potential permutations.

Supporting a move from data to knowledge is a change in focus from formal reports to more informal styles of communication, in particular storytelling. Stories and anecdotes, describing relationships between people and events, are generally the most effective ways to communicate understanding and to help people make sense of our world and their activities. They can be especially effective when we provide information in a way that uses our five physical senses and uses metaphor and imagery to appeal to our spiritual senses too.

Summary

Reader: '*I might need to read that through again a few more times. Remind me where we've got to now.*'

Author: 'Well, I think I've made a good case for thinking about HCM in complexity terms. As I stated earlier, I don't believe we can think of HCM purely as a strategic approach to the maximization of human capital. We also need to pay attention to the way that human capital is created and, given that this is about people, this seems to me to require an acknowledgement that we are dealing with complexity. This involves treating people as individuals; understanding that the future cannot always be predicted; recognizing that measurements of today or yesterday may provide a poor guide to tomorrow; and realizing that organizations need to be ready to take advantage of often new and surprising opportunities.

Complexity does not mean that measurement is unimportant but, linked to Chapter 1, it emphasizes the need to focus on knowledge that can form the basis for productive conversation rather than on pure data. It also means that we need to be clear what we want from our measures. Simply mining data to look for correlations – an approach I refer to as going on a fishing trip as you just want to catch something but don't care too much about what you catch – is likely to result in correlations that may or may not have strategic significance and could be dangerous to use as lead indicators of future performance. In summary, the need is to measure less rather than more, and get deeper into the meaning behind results rather than just focusing on what lies on the surface.

The other reason for introducing systems thinking and complexity is to signal that things in business may need to change both more extensively and more quickly than we might think. At some point, struggling to make things fit into an existing model no longer makes sense. The sigmoid curve shows that our current constructions of the way things are

Table 2.1: The Evolving focus of strategy and the role of Human Resources.

	Competition for Products and Markets	Competition for Resources and Competencies	Competition for Talent and Dreams
Strategic objectives	Defensible product-market positions	Sustainable competitive advantage	Continuous self-renewal
Major tools, perspectives	■ Industry analysis; competitor analysis ■ Market segmentation and positioning ■ Strategic planning	■ Core competencies ■ Resource-based strategy ■ Networked organization	■ Vision and values ■ Flexibility and innovation ■ Front-line entrepreneurship and experimentation
Key strategic resource (see Chapter 4)	Financial capital	Organizational capability	Human and intellectual capital
Perspective on employees	People viewed as factors of production	People viewed as valuable resources	People viewed as 'talent investors'
HR's role in strategy (see Chapter 5)	Implementation, support	Contributory	Central
Key HR activity (see Chapter 5)	Administering of recruitment, training and benefits	Aligning resources and capabilities to achieve strategic intent	Building human capital as a core source of competitive advantage

Adapted by permission of *MIT Sloan Management Review* from 'Building Competitive Advantage through People' by Christopher A. Bartlett and Sumantra Ghoshal, Winter 2002 vol. 43 No 2. Copyright © 2002 by the Massachusetts Institute of Technology: all rights reserved.

organized in business will inevitably have to change. And the time to make this change is before we have to. Of course, given complexity, there is no way we can prove the need to make this change. But there is plenty of evidence to suggest that the way we are doing things now is not working particularly well. For example, various different surveys show that there are more disengaged people working in our organizations than there are people who are highly engaged.

A strategic approach to people management means recognizing that people work in an environment of complexity rather than causality which means that managers need to focus on the way that people participate in organizational dynamics. This of course means that people need to be more central to strategy, emphasizing the importance of complexity, and so on. So there is potentially a virtuous circle (positive feedback) here and if this does exist it's going to help accelerate change.

I would like to think that HCM points to another way of doing things, based upon a different paradigm about organizations, in which the driver of what we do and how we do it really is about developing people and human capital. For me, the main paradox that results from a complexity view of human capital is that managing for capital requires us to get even closer to our people.'

Reader: 'So is an appreciation of complexity necessary for using HCM?'

Author: 'That's a good question. I do feel that complexity is very central to gaining an understanding of HCM. But there are other ways to arrive at the same conclusions. For example, it's worth noting that without referring to either systems or complexity, Bartlett and Ghoshal (2002) come to very similar conclusions about the need for change. As shown in Table 2.1., they identify three levels in the evolving focus of strategy and the resulting role of Human Resources. These three levels obviously have a high degree of correlation with my discussion on causal chains, dynamic systems and complex processes.'

References

Argyris, C. and Schon, D. (1978). *Organizational Learning: A theory of action perspective*. Addison Wesley.

Barney, J.B. (1991). 'Firm resources and sustained competitive advantage', *Journal of Management*, **17**(1), 99–120.

Bartlett, C.A. and Ghoshal, S. (2002). 'Building competitive advantage through people', *MIT Sloan Management Review*, **Winter**, 34–41.

Boxall, P. and Purcell, J. (2003). *Strategy and Human Resource Management*. Palgrave Macmillan.

Brockbank W. (1997). 'HR's future on the way to a presence', Human *Resource Management*, **36**(1), Spring, 65–9.

Collis, D. and Montgomery, C. (1995). 'Competing on resources: strategy in the 1990s', *Harvard Business Review*, July–August, 118–28.

Damsio, A. (2006). *Descartes' Error: Emotion, Reason and the Human Brain*. Vintage.

Davenport, T.H. (2006). 'Competing on Analytics', *Harvard Business Review*, January, 98–107.

De Geus, A. (1988). 'Planning as learning', *Harvard Business Review*, March–April, 70–74.

Flyvbjerg, B. (2001). *Making Social Science Matter: Why Social Inquiry Fails and How it Can Succeed Again*. Cambridge University Press. Translated by Steven Sampson.

Ghoshal, S. and Bartlett, C.A. (1998). *The Individualized Corporation: A Fundamentally New Approach to Management*. Harper Collins Publishers.

Grant, R.M. (1991). 'The resource-based theory of competitive advantage: implications for strategy formulation', *California Management Review*, **33**(3), 114–135.

Gratton, L. (2000). *Living Strategy: Putting people at the heart of corporate purpose*. Pearson Education.

Gratton L. (2004). *The Democratic Enterprise: Liberating your business with freedom, flexibility and commitment*. Pearson Education.

Gratton, L. and Ghoshal, S. (2002). 'Improving the Quality of Conversations', *Organizational Dynamics*, **33**(99), 209–23.

Grossman, R. (2005). 'Blind investment', *HR Magazine,* January, 40–47.

Grove, A. (1999). *Only the Paranoid Survive*. Time Warner.

Hamel, G. and Prahalad, C.K. (1989). 'Strategic intent', *Harvard Business Review*, May–June, 63–76.

Hamel, G. and Prahalad, C.K. (1993). 'Strategy as stretch and leverage', *Harvard Business Review*, March–April, 75–84.

Handy, C. (1994). *The Empty Raincoat*. Harvard Business School Press.

Heller, R. (1972). *The Naked Manager: Games Executives Play*. McGraw-Hill.

Herzberg, F., Mausner, B. and Snyderman, B. (1959). *The Motivation to Work*. John Wiley.

Holbeche, L. (2001). *Aligning Human Resources and Business Strategy*. Elsevier Butterworth-Heinemann

Lenz, R.T. and Lyles, M.A. (1985). 'Paralysis by analysis: Is your planning system becoming too rational?', *Long Range Planning*, **18**(4), 64–73.

Lewin, K. (1947). Group Decision and Social Change. In: *Readings in Social Psychology* (T.M. Newcomb and E.L. Hartley, eds). Henry Holt & Co. pp. 340–44.

Lovallo, D.P. and Sibony, O. (2006). 'Distortions and deceptions in strategic decisions', *The McKinsey Quarterly*, **1**, 19–29.

Maister, D.H. (2001). *Practice What You Preach: What Managers Must Do to Create a High Achievement Culture*. The Free Press.

Maslow, A.H. (1954). *Motivation and Personality*. Harper and Row.

McGregor, D. (1960). *The Human Side of Enterprise*. McGraw-Hill.

Mintzberg, H. (1994). *The Rise and Fall of Strategic Planning*. Prentice Hall International.

Nalbantian, H.R., Guzzo, R.A., Kieffer, D. and Doherty, J. (2004). *Play to Your Strengths*. McGraw-Hill.

Pascale, R.T. (1996). 'Perspective on strategy: the real story behind Honda's success', *California Management Review*, **38**(4), 80–91.

Pascale, R.T., Milleman, M. and Gioja, L. (2001). *Surfing the Edge of Chaos: The Laws of Nature and the New Laws of Business*. Random House.

Pickard, J. (2000). 'A design for Life', *People Management*, 12 October, 48–51.

Porter, M. (1985). *Competitive Strategy*. The Free Press.

Prahalad, C.K. and Hamel G. (1990). 'The core competence of the corporation', *Harvard Business Review*, May–June, 79–91.

Quinn, J. (1978). 'Strategic change: Logical incrementalism', *Sloan Management Review*, Fall, 45–60.

Senge, P. (1990). *The Fifth Discipline: The Art & Practice of The Learning Organization*. Century Business.

Stacey, R.D. (2000). *Strategic Management and Organizational Dynamics: The Challenge of Complexity*. 3rd edn. Pearson Education.

Sull, D.N. (2005). 'Strategy as Active Waiting', *Harvard Business Review*, September, 120–9.

Ulrich, D. and Brockbank, W. (2005). *The HR Value Proposition*. Harvard Business School Press.

Ulrich, D. and Lake, D. (1990). *Organizational Capability: Competing from the Inside Out*. John Wiley & Sons.

Warren, K. (2000). 'The softer side of strategy dynamics', *Business Strategy Review*, **11**(1), 45–58.

Warren, K. (2002). *Competitive Strategy Dynamics*. John Wiley & Sons.

Warren, K. and Kourdi, J. (2003). *People Power: Developing the talent to perform*. Vola Press.

Weatherly, L. (2003). *Human Capital – The Elusive Asset: Measuring and Managing Human Capital: A Strategic Imperative for HR*. SHRM Research, Quarter 1.

3

Best People Management Practices

Introduction

Reader: *'OK, so same question: if HCM needs to be focused on creating value rather than on measuring the value, how does that value get created?'*

Author: 'That's what we're going to be looking at, particularly in the next three chapters. In this one, I want to take a look through the most significant research into best people management practices to see what insight this may provide into what will make the difference and help move us on to the next sigmoid curve. I want to look at the types of people management activity that have the greatest impact on performance and in particular those types of activity that seem best suited to the complex environment I described in Chapter 2.'

Reader: *'I didn't really think the research evidence was strong enough to draw many conclusions from it though.'*

Author: 'Well it's certainly ambiguous. But as I think is now fairly well known, more than 30 studies since the early 1990s, primarily in the USA and UK, have researched the links between people management and business performance. And there is some strong evidence that there are correlations.

One reason for there not yet being clear proof is that many different methodologies have been used for these reviews. Depending upon your own particular biases, this either makes it difficult to compare the reviews and draw robust conclusions or, because the different approaches provide the same type of findings, reinforces the overall conclusions.'

Reader: '*So why do you say that the conclusions are ambiguous?'*

Author: 'There are a couple of reasons. For one thing, most of the reviews have only looked at single people management practices, not the effects of an integrated 'HR system' which is where I think we need to focus when we're talking about HCM. More importantly, there is quite a lot of evidence for correlation, but much less that demonstrates causation. Only a few of the reviews have been truly longitudinal. That means that, as well as a correlation between the data, the people management data needs to come from before the business performance data. And that other factors that could have led to changes in business performance need to be controlled or ruled out. The lack of evidence for causation inevitably raises questions over whether companies are successful because of effective people management practices, or because their positive financial results enable them to invest more in their people.

Interestingly, a complexity perspective helps to understand some of the results. For example, complexity recognizes that the difficulties in delivering proof of impact are not weaknesses in theory but simply reflect the idiosyncratic nature of business and the ambiguity inherent in the issues that are involved. Given this, and given people's ability to find data that will support what they want to believe, I am not sure we ever have enough proof to convince those who do not want to be convinced. I like one of Stephen Overell's quotes (2003):

The value of good people management is and will always be a matter of faith, conviction and of basic intuitive rightness, irrespective of clever proofs that may one day emerge.

Some of the studies also seem to suggest that there is a level of covariation between people management practices and business performance and that these act as a virtuous circle, reinforcing one another and increasing the overall effect. Again, I think a systems or complexity viewpoint helps explain why that is.

Plus, of course, complexity would argue that we are never going to be able to predict changes in business performance in the way some people hope. It suggests that instead of looking at these large-scale reviews we'd be better off having conversations about potential permutations and learning about the links within an individual organization. Because of this, longer-term but smaller-scale research producing deeper, more meaningful but less reliable research may be the most appropriate form of research. This would includes in-company studies, such as that conducted at RBS and Standard Chartered, and small-scale research projects like Lynda Gratton's Leading Edge Consortium which has involved seven major companies and a large hospital. And, of course, nothing will ever beat doing this type of research in your own organization for yourself ...'

Basic People Management Practices

The first level of research I want to look at suggests that there are some basic people management practices that generally contribute to organizational performance. For example, the CIPD's Future of Work research led by David Guest at King's College London (Guest *et al.*, 2000) has found that profits per employee increase with the number of people management practices in place. Note, though, that in research for the CIPD's black box report, Purcell *et al.* (2002) found that dissatisfaction with existing HR policies has a greater demotivating effect than the absence of the same HR policies. The net conclusion would seem to be that the more practices there are the better, as long as they are executed well.

Guest's research also highlights the way that practices are enhanced by operating in combination with other practices. This supports other research which has found that, in general, the adoption of single practices does not deliver the same level of improvements as do changes in the whole 'HR system'.

These conclusions are broadly supported in two pieces of research by Michael West, currently at Aston, and the consultancy, Watson Wyatt.

Research by Michael West

Mike West and colleagues followed a small number of single-site man-ufacturing companies over a five-year period, looking at which man-agement actions really made a difference to a company's performance. The study found that 'the acquisition and development of skills (selec-tion, induction, training and appraisal) and job design (job variety and responsibility, skill flexibility and teamworking) are significant predic-tors of both change in profitability and change in productivity' (West et al., 1997). In total, 19 per cent of the variation between companies in changes in profitability was a result of differences in an organization's people management practices.

The next most important management action was research and devel-opment, which accounted for 8 per cent of the variation in profitability. Strategic positioning, investment in quality and money invested in tech-nology resulted in even lower impacts. The fact that none of these management actions had very high impact supports the view that improvements in profitability and productivity are mainly caused by factors emerging from the system as a whole.

West went on to research people management in the world's third largest employer, the UK's National Health Service (NHS). Surveying HR directors from 61 acute hospitals in England and controlling for hospital size, number of doctors per bed and local health needs, West's team found strong associations between the extent and sophistication of appraisals, training and teamworking and lower patient mortality. A hospital that appraises around 20 per cent more staff and trains around 20 per cent more appraisers is likely to have 1090 fewer deaths per 100 000 admissions or a decrease in over 12 per cent of the expected total (West et al., 2002).

Research by Watson Wyatt

Watson Wyatt has developed a Human Capital Index (HCI) that quan-tifies a company's people management policies and practices and has been shown to link to, and inform, the company's market value (Watson Wyatt, 2002).

Watson Wyatt's 1999 study used multiple regression analysis on data from 400 US- and Canada-based organizations to identify 30 key people management practices that were associated with a 30 per cent increase in market value. In 2000, similar research was conducted on 250 companies from 16 countries across Europe and this found 19 key HR practices to be associated with a 26 per cent increase in market value. These studies only demonstrated correlation, but in 2001 Watson Wyatt repeated their study with 500 North American companies and compared two different correlations for 51 companies that had participated in the 1999 and 2001 surveys:

- Correlation between the 1999 HCI score and 2001 financial performance was 0.41.
- Correlation between 1999 financial performance and 2001 HCI scores was 0.19.

The fact that the first correlation was statistically larger shows that the main direction of causality is from better people management practices to financial performance. However the second correlation indicates that the relationship applies in the other direction too.

Watson Wyatt's 2001 research identified 43 specific people management practices in five dimensions which in total were associated with a 47 per cent increase in market value. The practices were not just better or better-funded programmes but completely different practices from those used by lower performing organizations. Table 3.1 shows how

Table 3.1: Watson Wyatt's 2001 research	
Dimensions	*Impact on market value%*
Total rewards and accountability	16.5
Collegial, flexible workplace	9.0
Recruiting and retention excellence	7.9
Communications integrity	7.1
Focused HR service technologies	6.5
Prudent use of resources	−33.9

much a one-standard deviation increase in all of the practices within each of these dimensions could be expected to increase a company's market value.

As the table shows, the research also raised a need for caution over six conventional practices that can diminish shareholder value. These are included in one dimension, identified in the table as 'prudent use of resources'. These practices include training employees for future jobs and giving employees the opportunity to evaluate their peers. Watson Wyatt stress that it is not these practices themselves that are at fault, but the fact that the majority of organizations implementing them do not align them with strategy or execute them properly.

Of course, we know that it is generally possible to find data to support any particular argument and you may find it interesting to speculate whether Watson Wyatt would have found the same conclusions if they were a training provider rather than a reward consultancy (see also McBassi's perspectives in Chapter 11).

Best and Best Fit People Management Practices

Going beyond the basics involves entering into an ongoing debate about whether there are universal best practices that can be applied irrespective of the circumstances, or whether it is more effective to seek best fit for a particular organization. We will review these two approaches, plus another three alternatives.

Best Practice

Best practice is a specific, universal perspective that assumes there is one best way of doing things, one set of practices and one way of performing them that if always followed will mean that any organization can improve its performance. One difficulty or, potentially, advantage in this perspective is that there is little consensus about what makes up the set of best practices. There is, however, greater agreement that the effect of best practices is cumulative – the more best practices that are applied and the more effective the practices, the better the results. A further finding is that best practices act together systemically, reinforcing one another and not working at cross purposes (like training for team skills but paying for individual performance).

Bundling Approach

A more flexible version of best practice acknowledges that there is more than one specific combination of appropriate practices which are known as 'bundles' and that these combinations will vary according to context, for example:

- generic strategy (differentiation, focus or cost leadership);
- workforce strategy, for example high involvement or high commitment (soft HRM), or high performance (hard HRM);
- industrial sector or type of organization (public company, private company, public sector, voluntary sector);
- organization structure (for example Mintzberg's simple structure, machine bureaucracy, professional bureaucracy, divisionalized structure and adhocracy);
- organization life-cycle stage (birth, growth, maturity and decline);
- specific organizational and broader environmental context;

The Work Foundation (Fauth and Horner, 2005) also emphasizes the importance of responding to the organization's current level of performance, finding that in order to move from poor to stable performance:

- organizations should make improvements like changing their CEO, introducing appraisals for managers and increasing product specialization;
- they should not downsize, focus on responding to legislation or introduce individual performance-related pay.

To move from stable to high performance:

- organizations should make improvements, like improving upward communication, introducing appraisal for non-managers and increasing product innovation;
- they should not change their CEO or launch a culture change programme but they should not avoid change either.

Although most examples of 'bundling' only deal with a small selection of these possibilities, this list of contextual factors shows that there could potentially be an almost infinite number of possible bundles to choose from.

Best Fit

Best fit is a flexible perspective that, in contrast to best practice, assumes that the appropriateness of people management practices is contingent on external or vertical fit with the business strategy. It recognizes that what works in one organization will not necessarily work in another. For example, as Peter Reilly, a director of the IES, explains:

> There's been a lively debate about best practice. In general, I don't like the focus on best practice as I think it often substitutes for good thinking. So I tend to go with the contingent view that what's important is how you put together your own people strategy given your own particular context. Given this, each organization needs to develop its own model describing the impact of people management. What are the raw materials, the bundles of activities, which will improve its performance? So, for example, Ulrich talks about capability times commitment. Penny Tamkin from the IES talks about access, ability, attitude and application [see Tamkin, 2005]. Organizations need to understand their raw materials, deploy them in the right sort of way, align them with the business strategy and then grow them.

The research evidence to support this position is ambiguous but conceptually it seems right that a strategic approach to people management should emphasize the need for fit between business strategy and people management. We have already seen that Porter's competitive positioning stresses the need for strategic fit between the business strategy and an organization's activity systems. Resource-based strategy requires an organization's capabilities to be matched with the opportunities available in the external environment. Purcell (1999) uses this to point out an inconsistency between a belief in best practice and resource-based strategy:

> How, then, can the universalism of best practice be squared with the view that only some resources and routines are important and valuable by being rare and imperfectly imitable?

Peter Cappelli at Wharton, author of *The New Deal at Work* (1999), links best fit with Hamel and Prahalad's core competencies and notes that there are many companies with best fit strategies:

> There are examples in virtually every industry of firms that have very distinctive management practices ... Distinctive human resource

practices shape the core competencies that determine how firms compete. (Cappelli and Crocker-Hefter, 1996)

Quoted more recently, Cappelli notes:

There aren't best practices that work across the board. It's about fitting people practices and management to the strategy. In some companies, it's smart to invest in people; in others, it may make sense to just churn them through. (Grossman, 2005)

In addition, it is well understood that strategic management is about being distinctive, not being the same. Best fit should contribute directly to this distinctiveness and the provision of competitive advantage. Gratton and Ghoshal (2005) also suggest that organizations need to go beyond best practice. They describe how RBS, Nokia and BP use standard best practices but have also developed idiosyncratic 'signature processes', reflecting the history and values of the organization. Rather than starting with shared knowledge from outside the organization, the development of these processes was led by internal executives. Because of this, the signature processes have successfully harnessed people's passion and energy which has helped drive organizational performance.

Configurational Approach

The configurational version of best fit argues that, to drive alignment, practices must be internally or horizontally consistent as well as externally contingent and congruent with the business strategy. This approach also recognizes that organizations are systems so unless the organization has found a key leverage point, trying to use a single lever to generate change is likely to fail. This is because the system as a whole is likely to act to maintain the status quo.

The approach posits that in order to support a business strategy, an organization needs a unified set of coherent and consistent people management practices that support each other; other management practices; business processes; technological systems and the organization's structure. This need for horizontal alignment can also be extended to external labour markets and employment legislation as well as current employee requirements.

Because there are an infinite number of potential business strategies there are also an infinite number of possible configurations in people management practices. This means that, with the bundling and configurational approaches, there are only very fine distinctions between best practice and best fit.

Flexible Approach

One criticism of best fit is that, given the complexity within and outside an organization, the rigidity some believe is inherent in a contingent perspective will inhibit ongoing effectiveness. For example, the CIPD's Armstrong and Baron (2002) state:

> An excessive pursuit of 'fit' with the *status quo* will inhibit the flexibility of approach essential in turbulent conditions.

The flexible approach recognizes that too much or too fixed an alignment can potentially be a problem. Fit has to change as fast as the environment. This requirement could be seen as an integral part of any best fit approach, since to maintain best fit when the environment changes people management strategy will in any case need to be readjusted to the new environment and any resulting changes in the business strategy. But it is also worth recognizing that flexibility and agility are central requirements if best fit is not going to result in hard wiring a position that will only be relevant in the short term. Boxall and Purcell (2003) explain this need for flexibility:

> A more helpful model for practice is one in which fit with existing competitive strategy is developed *simultaneously* with flexibility in the range of skills and behaviours that may be needed to cope with different competitive scenarios in the future…HR strategy *should* give effect to the firm's current competitive goals, by recruiting, developing and retaining people with the sort of skills and motivations needed in the firm's competitive sector. However, it is also highly desirable that HR strategy encourages staff to think 'outside the square', that it helps to build the sort of skills needed for new business capabilities in the future.

The Work Foundation provides four case studies of organizations aligning practices with changed business strategies. They acknowledge that given uncertainty, competition and limited resources, alignment is likely to be a tortuous process. However, one reason it is important to try to drive in alignment, even if this means that people management practices lag some way behind the business, is that these practices act as powerful symbols of what is important. Gratton (in Gratton *et al.*, 1999) explains that these symbols have more importance than organizational rhetoric in creating the reality in which people are managed and rewarded:

> Corporate mission statements may extol customer delight or product innovation, but when the communication fanfare is over and the customer-focus workshops have been completed, what is left? A group of people trying to make sense of the paradoxes and mixed messages with which they are faced ... Faced with this plethora of contradictory messages the employees, in their quest for 'sense-making', look at which behaviours are rewarded, which skills are promoted, and who is developed. It is the messages from reward, appraisal, and training processes, not simply the corporate rhetoric, which form the basis of sense-making and which give the steer on how to behave. If these people policies and processes lack linkage and fail to reinforce business strategy, then the performance of the business will suffer.

The Work Foundation conclude that:

> Some argue, with some justification, that it is possible to become too obsessed with strategic alignment as an end in itself. And if people in an organization are having to think about this 'fit' with any frequency, then it is probably missing the point. The notion of organizations as flexible adaptive systems can have resonance here, and is being embraced by a number of academics and practitioners as they seek to break free from the concept that organizations have to get all their structural and strategic 'ducks in a row' before change can even start. (Turner, 2004)

This is an important point, particularly as we tend to be able to see good fit with hindsight rather than foresight. Fit should not be something that people have to have conversations about, it is something that should be developed through the right sort of conversations.

Best and Best Fit People Management Practices Research Evidence
Important research into best fit approaches includes a study by Miles and Snow (1984) that identified differences between the business strategies followed by 'defenders', 'prospectors' and 'analysers' and their approaches to staffing and development, performance appraisal and

pay policies. Similar research was conducted by Schuler and Jackson (1987) who reviewed existing literature looking for evidence of links between competitive strategy (Porter's cost leadership and two types of differentiators – innovation and quality enhancement), desired employee behaviours and particular people management practices. The study found that different competitive strategies require different blends of employee behaviour and this requires people management practices that support the development of these behaviours. For example, a cost-reduction strategy would need to reward people working in repetitive jobs with narrow job descriptions for output and predictable behaviour. There would be little training and limited career paths. To support the innovation strategy, on the other hand, a company will need high levels of creative, risk-oriented and cooperative behaviour. The company's people management practices would therefore need to encourage co-operation and creativity and provide considerable opportunities for career development. Appropriate activities would include:

> Selecting highly skilled individuals, giving employees more discretion, using minimal controls, making greater investment in human resources, providing more resources for experimentation, allowing and even rewarding occasional failure, and appraising performance for its long-run implications. (Schuler and Jackson, 1987)

A third study was conducted by Jeffrey Arthur (1992), who studied 30 US steel mini-mills, some of which followed a control strategy emphasizing rules and procedures with little employee participation. Others followed a commitment strategy with more participation, training and higher wages. Mini-mills using the commitment strategy had significantly lower employee turnover, higher levels of productivity and quality, and lower scrap rates. Arthur found some, although not statistically significant, evidence for best fit, with the better performing differentiated mills using a commitment-oriented people management approach and the best performing cost-leadership mills using control-oriented people management. This implies that following a cost-leadership strategy reduces the need and incentive to engage in generic best practices.

Some of the best-known best practice research has resulted in similar findings which, to me at least, underline the primacy of the best fit approach.

Research by Jeffrey Pfeffer

Pfeffer (1998) reviewed financial outcomes in each of the top five companies in different industry sectors to identify seven basic dimensions these all had in common and that he believes characterize the people management processes that improve organizational performance:

1. Employment security.
2. Selective hiring.
3. Self-managed teams or teamworking.
4. High pay contingent on company performance.
5. Extensive training.
6. Reduction of status differences.
7. Sharing information.

Pfeffer also questions some of the management processes traditionally thought to be best practices. For example, he believes reward should focus on organizational performance rather than individual effort. He warns against the use of short-term or fixed contracts and the increased reliance on a contingent workforce as this sends the message to employees that they are readily dispensable and are not considered strategically important to the business. Pfeffer responds to Arthur's argument that a cost-leadership strategy means that it does not have to support its people so effectively:

> Although it may be true that certain types of strategies virtually necessitate the use of high-commitment work practices, there is little evidence that such work practices don't also help firms following other strategies such as cost minimization ... Obviously, how one would implement these practices will vary significantly, based on a given organization's strategy and its particular technology and market environment. What teams and incentive compensation might look like in retailing would probably differ from what one would observe in a manufacturer of arc welding equipment. In this sense, one would want to think systematically about the particular skills and behaviors one needs to execute the particular strategy in a specific market environment and obviously adjust the implementation of these practices to fit those requirements. However, there is an important distinction between the contingent nature of the *implementation* of these practices, which everyone would agree is necessary, and the idea that the practices themselves do not provide benefit in many, if not most, situations (Pfeffer, 1994).

Not only do Singapore Airline and Virgin Atlantic, pursuing strategies of service differentiation, value their employees: So, too, does Southwest Airline, with the lowest costs – and the lowest fares – in the domestic airline industry. Southwest emphasizes training, selective recruiting, profit sharing and stock ownership and has never had a layoff or furlough in its history – all elements of high-commitment work systems (Pfeffer, 1998).

All Pfeffer is saying is that his seven practices are consistently good things to have in an organization – he is not saying these practices need to be applied in the same way. In fact, he provides a diagnostic alignment process to drive horizontal and vertical alignment that starts with the business strategy in the same way as best fit (Pfeffer, 1994):

1. Determine the organization's strategy or strategic intent
2. What skills and behaviours are necessary to implement the strategy
3. List the organization's management practices
4. Assess external congruence (vertical alignment) and internal consistency (horizontal alignment).

Pfeffer (1998) also responds effectively to the challenge over whether alignment is really a good thing or whether it limits flexibility. Firstly, external congruence:

'If the organization's practices are so externally congruent, doesn't that very congruence and the interconnectedness among the elements make change difficult?'

Answer: 'I haven't observed that fundamental organizational change to meet new market demands occurs without friction or delay even in firms that have poorly designed management practices.'

Secondly, internal consistency:

'What if the strategy is incorrect or must be changed due to changes in the competitive environment? Wouldn't the internal consistency of the various aspects of the organization make such change more difficult?'

Answer: 'The premise of the question seems to confuse chaos with change. An organization that has training in teamwork but no team-based incentives, little implementation of self-managed teams, and little sharing of the information necessary to utilize the teamwork training is not necessarily better able to change. Such an organization simply has many processes operating at cross purposes and in ways inconsistent with obtaining profits through people.'

Research by Mark Huselid

Huselid calls his version of best practice a 'high-performance work system' (HPWS) and notes (Becker *et al.*, 2001) that an HPWS:

- links its selection and promotion decisions to validated competency models;
- develops strategies that provide timely and effective support for the skills demanded by the firm's strategy implementation; and
- enacts compensation and performance management policies that attract, retain and motivate high-performance employees.

Over the last decade, Huselid and his colleagues have used biannual large-scale surveys to study the relationship between HPWS and the performance of around 3000 publicly held companies in terms of sales revenue, shareholder value and profitability. A questionnaire sent to senior HR practitioners has been used to develop a High-Performance HR Index and financial data has been gathered from subsequent years to ensure results demonstrate causation not just correlation. The research has found that the people management practices, outcomes and business results of high-performance to low-performance firms are all very different. Becker *et al.* (2001) explain:

> They devote considerably more resources to recruiting and selection, they train with much greater vigor, they do a lot more performance management and tie compensation to it, they use teams to a much greater extent and they are much less likely to be unionized. Indeed, the most striking attributes of these comparisons is not any one management practice – it is not recruiting *or* training *or* compensation. Rather, the differences are much more comprehensive – and systemic.

HPWS firms employ roughly double the number of HR professionals per employee as other firms. In addition, their HR professionals are more likely to be rated positively in both their traditional and strategic roles. HPWS firms are also more likely to have developed a comprehensive measurement system for communicating non-financial information to employees.

HPWS firms are also likely to exhibit dramatically higher perform-ance (Becker *et al.*, 2001):

> Employee turnover was close to half, sales per employee were four times as great, and the ratio of firm market value to the book value of assets ... was more than three times as large in high-performing companies.

By correlating the High-Performance Index with a company's finan-cial performance, Huselid has found that if a company increases its Index score by one standard deviation (about 14 per cent better) rev-enue is increased by to up to $42 000 per employee per year. Becker and Huselid (2001) comment on these findings, stating:

> While these results provide dramatic evidence of the potential financial benefits of a properly designed HR system, we like to remind managers that understanding that value is really only part of the battle. A few simple tweaks in the HR system will not immediately send a firm's stock price soaring. Remember that our HR Index describes an entire HR system. Changing a firm's system to the extent needed to produce such effects is a huge undertaking, requiring time, insight, and considerable effort. If it could be done overnight, HR systems could be easily imitated and would lose much of their strategic character.

Becker and Huselid also emphasize the inimitability of an HPWS that is the precondition for a resource-based strategy and hence com-petitive advantage. Although Huselid's research provides very little real evidence that internal and external fit increases performance, Huselid and his colleagues infer that a company's HPWS needs to be aligned with its business strategy, like best fit:

> Organizational HPWS are highly idiosyncratic and must be tailored carefully to each firm's individual situation to achieve optimum impact ... 'Best practices' ... are only a point of departure. While becoming 'best in class' may be a necessary condition for ultimately improving firm performance, it is not a sufficient condition. The more crucial strategic decision is ... how the total HRM system is designed, such that it supports key business priorities. Without the latter, the HRM system will be just a 'best in class' version of an HRM function in crisis. (Becker *et al.*, 1997)

> 'In fact, a key distinguishing characteristic of a High-Performance Work System is not just the adoption of appropriate HR policies and

practices ... but also the way in which these practices are deployed. In an HPWS, the firm's HR policies and practices show a strong alignment with the firm's competitive strategy and operational goals. Moreover, each HPWS will be different. No single best example exists; each organization must customize its system to meet its own unique strengths and needs ... high-performing firms are characterized by greater use of incentive pay. However, the behaviors and outcomes that are being reinforced will differ substantially across firms and strategies. (Becker, Huselid and Ulrich, 2001)

Figure 3.1 provides a graph from Huselid and Becker's 1996 index (Becker and Huselid, 2001) demonstrating the extent to which a firm's HR system is consistent with Huselid's principles of an HPWS plotted against market value per employee. Two things are very noticeable. Firstly, the financial returns from HPWS are considerable. Secondly, the returns from investment are not linear – there appear to be three distinct phases of experience with improvements at both the low and the high end of the distribution giving rise to benefits that are nearly four times as great as changes within the larger middle ground of the distribution.

Huselid believes that the area of the graph between the lowest and the twentieth percentile ranking marks companies with poor people management practices. Improving these practices provides a quick and significant return so that 'the HRM system creates value simply by getting out of the way'. In the broad, middle range, from the twentieth to the

The strategic impact of the HR system

Source: Becker, B.E. and Huselid, M.A. (2001). 'The Strategic Impact of HR' Balanced Scorecard Report. Harvard Business School Publishing. May-June.

Figure 3.1 The strategic impact of the HR system

sixtieth percentile, companies have already developed relatively good people management practices. Simply getting them even better has little marginal impact on firm performance. The approach does no damage but does not yet indicate a strategic approach to people management. Finally, above the sixtieth percentile the pay-offs begin to rise as quickly as they did below the twentieth percentile, but for different reasons. In this range, companies have comprehensive HR systems that are aligned with their company strategy and are internally consistent. It is in this third group that Huselid believes HR begins to emerge as a strategic asset. These companies:

> Not only have adopted the appropriate HRM practices and implemented them effectively throughout the firm but also have begun to integrate the HRM system into the strategic 'fabric' of the firm … combining the appropriate HRM policies and practices into an internally coherent system that is directly aligned with business priorities and operating initiatives most likely to create economic value. (Becker *et al.*, 2001)

Huselid emphasizes the need to ensure best fit in people management practices by linking this back to the need to create differentiation. He criticizes companies that understand the need to differentiate themselves in terms of corporate strategy, but then manage their employees in a way that is wholly generic:

> Competitive advantage is created by being different in ways that are meaningful to customers. For that reason, it is important for firms to embrace the difference, to go against the grain, to value differentiation externally and internally. Such a perspective has distinct implications for internal workforce practices, and part of our message is to urge firms to tread cautiously in applying the 'best practices' of others to their own circumstances. (Huselid *et al.*, 2005)

Comparing Best Practice and Best Fit

Although best practice and best fit seem to be contradictory perspectives, they are not in fact opposites. The bundling and configurational approaches have already shown how close these two perspectives can become. In fact, the differences between them are mainly about level of detail and the way practices are applied and implemented, the 'how' rather than the 'what'. Best practices can be seen to describe a level of HR architecture or broad policy matters which Guest *et al.* (2000) refer to as 'the principles underlying the choice of practices' and which it may make sense for all organizations to use. A company may then choose to emphasize certain elements of these practices more than others and will certainly implement them in different ways which introduces a level of alignment. Huselid and Becker (1995) support this distinction, stating:

> We believe that the HR management system–firm performance relationship is characterized by both a 'best practice' and 'alignment/ contingency' dimension, and that both dimensions have a powerful influence at different levels of analysis … For any particular element of an HR system's architecture, there may be a variety of specific HR *policies and practices* that are an appropriate fit with the firm's strategy and operational demands. This implies that two firms could have a similar HR architecture with respect to a reward-performance linkage, though manifestly different pay practices.

The CIPD's Armstrong and Baron (2002) note that fit needs to be achieved first and then best practices selected to support this:

> It is accepted by most commentators that 'best fit' is more important than 'best practice'. There can be no universal prescriptions for HRM policies and practices. It all depends. This is not to say that 'good practice' or 'leading-edge practice' – i.e. practice that does well in one successful environment – should be ignored … The starting point should be an analysis of the business needs of the firm within its context (culture, structure, technology and processes). This may indicate clearly what has to be done. Thereafter, it may be useful to pick and mix various 'best practice' ingredients, and develop an approach which applies those that are appropriate in a way that is aligned to the identified business needs.

However, in reality, these best fit approaches may actually be very small aspects of an overall people management strategy. Davenport (1999) offers two theories to explain this:

> *God Is in the Details.* Nuances make all the difference. Subtle shadings in the definitions of human capital elements are magnified when applied in a strategic context. Two companies may both look for a 'bias for action' in the people they hire, but they may mean something quite different. In my pharmaceutical company, it may mean 'self motivated application of technical knowledge to develop new products'. In your investment bank, you may define it as 'taking steps to close a deal without waiting for unnecessary analysis or approvals from upstairs.' The Details theory recognizes that industry characteristics, competitive

landscape, culture, and a host of other factors color the definitions of human capital elements. Just as the DNA codes of a wolf monkey and Wolfgang Amadeus Mozart differ by only 2 percent, so may small differences in the definition of human capital elements have profound effects on strategic outcomes.

Execution Makes the Difference. Two companies may use similar words and phrases to define their human capital needs but take widely divergent approaches to filling those needs. Differences in hiring practices, learning strategies, work environment, reward policies, and communication can have a significant influence on the effectiveness with which organizations manage their human capital. To paraphrase Thomas Edison, the genius of human capital may reside in the perspiration of execution rather than in the inspiration of the definition.

Conversations in Best People Management Practices

Best Fit at Siemens

Siemens provides a broad range of technology and services from designing traffic lights to manufacturing superconducting magnets and from managing back-office processes to maintaining a fleet of electric trains. The company employs 21 000 people in the UK. I spoke to Peter Merrick, Corporate Personnel Director for Siemens plc:

Author: 'How do you ensure that your people strategy is aligned with Siemens' business strategy, for the group and the individual businesses within it?'

Merrick: 'We have a separate business strategy, people strategy and HR strategy, but these all need to be aligned and reviewed regularly, so the people strategy is based upon what we want to achieve as a business. But the people strategy also influences the business strategy – HR needs to contribute to the way the business is run. For example, there are chronic skill shortages in power generation in this country and this imposes limits on our growth in our business in this area, there's a caveat about what's feasible. As another example, we're developing a kernel of specialist skills in our research institute. We find that having these research skills gives other parts of the organization an entrée too. For example, our research people have developed a tool for railway maintenance that has helped us build relationships and has given us opportunities to introduce the transport division and sell rolling stock.

The people strategy varies according to the business. The essence is still the same but we'll deploy it in different ways depending on what the business is. We've got about 5000 people in manufacturing and the rest of the organization are in sales, after-sales and consultancy. These are all areas where client relationships are key so we need to build an engaged workforce – that's how we're trying to differentiate ourselves from our competitors.

In power generation turbines, our engineers need to be able to respond at the drop of a hat to provide an emergency service or just planned maintenance for sites in India or China. In our railway depots where we service rolling stock, our workforce need to focus on getting stock in and getting it out in the minimum of time. Engagement is very important to us in both groups but how we develop it is different. In manufacturing, engagement isn't as important. The reality is that there's a different set of tools and techniques. In our vehicle factory we make control panels for Range Rovers. We complete one panel every 367 minutes and if we slip up or miss a slot we get fined £10k. So these staff need to be very customer focused and HR is about ensuring they understand the criticality of delivering on time and that they're participating in quality groups and so on.'

Author: 'So does HR's role look different according to the business and its people strategy?'

Merrick: 'Our businesses and the labour markets they operate in are very different. So in our reward framework for example, all that I can say is that we want a link to performance, we want a certain position in labour market benchmarks and that we want a variable element to drive performance.

After that I start to dry up, apart from saying that I want the HR business partner in the business to apply the framework effectively in their business.

The roles of the business partners are all still largely the same – the headings are the same, but the way these are applied is different. The business partner needs to deliver whatever is appropriate locally. Within human capital management, we're looking at a competency system to help us measure people's capability. But the business partner shouldn't be thinking about this if they're in a business that is threatened with going under. They should be talking about a weekly incentive system to keep the business afloat over the next three months.

The strategy can be more or less sophisticated – it is still the skill set of the HR person that makes the difference. I've tried to develop a metrics and measurement culture to ensure that they all keep business focused. Some of the business partners still haven't got anything in the way of human capital systems or measures but they've developed credibility in the business based on their intelligence, experience and personality. Others have got this credibility and the measures as well and they do even better. And others have got measures and still don't have much impact.'

Best Fit at Motorola

Best known for its mobile telephones, Motorola is a Fortune 100 global communications company that provides seamless mobility products and solutions. The company's three divisions are Connected Home Solutions, Networks and Enterprise Solutions, and Mobile Devices. Motorola believes that the technologies within these divisions are converging, and to take advantage of this, the company is focused on becoming 'One Motorola', emphasizing the need for collaboration across its businesses.

Motorola is also well known for coining the term 'six sigma' to define its approach to quality improvement. When first developed, six sigma was about standardizing the way that defects were counted in a product or process. However, during the last 20 years, Motorola has evolved six sigma into a fully integrated management system that is 'the way work gets done'. The approach is based upon an analytical, fact-based and systematic problem-solving methodology known by the acronym DMAIC:

- Defining the business problem to determine what needs to be improved.
- Measuring the current state against the desired state.
- Analysing the root causes of the business gap.
- Improvement solutions brainstormed, selected and implemented.
- Controlling the improvements by establishing monitoring mechanisms and clear accountabilities.

I talked to Mark Doughty, HR Director, Organization Development, EMEA, and Vanessa Loughlin, Director, Leadership and Diversity, EMEA. I mentioned that I had heard Dave Ulrich talk about Motorola, along with Dell, HP and Sony Ericsson, as good examples of organizations that look at what their business is trying to do, develop people management deliverables to support this and then develop people management practices that lead to these deliverables.

Author: 'How does HR at Motorola go about developing an HR strategy that is so aligned to the business?'

Loughlin: 'HR people tend to construct themselves as separate from the business which leads them to take an internal focus and a lot of HR for HR. There's a different orientation in this company. Our HR people need to have a commercial orientation, they need to understand how the business makes its money – it's part of our core DNA. They need to think like the business, not just HR. We're specialists, our role is about optimizing our people, so we bring different language with us, but it's about couching things in the terms of our managers so they understand us better.

We're leading the organization towards the strategy, pushing it towards One Motorola. So for each of our talent groups, in marketing or whatever, if our succession plans indicate we need to do a search, we'll run a generic research programme on behalf of the businesses and share the costs. Then when we find the people who are at the top of their class in this field, we'll talk to the businesses about how we continue, who wants to take who out for dinner.

HR's part of, and integrated with the business – it's not a separate thing. The HR strategy is derived from the business strategy. We start with the business strategy and then this fans out – there's a product-oriented plan, a people-oriented plan, a sales-oriented one and so on. It's not about 'here is the business plan and by the way, what are the implications for HR?' This ensures there's a line of sight between the business strategy and what we're doing for our people. We're working to even more fully integrate the people planning process through the strategic cycle, using mechanisms managers are familiar with, using the existing rhythm of quarterly and weekly meetings. This helps ensure the process isn't seen as a bolt-on, it makes it easier to integrate it and institutionalize it, to help managers see that people are part of the business plan.'

Doughty: 'We go out and hunt for both transactional and strategic work. This is where the metrics piece comes in. As an example; about 18 months ago we identified that 23 per cent of our sales people generated 67 per cent of our revenue. Our thought processes then took us to ask more questions, for example, is this related just to one account or one country, is this length of service related or account specific and so on, and also back to our business strategy. Our business model is changing away from box shifting towards solution selling; lower volume but higher value and margin. Someone may be a great box shifter today, but will they be a good relationship manager tomorrow?

We asked about how the relationship between our salespeople and revenue would change in a Strategic Account Management environment and drew some hypotheses about the impact on our strategy and the impact on the business. What we found was that there is a fairly regular distribution curve in which four quartiles emerge: people who can't do relationship selling; people who could do it; people who can do it and people who can't not do it. About 23 per cent of our salespeople are in the top quartile and they earn between four and seven times more margin of those in the second quartile. And if everyone in the third quartile had the performance of people in the top quartile this would provide an extra $1 billion revenue per year. We go through periods of open and frozen headcount – times we can recruit and other times we can't. Our analysis led us to a paradigm shift – that when we can find salespeople who get it, we should buy them. Whether we've got positions available at that time doesn't matter. It's an example of effective use of data, but also of how we take action that's linked to the business strategy.'

Author: 'Motorola is obviously famous for its ongoing focus on six sigma, does HR use this approach within its own activities?'

Doughty: 'We're introducing an organizational alignment diagnostic for our in-business folk to use with their business teams to evaluate their business, or their country. It consists of 11 levers, for example, the strategy, which is the most important lever; talent; the organization and so on. If you think about the sigmoid curve, the diagnostic can be used at the top of the curve, for example to react to the signals that change is needed; it can be used in the middle of the curve – when all the signals suggest that there is no need for change – well, sometimes we go to the doctor's, just because it's generally good for our health; and the tool can be used at the bottom of the curve, to help anticipate what's in front of us and accelerate the opportunity. There are five stages to the diagnostic tool.

The first stage is to create a burning platform. It's about taking time out to look at a range of metrics, trends and benchmarks; and to put a value on the potential that could be lost. For example, our average turnover is 5 per cent, but in Russia it's 20 per cent. We've got 120 people so this is 24 people leaving every year. The average recruitment cost is $45 000 per person so this is a cost of over a million dollars per year. This is done, not secretly, but covertly.

The second stage is the development of a strategic future state; working with the country and regional managers to scope out the vision, customer value and employee value with each country represented, each business represented, on a one-pager. The third stage is to look at the 11 levers and to set measures for each one. What are the indicators of high performance, what is the evidence or observations of this, and therefore is this lever a strength or a weakness?

The fourth stage is to bring this forward to the front of the plan in a deep dive summary. And in the fifth stage we identify the top 12 critical success factors; then six critical actions – what are the things you're actually going to do to implement the actions? Then we identify predictive values for the top six actions – what's the potential financial impact of what you're going to do? So you can see that there's a six sigma or DMAIC orientation built in.'

Loughlin: 'I've got a six sigma green belt on my team who helps me ask the right questions. We used six sigma for developing our overall talent supply system – looking at what it is; the strategy; the operating plan; workforce segments and so on. It influences the questions you ask and the baselines you set. Again, the orientation is six sigma. You can use six sigma for any process. The key is to apply it sparingly and to build it in.'

Author: 'You mentioned benchmarking as part of your organizational alignment diagnostic – can you tell me more about Motorola's approach to this?'

Loughlin: 'We won't go out to look at what everyone else is doing just because we want to do something new. There has to be a specific reason that would mean we wanted to explore how other companies do something. We may want to get an idea about something, so we'll talk to our networks or a research company – Corporate Leadership Council (CLC) or Corporate Research Forum. If we want to do it, we'll want to do it quickly, so we'll try to identify who does it better than us, then call around a few people, quite informally.

For example, we wanted to get better at onboarding executives and CLC have a good case study on Amex for this. So we sent in a team to them and shared what we are doing on a reciprocal basis so we could learn some more. We did something similar looking at a company who were doing some good things around development experiences too.'

Doughty: 'Or we may just want some metrics, going back to six sigma. We may want to look at expenditure or cycle time and get a feel for what the measures are in other organizations. If theirs is 20 days and ours is 50 that would feel uncomfortable. You need the baseline to say whether it feels right or wrong, and so you're not just completely internally referenced. But I wouldn't pay to get this information. Most of this is out there. I'd talk to a few people and ask them what they recommend, and check it out on the internet.'

Loughlin: 'We don't have a lot of time for benchmarking studies. We're a consumer business. People want answers tomorrow and the solution implemented the day after tomorrow. We don't have three months to think it through.'

Best fit at Yahoo!

Yahoo! consists of three main concerns – Media, which is Yahoo!'s original business, Marketplace, based around its 2004 acquisition, Kelkoo, and Search, based around the 2003 acquisition, Overture. I talked to Helen Russell, Vice-President, Human Resources, Yahoo! Europe who joined the company in September 2005.

Author: 'I know that you joined Yahoo! with the aim of achieving a closer alignment between HR and Yahoo!'s business strategy. How have you been going about this?'

Russell: 'Our leaders here are all entrepreneurs, they've started up their own companies and typically they don't do HR. But that's changed now and HR and the business are totally in-synch. I speak to my boss at least twice a day and it's because he has things he needs to discuss with me not because he's feeling forced upon. We've used metrics to educate the guys that there is value in HR. The search business is all about algorithms and everything has numbers attached to it so using metrics helps to get people's attention. When I joined, it was suggested that I ask the business what sort of reports they wanted. I said no, they wouldn't know what would be useful for them to know, so I put some reports together and explained to them the value of these reports.'

Author: 'So can you give me any examples of things you've done which are about creating alignment between business and people management strategy?'

Russell: 'The current strategy is about improving operational efficiency and scalability, putting in more control, red tape, processes and systems to help us grow. So as well as improving HR's own effectiveness, for example through some really basic things like outsourcing our European payroll, I've put some metrics together to help the executives have greater clarity and visibility on how to run an operationally-based business. The most effective part of the business has a span of control of one to seven and its organizational depth has most of the people at about level four. This gives us the basis to encourage the rest of the business to operate more like this. We also have a consensual and democratic culture. We want to ensure that this culture spans all the way across the business so we've created some transversal roles − we've called one of these engagement, which is about creating customer engagement consistently across the business.

There's a phenomenal war for talent for individuals and teams in this sector, it's a very aggressive space. There's a humungous amount of calls and poaching. So we need to focus on recruitment and retention and this does mean we sometimes have to increase salaries above what we would ideally offer. We can't afford to procrastinate in recruitment so we have swift, clean recruitment processes that mean we can turn offers around in a day. We know we can never give our employees the annual increases that would compare against the 25 per cent they could get from going and joining Google or MSN, but we need to be able to give people as much opportunity to progress internally as we can. One of the things I've done is targeting our recruiters on ensuring that 30 per cent of vacancies are filled with internal hires and I've asked the President to help me lobby the business to embrace this approach.

We get hung up on what makes people stay with us in the same way a lot of companies get hung up on why people leave. We ask people about what makes them want to work the long hours they do and it's always the same answer – the thing that makes the difference is our fun culture. I know a lot of companies that have 'fun' as a core value, but you don't usually see it in practice. Here, it's really true – we've just had our work conference in Tenerife and this included a beach volleyball competition, our Music group presenting a session that had Coldplay expressing their gratitude for promotion and this week we have Tom Cruise as guest speaker in our Sunnyvale campus. For a 23-year-old employee this stuff is really cool. And it's something we can do because our business is so broad and we do so much more than just search – we have music and movie properties too.

I'm also trying to ensure that we keep things simple. Last year after I arrived we had a guy wandering around dressed as Elvis to promote the opportunity to win a holiday for making a referral. It says a lot for our fun culture that we could get an Elvis guy to walk round the office but it was too complex, people just talked about there being someone walking around dressed as Elvis and didn't see the connection to the referral program. Now they know that can get 2500 Euros for referring someone who then joins us, period. Our average age is 29 so our managers don't need sophisticated competency frameworks, just basic management training. We were trying to serve nouvelle cuisine to people who just want great hot dogs.'

Summary

Reader: *'So are there any particular points you would want to high-light from these case studies?'*

Author: 'I think the three case studies demonstrate some important points about best fit. The Siemens case study shows how fit varies according to business unit within a diversified group. In contrast, Motorola's experience demonstrates how a particular fit can apply across a number of business units. (These are relatively similar businesses but I think there is also an element of best practice bundling here.) In this case study, fit refers to both the way Motorola manages and develops people to support 'One Motorola', and more significantly, to how the company's philosophy to managing people mirrors the approach and the language of the business, through the use of the six sigma/DMAIC process. I am not suggesting that all companies should use DMAIC or that six sigma is the best way to manage people for human capital. Indeed, although I support some of the perspectives of this approach, particularly its focus on the future state, I have some concerns about its heavy focus on measurement and in particular, the way it seeks to quantify future benefits. However, in the same way that RBS's and T-Mobile's approaches are well aligned with those businesses and their competitive environments, Motorola's DMAIC approach seems to be very well aligned for them. So to me, this is an example of best fit in HCM, rather than an example of what HCM must be.

Lastly, the Yahoo! case study demonstrates how a broad range of processes including organization development, recruitment, retention and reward have all been very specifically focused on Yahoo!'s stage of development, employee base and business strategy. So they are three very different case studies. But I think, and although it is difficult to prove it statistically, that together with the research we covered earlier they do seem to provide convincing evidence for best fit. The key to me is Huselid's graph. Although again there is no proof, it seems clear to me that there is something different going on below the twentieth and above the sixtieth percentiles. These are qualitative changes, they are not just about more of the same thing.'

Reader: *'They mark the change from basic practice, to best practice, to best fit?'*

Author: 'Yes, I think that's right. The interesting thing at these change points, or inflection points, is that a small change in activity makes a big change in impact. I don't think these points mark a whole new set of practices. I think the twentieth percentile mark indicates a point where all the right basic practices are in place, For example, all of the good practices from Watson Wyatt's research. After this point, organizations are starting to combine practices systemically, to form coherent bundles of activities. It suggests you can't really form the bundles until you've got all those basic practices in place.

It's the same sort of change at the sixtieth percentile point. It's where a coherent set of practices start to become linked to business strategy and a certain amount of differentiation is introduced. Again, it implies that you don't get benefits from these vertical linkages until there is a bundle of best practices in place to support them. It's an example of the Pareto principle. Best practice should always form the bulk of people management practice but it is the smaller amount of more specific practices that provide the greatest benefit.'

References

Armstrong, M. and Baron, A. (2002). *Strategic HRM: The key to improved business performance*. Chartered Institute of Personnel and Development.

Arthur, J.B. (1992). 'The link between business strategy and industrial relations systems in American steel mills', *Industrial and Labor Relations Review*, **45**(3), 488–506.

Becker, B.E. and Huselid, M.A. (2001). 'The strategic impact of HR', *Balanced Scorecard Report*. May–June, 3–5.

Becker, B.E., Huselid, M.A. and Ulrich, D. (2001). *The HR Scorecard*. Harvard Business School Press.

Becker, B.E., Huselid, M.A., Pickus, P.S. and Spratt, M.F. (1997). 'HR as a source of shareholder value: research and recommendations', *Human Resource Management* **36**(1) Spring, 39–47.

Boxall, P. and Purcell, J. (2003). *Strategy and Human Resource Management*. Palgrave Macmillan.

Cappelli, P. (1999). *The New Deal at Work: Managing the Market-Driven Workforce*. Harvard Business School Press.

Cappelli, P. and Crocker-Hefter, A. (1996). 'Distinctive human resources are the firm's core competencies', *Organizational Dynamics*, **24** (3), 7–21.

Davenport, T.O. (1999). *Human Capital – What It Is and Why People Invest It*. Jossey-Bass Publishers.

Fauth, R. and Horner, L. (2005). *Workplace Trends Survey 2005*. The Work Foundation.

Gratton, L. and Ghoshal, S. (2005). 'Beyond Best Practice', *MIT Sloan Management Review*. **46**(3), Spring, 49–57.

Gratton, L., Hope Hailey, V.H., Stiles, P. and Truss, C. (1999). *Strategic Human Resource Management: Corporate Rhetoric and Human Reality*. Oxford University Press.

Grossman, R. (2005). 'Blind Investment', *HR Magazine*, January.

Guest, D.E., Michie, J., Sheehan, M., Conway N. and Metochi, M. (2000). *Effective People Management*. Chartered Institute of Personnel and Development.

Huselid, M.A. and Becker, B.E. (1995). *The Strategic Impact of High Performance Work Systems*. Rutgers University.

Huselid, M.A., Becker, B.E. and Beatty, R.W. (2005). *The Workforce Scorecard*. Harvard Business School Press.

Miles, R. and Snow, C. (1984). 'Designing strategic human resources systems', *Organizational Dynamics*. Summer, 36–52.

Overell, S. (2003). 'Time to reflect on HR's influence', *Personnel Today*, 2 September, 11.

Pfeffer, J. (1994). *Competitive Advantage through People: Unleashing the power of the work force.* Harvard Business School Press.

Pfeffer, J. (1998). *The Human Equation: Building profits by putting people first.* Harvard Business School Press.

Purcell, J. (1999). 'Best practice and best fit: chimera or cul-de-sac', *Human Resource Management Journal*, **9**(3), 26–41.

Purcell J., Kinnie, N., Hutchinson S., Rayton, B. and Swart, J. (2002). *Understanding the People and Performance Link: Unlocking the Black Box.* Chartered Institute of Personnel and Development.

Schuler, R. and Jackson, S. (1987). Linking competitive strategies and human resource management practices. Academy of Management Executive. **1**(3), 207–219.

Tamkin, P. (2005). *The Contribution of Skills to Business Performance* (Publication RW39). Department for Education and Skills.

Turner, N. (2004). *Achieving Strategic Alignment of Business and Human Resources.* The Work Foundation.

Watson Wyatt (2002). 'Human Capital Index: Human Capital as a Lead Indicator of Shareholder Value'.www.watsonwyatt.com.

West, M.W., Borrill, C., Dawson, J., Scully, J., Carter, M., Anelay, S., Paterson, M. and Waring, J. (2002). 'The link between the management of employees and patient mortality in acute hospitals', *International Journal of Human Resource Management*, **13**,(8), December, 1299–1310.

West, M., Patterson, M., Lawthom, R. and Nickell, S. (1997). *Impact of People Management Practices on Business Performance.* Institute of Personnel and Development.

4

Intangible Capability through People

Reader: *'So what are we talking about here?'*

Author: 'The formal definition of intangibles is that they are things which are incapable of being realized or defined. They're without physical substance, they're non-monetary and they cannot be seen or touched. They behave in a very different way to tangible assets. So, for example, physical resources can only be used for one activity at a time. Intangibles can be deployed for various purposes at the same time. Tangible assets depreciate with use and get used up through production, so they have limited numbers of applications. Intangibles have multiple applications without any reduction in their value and some intangibles like knowledge even appreciate and develop the more they are used. The law of decreasing returns means that the more a tangible asset is used, the lower the marginal return. So tangible assets need to be controlled and managed with a scarcity mentality. Network effects mean that the more some intangibles are used, the higher the return. You're best off with an abundance mentality to manage these: a mental model that assumes there are always opportunities for adding and creating value.

Largely because of these reasons, intangibles are becoming more important. For example, it is mainly because of intangibles that the stock market values most companies at high multipliers of their book values.'

Reader: *'And intellectual capital – is this the same thing?'*

Author: 'Not quite. Patents, for example, could be considered to be intellectual capital. But they're quite tangible assets. But the two terms are used more or less interchangeably and are close enough for us. In general, I prefer the term intangibles to intellectual capital, Largely because I think the capital is as much emotional as it is intellectual. And I also borrow the term capability from resource-based strategy and talk about intangible capability to underline the fact that intangibles only bring value to an organization when they are aligned with business needs. Huselid and Becker (1995) make the same point in connection with their high-performance work system, or HPWS, which I described in Chapter 3:

Our view is that HR strategies that successfully develop and implement a coordinated HPWS create invisible assets ... that both create value and are difficult to imitate. These asset values are maximized when the HPWS is so embedded in the operational systems of the organization that it enhances a firm's capabilities.

I also use the term intangible value to describe the worth of the intangible capability. This value is very hard to measure – for example, the value of creativity can be seen in its impact in developing new products. But it's essentially an idiosyncratic process with unpredictable outcomes. I think there's a close link between intangibles, complexity and the need for knowledge. Quantitative and especially financial measures can never truly reflect the full richness of people's contribution to corporate performance. However, the qualities that make intangibles difficult to measure are the very same ones that make them difficult to imitate and explain their importance in resource based-strategy. And the importance of human capital in HCM ...'

Financial Capital and Intangible Capability

A firm's market value is based largely on two factors: financial capital and intangible value. This section will review both of these factors to help understand why intangible capability is becoming increasingly important.

Financial Capital and Porter's Value Chain

Fifty years ago, financial capital was the critical strategic resource for organizations. Companies were successful if they could arrange preferential access to financial capital. Senior managers were responsible for acquiring, allocating and using this capital effectively. Most management models developed at this time, for instance the Boston Consulting Group (BCG) matrix, were designed to help managers allocate capital, for example to decide which businesses to grow and which to harvest. Another highly influential tool developed during this period was Porter's value chain which describes how raw materials enter the organization; go through a series of processes that convert these materials into finished goods; and how these goods are then provided to customers. The value chain describes a physical process but the scarce resource that enables a business to make this transformation is financial capital and the value that is added to the product results in margin – a return on the financial capital that has been invested. Return on investment (ROI) is also an important and easy to use tool as both inputs and outputs have a defined financial value. The key to achieving a high ROI is mass production – maximizing economies of scale to produce goods as efficiently as possible and maximize margins. People are supporting actors in the value chain. Their role is to perform transactional, routine, defined work and people management is expressed as a secondary activity.

Although the value chain is still relevant and is still in use today, it originates from an industrial perspective, focusing on the interplay between goods and capital. It is also worth noting at this point that the earliest versions of our current financial reporting standards were also developed at this time. These standards were developed to monitor the incomings and outgoings of the physical and financial assets and resources described in Porter's value chain. Other more recently developed financial management models come from the same perspective. For example, economic value added (EVA) suggests that a company should only fund a project if its return on financial capital is greater than the cost of that capital.

But financial capital is no longer the scarce resource that constrains growth. Global capital markets move money around so quickly that having preferential access to capital no longer brings competitive advantage. In addition, increasing industry capacity has reduced the demand for financial capital. Many companies have more financial capital than they are able to use in the activities described in Porter's value chain to generate margin at sufficiently high returns for their shareholders. When this is the case, companies spend their excess capital on mergers and acquisitions. If even this does not generate sufficient returns, companies buy back their own shares. This is increasingly common, so, for example, while completing this book, two high profile acquirers, Vodafone and RBS, announced they were cutting back on their plans for global acquisitions and would be paying money back to their shareholders through share buy-backs and raised dividends.

In addition, the transformation of value described by Porter's value chain is not the only way that value can be added in a business, and given the changing importance of different forms of capital, it is no longer even the most significant. In today's economy, success depends on accumulating intangible value rather than financial capital. This means that the need to provide EVA still holds true but it is no longer an appropriate focus for business strategy.

Intangible Capability

The components of intangible capability can be separated out in several different ways. The model described here is the one used by the CIPD and is the approach that seems to me to best capture the value of people and the way they are organized. The model suggests that market value is influenced by two main things within an organization: financial capital and intangible capability of which customer capital is a major part.

Customer Capital and the Customer Value Chain

Customer capital is the value of a company's franchise: its ongoing relationships with the people with whom it does business, supported by its branding and corporate reputation. The value provided by customer capital has become increasingly important. Of course, financial capital and the investors' perspective are still important too. If a company does not have enough financial capital it cannot meet its customer needs and if it does not provide a sufficient return to its shareholders, customers will suffer because the company will fold. But to succeed in meeting investors' requirements for return on financial capital, companies need to focus on their customers.

For many organizations, the key value chain therefore becomes a customer-driven one. In this chain, a demand for a product or service the company can meet is identified by the organization and goes through a series of processes to provide a solution that satisfies this demand. Value is added through the processes by consistently meeting the customer's demands and this results in lifetime value – a return on customer capital. People now play a central role in the primary activities of the value chain, using customer information to deliver personalized services to consumers. This is the basis of customer relationship management (CRM), although this approach, like HCM, seems to have become dominated by technology solutions rather than strategic approaches to particular requirements. The customer value chain is also the basis of Bain & Company's work on customer loyalty. One of their directors, Frederick Reichheld (1996a) has noted that:

> The average US company now loses half its customers in five years, half its employees in four, and half its investors in less than one.

Reichheld argues that although loyalty is not fashionable and can be seen as anachronistic given the change and complexity in today's society, it still results in substantial benefits for those organizations that can achieve it. Loyalty sets up a positive feedback loop based on loyal customers, motivated, long-term employees and loyal investors (Reichheld, 1996a):

> Profits are not at the heart of this new model. They are critically important, of course, as an end in themselves and because they are the source of the incentives that keep employees, investors, and customers loyal. But the course of all cash flow, including the cash flow that eventually becomes profit, is the rising spiral of value that springs from the creation of superior value for customers.

Together with Earl Sasser from Harvard, Reichheld has estimated that a 5 per cent increase in customer loyalty can produce profit increases ranging from 25 to 85 per cent and concludes that the quality of market share, measured in terms of customer loyalty, deserves as much attention as the quantity of that share (Reichheld and Sasser, 1990). Taking the credit card industry as an example, Reichheld (1996b) has shown that given customer acquisition costs and the additional value of repeat purchases and referrals, a customer who stays with a company for two years would generate $26 of profit whereas customers who stay for 10 and 20 years would generate $760 and $2104 net profits respectively.

The value of customer capital has been seen most clearly during the dot-com boom when it stimulated a war between internet-based companies attempting to grab the largest possible share of the rapidly growing market. One of the reasons for the subsequent failure of many of these companies was that the market had not thought hard enough about what was being offered to customers in order to understand if the dot-coms could create lifetime value from their growing market shares.

One of the first attempts to map out the customer value chain was made by Leonard Schlesinger and James Heskett at Harvard in response to what they saw as endemic poor service quality. In what they called a 'service profit chain', updated to 'value profit chain' in a more recent book (Heskett *et al.*, 2003), the authors mapped out a process in which internal service quality leads to employee satisfaction which leads in turn to employee retention, external service value, customer satisfaction, customer retention and on to improvements in profits (Schlesinger and Heskett, 1991). External service value is the key link in this chain and Heskett *et al.* (1994) note that delivering this requires personalized service:

> Value is always relative because it is based both on perceptions of the way a service is delivered and on initial customer expectations. Typically, a company measures value using the reasons expressed by customers for high or low satisfaction. Because value varies with individual expectations, efforts to improve value inevitably require service organizations to move all levels of management closer to the customer and give frontline service employees the latitude to customize a standard service to individual needs.

This shows that in this customer value chain, mass production has been replaced by mass customization – manufacturing a product or delivering service in response to an individual customer's needs and doing so as efficiently as possible.

Interestingly, one of the organizations criticized by Heskett for failing to provide service quality was Sears, Roebuck & Co., a large US retailer which clearly took Heskett's advice to heart and quickly became a well-known case study for the customer value chain. More recent case studies detailing this sort of approach include RBS, Standard Chartered and Barber *et al.* (1999).

Customer Value Chain at Sears. In response to a series of heavy losses in the 1990s, Sears developed a new vision in which it would become a compelling place for investors to invest. For this to happen, the company would first need to become a compelling place to shop, and this would rely on having highly motivated employees, which would depend on being a compelling place to work. This vision became known as the three compellings, or the 3Cs.

Gathering data to support this vision, Sears developed a set of measures that became the basis for a business model known as the employee-customer-profit chain. For a compelling place to invest, Sears selected financial measures linked to revenue growth, sales per square foot and inventory turnover. For a compelling place to shop, measures related to meeting customer needs and customer satisfaction were selected. The original measures chosen to support a compelling place to work were about personal growth and development and empowered teams. However, in validating the initial set of measures, Sears found that it was actually employees' attitudes towards their job and the company that had the greatest effect on their behaviour. In fact, responses to just 10 of the 70 questions in their employee survey had a greater impact on behaviour than all the other data that had been examined put together (Rucci *et al.*, 1998):

> Conversely, the statisticians could find no direct causal pathway from two other measures we had put into our tentative model – *personal growth and development* and *empowered teams* – to any of our customer data. We believe that growth, empowerment, and teamwork matter, but clearly something about the way we measured them was flawed. However important they might be, the measures we had did not lie on a predictive pathway from employee attitudes to customer satisfaction to shareholder value. So in the next version of our employee-customer-profit

model, we replaced those initial measures with the 10 questions about the job and the company.

The result of this major programme was a significant financial turn-around and HR was widely identified as the single most important business group in leading the change efforts within the firm (Kirn *et al.*, 1999).

Whatever combination of the words service, customer, value and profit we want to use for it, the customer value chain is rather different to Porter's original value chain because it focuses on outcomes rather than the series of activities themselves. This is because the activities involved in providing service to customers often take place in parallel. The actual value chain is therefore a lot messier and more complicated than Porter's one. It would of course still be possible just to see the customer value chain as an extension of Porter's chain with more focus on customers (and some additional focus on employees). But as the customer value chain has a different focus – service rather than products – and its own output loyalty and customer capital not margin and financial capital – it deserves to be treated as a separate source of value in its own right.

Human, Organizational and Social Capital

Human Capital. As well as customer capital, the other constituents of intangible capability are human, organizational and social capital. Human capital exists as a resource and a capability, at individual and organizational levels. Individual human capital can be acquired by attracting and selecting staff with the right skills and experience. It can be developed through learning. Human capital can be converted into an organizational resource by aligning people with the organization, engaging its owners and investors, so that they will choose to make it available to the organization. This can then be leveraged by applying it to meet business requirements. These activities are illustrated in Figure 4.1.

Organizational Capital. Organizational or structural capital is the infrastructure that supports people to do their work. It includes elements like the fitness of the organization structure, operational and management processes, procedures, routines, general use of information, IT systems and databases, existence of a knowledge centre, explicit knowledge and

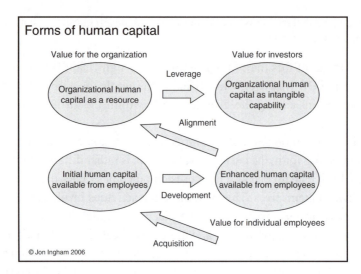

Figure 4.1 Forms of human capital

know-how. Some of these elements may be legally protected and become intellectual property rights, legally owned by the firm, for example patents, copyrights, design rights, trade secrets, trademarks and service marks. Organizational capital has the advantage of being fully owned by the company – it remains in place when the employees leave and is therefore to some extent easier to manage and change than human capital.

Social Capital. Social or relational capital is an emergent property arising from the organizational system – the organization and the people working in the organization. Social capital includes the network of relationships and features of social life within an organization, the knowledge tied up and shared in these relationships, the ability to work together with other people in value creation, the corporate culture, beliefs lived and values demonstrated by employees. It provides the glue that holds organizations together. Social capital is even less tangible than human capital and demonstrates even more attributes of complex systems. How is this for a paradox: social capital is not owned by the people but leaves when they leave and is not contained within the organization but does not exist in the same way without it:

> Social capital is owned jointly by the parties in a relationship, and no one player has, or is capable of having exclusive ownership rights. (Nahapiet and Ghoshal, 1998)

Social capital cannot be managed but it can be influenced, mainly through conversation. I also think that there are some signs of a positive feedback loop here. As social capital along with other intangibles becomes more important, so it increasingly needs to be socially constructed which requires effective conversations. This increases the importance of social capital, which requires it to be socially constructed, ad infinitum.

The HCM Value Chain

Human capital and the other internal intangible capabilities listed above display the attributes of intangible value that were described earlier, that is they appreciate with use. This is one reason for human capital's growing importance in organizations. Another reason is that in the UK and many other countries, changing demographics mean that the availability of this resource is decreasing. So as financial capital is becoming more accessible, talent is becoming rarer, at least until we learn to use what is available more intelligently. Bartlett and Ghoshal (2002) summarize this shift, pointing to the 'exuberant and often irrational' funding of technology entrepreneurs before the dot-com crash as evidence that:

> There is a surplus of capital chasing a scarcity of talented people and the knowledge they possess. In today's economy, that is the constraining – and therefore strategic – resource.

A third reason for human capital's growing importance is the causal ambiguity of this scarce resource. This change emphasizes that people form the basis for competitive advantage and so HCM is a form of resource-based strategy, where the people are the scarce resources not aspects of this resource. As the CIPD report on *Evaluating Human Capital* (Scarborough and Elias, 2002) explains:

> Human capital is to a large extent non-standardized, tacit, dynamic, context dependent and embodied in people. These features provide a competitive advantage because they are causally ambiguous – the relationship between cause and effect is not readily identified. One corollary of these context-dependent and causally ambiguous features is the difficulty that competing firms experience should they try to replicate a firm's human capital base. It is extremely difficult to imitate another firm's deployment of human capital, and this may provide an

105

enduring source of competitive advantage. On the other hand, while rival firms cannot do this, there is every likelihood that a firm's own managers will not be able to either.

However, a key proposition within this book is that these factors are not the only or even the most significant reasons why human capital has become as important as it has. I believe instead that there is a third value chain driven by human, organization and social capital. This value chain and the value it provides are what I think we need to be talking about when we use the term HCM.

In this chain, the current potential of the business, including the value that people associated with the business may choose to invest in it, are the 'raw materials' that form the inputs to the value chain. These inputs go through a series of transformational processes that could be part of a major change programme. Alternatively, they could just be the activities undertaken by individuals and teams who are flexible and adaptive to change and who, by responding to emerging situations, transform the way that business is performed. The output of the processes is improved organizational capability which provides a return on human capital. This capability is also expressed as human, organizational and social capital but is now created value, intangible capability, not just a 'resource'. It is valuable, rare or unique, sustainable over time and not easily imitated. This capability provides the basis for business sustainability, differentiation, competitive advantage and transformation.

The progression from the customer to the HCM value chain is similar in nature to the progression from Porter's value chain to the customer-driven one. Businesses can always access financial capital if they have got profitable customers. Businesses can always find customers if they have got appropriately capable people. Again, this is not saying that either investors or customers are unimportant – but by moving focus to a deeper source of value it is possible to have a greater impact on the business. This is why Richard Branson at Virgin has always said he focuses on people first, customers second and shareholders third. Jack Welch at GE stated 'there are three key measures in business – customer satisfaction, employee satisfaction and cash flow, in that order' but later admitted he had listed customers and employees the wrong way round.

Again, we could just see this as an extension of Porter's value chain or of the customer value chain with more focus on employees but, also again, it is really something different. This chain has its own focus and its own output, the potential for sustaining and transforming the business, rather than margin or loyalty. In particular, unlike the two previous value chains, the output of the HCM value chain does not have a direct financial impact (see Chapters 5 and 6). This is simply as a result of the fact that we are working with intangibles. Porter's value chain delivers a current financial impact. The customer value chain delivers this in the future. The people value chain provides the potential for a transformed level of financial impact.

HCM ensures that people are as prepared as possible to take advantage of opportunities in the business environment and it is down to the business to deliver on these opportunities. A metaphor for the HCM value chain is the work a football coach does with a team before a match. Organizational human capital refers to the resourcing and capability of the team. It is then down to the team captain to make as much as possible from the capability assembled on the pitch.

Thomas Stewart (1997), editor of the *Harvard Business Review*, supports the change in focus from financial to human capital and describes the operation of the HCM value chain from a knowledge management perspective:

> We grew up in the Industrial Age. It is gone, supplanted by the Information Age. The economic world we are leaving was one whose main sources of wealth were physical … Land, natural resources such as oil and ores and energy, and human and machine labor were the ingredients from which wealth was created. The business organizations of that era were designed to attract capital – financial capital – to develop and manage those sources of wealth … In this new era, wealth is the product of knowledge. Knowledge and information – not just scientific knowledge, but news, advice, entertainment, communication, service – have become the economy's primary raw materials and its most important products. Knowledge is what we buy and sell … The capital assets that are needed to create wealth today are not land, not physical labor, not machine tools and factories. They are, instead, knowledge assets.

Like the customer value chain, the relationships within the HCM value chain have been investigated in academic research. The comprehensive evidence of the impact of people management on organizational performance was discussed in Chapter 2. There has also been some research into the nature of the links between people management and performance. One recent study was conducted by John Purcell and researchers from Bath University. Their people and performance model, detailed in the CIPD report *Unlocking the Black Box*, identifies a series of people management practices that influence business outcomes by creating ability, motivation and the opportunity to make individual and team choices over the way that work is performed.

The researchers found that the most important practices are, in order, career development, training opportunities, job influence and challenge, involvement, appraisal processes and worklife balance. Other practices such as pay satisfaction were not seen as important. Supporting the findings on contingency covered in Chapter 3, the research found that the way practices need to be applied varies considerably according to sector. Purcell *et al.* (2002) noted that:

> We found in some companies, especially those with professional employees, such as an accounting consultancy, that satisfaction with careers, training and job challenge was particularly important. In clerical or manual work, satisfaction with involvement and team working was the vital ingredient.

The research found that people's ability, motivation and opportunity, together with line managers' actions and a strategic intent, or 'big idea', lead to job satisfaction and organizational commitment. These then lead to people exhibiting discretionary behaviours which Purcell *et al.* (2003) define as the extra effort, innovation and productive work that an individual can choose to make, noting:

> One way or the other, the employee chooses how conscientiously to undertake the job. Most jobs are built up of many tasks, so the level of complexity can be surprisingly high, even for seemingly routine ones. The choice of how, and how well, to do things is not necessarily made deliberately: it can be unconscious – just part of the way people behave in that organization. But discretionary behaviour can certainly be withdrawn, often in the sense of adopting an uncaring attitude. This may be a reciprocal response to a belief that 'the firm no longer cares about me, my future or my opinions'.

Models are deliberately designed to simplify reality and in order to show a simple, one-way causal chain of relationships; the people and performance model makes several high level simplifications. In particular, it completely ignores the way that ability has a direct impact on performance outcomes by itself as well as through its indirect impact through discretionary behaviour. Even the relationships that are included in the model are actually a lot more complicated than is indicated. For example, the line management behaviours that form the link from ability, motivation and opportunity to discretionary behaviour are in themselves discretionary behaviours:

> Managers vary, of course, but how much attention is given to the way managers deal with people management issues is itself a reflection of what they are allowed and encouraged to do. (Purcell *et al.*, 2002)

This implies that there is really a positive feedback loop in the system. The addition of more relationships and feedback loops soon mean that reality can no longer be modelled in the way presented in the CIPD report. Ralph Stacey (2000) comments that:

> Cyberneticists recognized that feedback means circular causality – event A causes event B which then causes event A. They argued that one can determine the direction this circular causality takes for any pair of events simply by observing which precedes which in a large number of cases. But when dealing with large numbers of interconnected pairs it all becomes too difficult. These internal structures are so complex that one cannot hope to understand them – they constitute a 'black box' ... Those arguing this position are assuming that there is always a specific cause for each specific outcome, the problem being that it is all too complex for us to understand ... there is another way to tackle this difficulty, it may be impossible to reduce our understanding to specific cause-and-effect links because the links themselves are lost in the detail of what happens; the alternative is then to think in terms of patterns in the behaviour of systems as a whole.

The progression from Porter's value chain to the HCM chain and the difficulty in understanding cause and effect links within this chain were also expressed by Richard Youngman, previously Dissemination Manager for PRISM, a multidisciplinary European initiative researching the management of intangibles, that reported in July 2003:

> In the 20th century we focused on margin, investment and asset productivity to achieve comparative advantage. This game has run its course ... A fundamental difference between the 20th and 21st century economies is that we can no longer rely on tangible assets and the representation of production as purely a physical process to provide us with a reliable guide to the rate and direction of economic change ... The winners in the 21st century will focus increasingly on *architecting* capabilities – the capability to innovate and the capability to act – and

109

managing risks such as reputational loss ... Growth and value creation are not merely a function of the external inputs introduced into the 'black box'. Growth drivers are internal. They are located in the interplay and complementarities achieved between tangible and intangible assets – few of which are owned by the firm ... Cause and effect in such a complex value chain are not only unknown, but arguably are not knowable. There is no direct relationship between a single intangible asset and a financial outcome. (Youngman, 2003)

The consequences of the HCM value chain are that people need to take a new, central role in corporate life as the primary means of differentiating a company from its competitors. A company's ability to generate human capital is an absolutely key, if not the key, business process. We have talked about mass production and mass customization and the HCM value chain suggests we also need to think about mass personalization. This is the individualization Tim Miller refers to in his Foreword and equates to Heskett's customization of a standard service for customer capital. In the HCM value chain, the customer value chain's war for market share – the market grab of the dot-com era is replaced by a war for talent. This means that organizations need to recognize that they are playing in talent as well as financial and customer marketplaces. The supply of human capital and its ability to create demand for new products and services becomes as or more important than the existing demand. Business strategy must be built on the capability of a business's people.

In addition, work needs to be performed differently – with a view to delivering the extra value that people can provide. Denise Kingsmill summed this up nicely, saying 'work should be more people shaped'. The result of doing this should be a significantly increased level of human capital value. This new way of working marks the transition to the new sigmoid curve.

Examples of Intangible Capability

In some ways, there is little new in these categorizations of value. For example, McKinsey's 7S model basically consists of different elements of human, organizational and social capital:

- human capital = staff and skills;
- organizational capital = strategy, structure and systems;
- social capital = superordinate goals and style.

The advantages of conceptualizing these areas as forms of intangible value are firstly that this ensures a focus on the outcomes of people management activities, rather than the activities themselves. Secondly, this emphasizes that given their different nature, the three types of capital each need treating in different ways.

More recently, Ulrich (Ulrich and Smallwood, 2004) has identified 11 intangible capabilities he believes are important to business effectiveness and that I have categorized as follows:

Customer capital
- Customer connectivity: building enduring relationships or trust with targeted customers.

Human capital
- Talent: attracting, motivating and retaining competent and committed people.
- Leadership: embedding leaders throughout the organization.

Organizational capital
- Speed: making important changes rapidly.
- Accountability: demanding high performance from employees.
- Learning: generating ideas with impact.
- Innovation: developing breakthrough products and processes.
- Efficiency: managing costs.

Social capital
- Shared mindset and coherent brand identity: ensuring positive, consistent perceptions of the company among employees and customers.
- Collaboration: working effectively across organizational boundaries.
- Strategic unity: articulating and sharing a strategic viewpoint.

Ulrich also describes how an organization needs to pick intangibles that fit with its business strategy, emphasizing, for example:

- Collaboration if the business strategy is about managing alliances.
- Learning if the strategy is about sharing knowledge across global business.

- Talent if the employer is trying to grow in new industries.
- Speed if the organization is trying to compete on cycle time.

The impact of Ulrich's capabilities has been reviewed in Huselid's research, described in Chapter 3. Huselid found that firms rated higher on these capabilities also invest more in R&D (an indirect measure of innovation), are more productive and more profitable. The ratio of market to book value was also found to be nearly four times larger in the highly rated firms (Ulrich and Smallwood, 2004).

The Work Foundation has recently conducted research placing 3000 companies in a league depending on how they handle customers and markets; shareholders and governance systems; stakeholder relationships; human resources practices and the management of innovation and creativity, which together form an overall Company Performance Index (CPI). During a 13 month period when the UK stock market grew by 14 per cent, companies at the top of the Work Foundation's index experienced a 26 per cent gain in market value and companies at the bottom of the index gained just a 6 per cent increase. The Work Foundation has identified five 'intangible factors of production' that translate the five process areas of the CPI into productive action. Again, using my categorizations, these intangibles are:

Human capital
- Leadership: visible and accessible leadership and management, combined with high expectations from those in decision-making roles.

Organization capital
- Structure: unique organizational structure resulting from geography, size and history, that enables continued success rather than being a specific driver of that success.
- Process: a higher degree of informality and continued dialogue supported by simple – though not simplistic – processes that allow faster decision-making.

Social capital
- Communication: openly sharing information between peers and networks or managers that need timely and accurate information in order to get the best job done.

- Culture and employee relations: a distrust of the status quo, valuing quality rather than quantity, a focus on the long term and on outcomes; a positive climate characterized – not codified – by pride, innovation and strong interpersonal relations.

The research found that there are radical differences in these intangibles between top scoring and bottom scoring firms. High performing companies have a higher degree of dialogue and value quality rather than quantity. Poor performers tended to have a bureaucratic and hierarchical culture, with leaders more concerned with a narrow range of financially driven output metrics than how top managers behave and interact with others.

The research (Work Foundation, 2005) concluded that achieving high performance is about developing best fit between a company's strategic choices over their business goals and the practices they choose to achieve these goals. It also noted that:

> The exact 'fit' will depend on a myriad of external and internal factors such as history of the organization, its geography, its sector and its position within that sector.

While these lists of human, organizational and social capital may appear to be very similar to a list of best practices, there is a crucial difference in that they are actually the results of best practices rather than the practices themselves. For example, developing leadership skills is a practice; the ability to lead change is an intangible capability.

But there can be overlap. For example, organizational capital exists to support people in the organization – either by enabling business processes, by supporting customer activities or by directly improving financial performance (for instance, an intangible capability to meet forecast projections). But organizational capital can also support people management so, for example, developing leadership skills could be organizational capital, as well as a practice, if the organization is as effective as GE in developing senior executives and ensuring smooth succession into top jobs. The key issue in understanding whether something has intangible value is whether it is something that is so strongly valued that investors would pay for the organization to have it. But how do managers or investors understand the financial value of these intangibles?

Accounting for Intangible Value

The Value of Financial Valuation

To emphasize the importance of intangibles, Baruch Lev, Professor in Accounting and Finance at New York University, points to the fact that companies' market to book value (the ratio of their capital market value to their net asset value as stated on their balance sheets) has increased dramatically since the 1980s. In research for the Brookings Institution, Lev (2001) has calculated that the mean market to book ratio of the Standard & Poor's 500 companies has increased from about 1.6 in 1980 to about 4.2 at the time of writing. It is generally accepted that the main reason for this change is that the market sees something of greater worth than the physical assets recorded in financial accounts. This additional value is due to the company's intangibles and there is a growing need to account for this intangible value.

As noted earlier, today's accounting systems were designed to report on tangible assets such as plant and machinery. They cannot handle the intangibles involved in HCM and Lev thinks that, because of this, organizations are constrained from investing appropriately.

Organizations may recognize their employees as their most important asset but our reporting requirements do not allow them to be considered like this. Spending a million pounds on training employees is treated as an expense and would have an immediate impact on earnings. If expenditure on training was treated as an investment, these costs would be treated as assets and capitalized on the balance sheet. So the same spending would be depreciated over the useful life of the training and earnings would be reduced gradually over this period. Treating this spending as an investment would also mean that it would be much more likely to be monitored over the period it is amortized for.

This asymmetrical treatment of tangible resources and intangibles, and the lack of information on investments in intangibles leads to volatility and mispricing of company's shares. Evidence for this conclusion is provided by Lev's finding that the mean market to book ratio of the Standard & Poor's 500 companies actually increased to as high as 7.5 at the stock market's peak in March 2000 before falling back to today's levels. Despite heavy downsizing, the initial overvaluation and subsequent dramatic decline in both share values and market to book values had little to do with an increase and ensuing reduction in intangible capability. Instead, these changes reflected the earlier over-valuation of many companies that had resulted from the difficulty in pricing them correctly.

More significantly for HCM, the market can also undervalue a company's intangibles. When this happens, companies are either led to under-invest in their people or will be penalized by the market. Providing better valuations of intangibles would not necessarily increase market value (remember Coloplast from Chapter 1) but would help keep share prices stable, reduce the risks associated with investing in a company and should result in lower cost of capital.

Although the trend has recently been reversed, senior manager's compensation has been increasingly tied to their company's share price and this means that accounting's asymmetrical treatment of tangible and intangible factors also affects the behaviour of people within the company. Lev believes these factors mean that it is much easier to spend on physical resources and to cut back on intangibles including people, or at least to focus on their short-term utilization rather than any long-term growth. He therefore thinks it important that intangibles be measured and valued, as this quote in Ernst & Young's *Measures that Matter* report (1997) demonstrates:

> To claim that tangible assets should be measured and valued, while intangibles should not – or could not – is like stating that 'things' are valuable, while 'ideas' are not.

Valuing Intangible Capability

The difficulty in valuing intangibles financially is that while costs are still fairly easy to identify, it is much harder to understand their benefits. Developing the point, Armstrong and Baron (2002) state:

> The result is that we are embedded in a situation in which human capital as cost is relatively easy to measure using hard metrics such as wages, cost of absenteeism, benefits, cost of training, etc. And yet the return on investment in human capital or its worth as an asset is much harder to measure because this value is rooted in things that can only be expressed using softer measures not always translatable into financial terms.

Table 4.1 provides a range of approaches for valuing intangibles that fall within two categories, identified as direct and indirect. Direct valuation

Table 4.1: Valuing intangible value

	Direct	*Indirect*
Top-down	Market value	Calculated intangible value
Integrated	Human resource accounting	Scorecard
Bottom-up	Cost-based Market-based	Income-based

involves assigning a self-standing financial value to intangibles. Indirect valuation requires an understanding of the impact of the intangible on financial results in order to be able to judge its value. Within each category, an array of methods are available that range from top-down (calculating the entire intangible value of the company) to bottom-up (calculating its constituent parts which if appropriate can then be pulled together to form an overall value) with integrated methods combining elements of the top-down and bottom-up approaches.

Direct Valuation

Direct valuation is the most commonly used of the two perspectives. Richard Youngman (2003) of the PRISM research initiative explains one reason for this may be that it falls within our existing mindsets:

> Many accept the notion that intangibles are central to creating value in the future but in practice, we tend to fall back on the norms we're comfortable with. We also look for solutions within the parameters of our current understanding and outlook. Consequently, we try to identify assets such as brands and patents, and value them like we would a building, separating them from their context. It is uncertain whether this is either possible or meaningful. Theory without measurement is a primitive kind of knowledge and it is not certain we fully understand what we're trying to measure when we set out to measure intangibles in this way.

The benefit of direct valuation is that, like metrics, it gets attention. The disadvantage is that it can be very superficial – all valuations rely on subjectivity and uncertainty so they lack reliability.

Top-down Approaches. The fact that market value is so much higher than book value is often used to argue that intangibles have a financial value which is the absolute difference between a company's market value and its book value. A slightly different value model is Tobin's 'q', developed by economist, James Tobin, where q is assessed as the difference between the market value of a company and the replacement costs of its fixed assets (Tobin, 1969). Other models attempt to deal with the non-linear relationship between market value and intangible value by introducing an additional element, 'market premium', recognizing investors' changing expectations about the future. From this perspective, intangible value can be calculated as the difference in market value and the sum of financial capital and market premium.

The major drawback of these approaches is that they involve defining intangibles based on what they are valued at by the market, rather than what they actually are. The approaches are not relevant for use in the public and non-profit sectors. If assumptions about market performance are wrong, valuations on intangible capability are also going to be incorrect.

Bottom-up Approaches. These methods estimate the financial value of intangible capability by assessing its various components. Cost-based approaches use the cost of acquiring intangibles. One version uses people's discounted future remuneration. An alternative uses costs for recruitment and development. In either method, costs need to be amortized by making an assumption about how long someone will stay in an organization. The main problem with cost-based approaches is that they go back to the traditional practice of treating people as a cost rather than as value. Plus, of course, we already have plenty of numbers for costs – so the approach really is not that clever.

Market-based approaches use the cost of buying an equivalent level of capability or contribution from an outside contractor, temporary agency, interim provider or consultancy. The method is limited to roles which are directly comparable to external services. Plus market-based prices will be higher than internal costs for same service. Calculations can also be difficult and time-consuming to make.

Tools like the Human Capital Monitor developed by Andrew Mayo (2001) can also be used to derive an overall quasi-financial measure of human asset worth which is calculated as employment cost multiplied by an individual asset multiplier (the weighted average assessment of capability, potential, contribution and stakeholder value) divided by 1000. This measure does at least focus on value creation but it does not really provide a proper financial valuation.

Integrated Approaches. Human resource accounting seeks to account for people by measuring both the cost and economic value of managing people. Flamholtz (1985) explains that this involves:

> Measuring the costs incurred by business firms and other organizations to recruit, select, hire, train and develop human assets. It also involves measuring the economic value of people to organizations. In brief, it involves accounting for people as organizational resources, for managers as well as financial accounting purposes.

People's economic value is calculated as a combination of productivity, transferability (flexible skills) and promotability multiplied by the probability that someone will stay with the organization. The approach is an integrated one because it can be used for teams and organizations as well as individuals. The main benefit of the approach is that it has the greatest potential validity of the direct valuation approaches. The disadvantages are that it is very complicated and not very robust, relying on substantial value judgements in making predictions about the future. Accounting standards do not allow these HR measures to be used as part of financial accounting.

Summary of Direct Valuation. The assumption in direct valuation is that intangibles have an absolute, fixed value. This can lead to some further questionable conclusions. For example, it can be taken to mean that intangibles account for an absolute part of market value and potentially the difference between book and market value. In this situation, it makes sense to quantify each type of intangible capability in order to justify market value and keep share prices high. This seems to be the thinking behind Armstrong and Baron's (2002) explanation that one of the motives for measuring human capital in financial terms is that:

> Human capital constitutes a key element of the market worth of a company, and its value should therefore be included in the accounts as an indication to investors or those contemplating a merger or acquisition of the total value of a business, including its intangibles as well as its tangible assets.

As this comment demonstrates, the assumption of direct valuation can be used to argue that financial accounting should be 'fixed' by putting intangibles on the balance sheet, enabling expenditure on people to be capitalized and quantifying the economic value of people to the organization. ROI calculations fit neatly into this perspective. Intangibles have a cost and a value, so ROI becomes a relatively simple calculation of measurable factors.

When people talk about the 'holy grail' of putting people on the balance sheet or calculating a return on investment in human capital, they are generally looking at intangibles from a direct valuation perspective. For example, discussing intangibles like employee skills, Robert Kaplan at Harvard Business School, and David Norton, a consultant, who together developed the Balanced Scorecard, argue that:

> Measuring the value of such intangible assets is the holy grail of accounting … If managers could find a way to estimate the value of their intangible assets, they could measure and manage their company's competitive position much more easily and accurately. (Kaplan and Norton, 2004a)

Writing on a similar track in SHRM's *HR Magazine*, Steve Bates (2003) refers to HR leaders who think they are getting closer to a holy grail of organizational measurement. Bates defines this holy grail as 'calculating with confidence the return on investment (ROI) of individual employees'. My views on this idea have not changed since my response was also published in *HR Magazine* (Finn and Ingham, 2004):

> Disagreeing with Steve Bates' article ('The metrics maze'), we cannot believe that attempting to measure the ROI of individual employees will ever result in anything other than overly mechanistic simplification and spending much valuable HR time on measuring the unmeasurable.

As with the original holy grail, I believe the search for an approach to direct valuation will also prove futile. It has already become less popular since the downturn in the stock market in March 2000 when it became clear that intangibles could not be measured as a simple difference between market and book values but involve a more complicated relationship than this. A powerful criticism is that direct valuation tries to cope with complexity by pretending it does not exist and this can be dangerous if it leads to managing in an inappropriate way. For example,

Kearns believes that there are two distinct questions that need to be answered in HCM and emphasizes that the questions need to be answered in this order (Kearns, 2004):

- What is the current value of our human capital?
- How much more value can we get from our human capital?

The focus here is on the direct valuation of human capital (value in monetary terms) and how this value can be increased. It is the value, the financial measurement, that is the focus of attention. From this perspective, HCM is about measuring the value and then managing the measurement. This is likely to lead to a very mechanistic approach to people management and it is this that is behind the perception that there is no 'human' in human capital management.

Compare this approach to one that reverses the order of the questions. Doing this may seem pedantic but it makes a big difference to ask: 'How much more value can we get from our people?', and then evaluate the additional value that has been created. Reordering the questions means that the focus is still very much on the people so the approach is about managing the people and then measuring the effectiveness of the management.

Indirect Valuation

Top-down Approaches. These indirect approaches for calculating intangible value rely on being able to calculate the additional earnings that are the result of intangibles. For example, Lev (2004) provides a methodology for calculating intangible-driven earnings by subtracting from earnings the average contribution of physical and financial assets in the company's industry. The value of intangible capital is then calculated as the present value of the forecasted stream of intangible-driven earnings.

The benefits of this approach are that it provides a more valid calculation of overall intangible value than market value. The disadvantage is that it is very sensitive to interest rates and to assumptions that are made in calculating discounting rates.

Bottom-up Approaches. These approaches seek to identify the additional value that is the result of individuals and teams. Income-based approaches are based on the revenue that a person could generate for an organization. In practice this is limited to roles that are directly responsible for income generation, for example in sales or consultancy. The approach also overstates value because it assumes that intangibles are the only factor driving the revenues of an organization. If you performed this calculation for all employees and added everything up you would just get the entire income for the organization. This tells you nothing new and assumes that tangible assets and other intangibles have no impact on revenue.

Another way of estimating the income value of individuals is to use an approach like Saratoga's measure of revenue per employee that is calculated by dividing 'adjusted profits' (revenue minus expenses for facilities, machinery, materials and suppliers, and minus payroll and benefits cost) by the number of employees. But this is an average rather than an individual valuation.

In fact, calculating a true value of an individual employee's contribution is much more difficult than either approach suggests. Lev notes that:

> Employees are part of a team. There are things that are very difficult, perhaps even impossible, to disentangle. If it can be done, it's beautiful. But I'm skeptical. (Bates, 2003)

Integrated Approaches. Given the difficulties inherent in the top-down and bottom-up approaches to indirect valuation, scorecards like Skandia's Navigator, described at the end of this chapter, and the HCM Value Matrix outlined in Chapter 6, may provide the most appropriate mechanism for valuing human capital. The use of scorecards helps to raise the whole level of valuation from pure data to information and knowledge. As Scarborough and Elias (2002) explain:

> The challenge facing companies, however, is to go beyond the strictly financial measures and identify and report on the dynamics and value within that company. There may be little point in providing more information on all intangibles per se. Stakeholders are likely to be interested only in those intangibles that will drive future value.

But these scorecard-based approaches still require a basis for describing what an organization is doing to develop its intangibles, and the intangibles themselves, as well as the financial value that will result from these activities and intangibles. Therefore, the focus within this perspective is really more about evaluation of human capital management than just the valuation of human capital itself.

Summary of Indirect Valuation. In this perspective, which takes more account of complexity, intangibles are just the cause, not the substance of the difference between market value and financial value. Intangibles have no self-standing value in themselves; their value is created through their potential impact on future earnings. Investors' expectations about these future earnings are what results in a company's market value. These expectations are influenced more by intangibles than tangible assets because the market believes that intangibles will have a much bigger impact on future earnings than tangible assets. So investors pay for the expected impact of intangibles, not the intangibles themselves. Microsoft's market to book value is higher than Ford's not because investors are valuing a higher level of intangible capability but because they expect a higher level of future earnings. Microsoft does have a much higher proportion of intangibles but its market value reflects the expected impact of this human capital, not its absolute current value.

But the expectations of investors are subjective. Market value is only indirectly affected by intangibles and is also subject to a number of external factors including the political and economic climate, actions of competitors, changes of technology and general rumour. As I mentioned previously, some models introduce an additional element, 'market premium', into company valuation. This market premium is based solely on investors' subjective perceptions about the future and means that it is now the adding together of financial capital, intangible capability and market premium that results in market value. However, it seems much more likely that the whole entirety of market value, not just a smaller market premium, is the result of investors' subjective expectations. Intangible capabilities are the main driver for these expectations, but they cannot be the basis of an absolute calculation of intangible value.

An indirect approach to measuring intangibles recognizes that intangibles and the processes that are used to develop them only result in increased financial value through their contribution to business activities. For example, Kaplan and Norton (2000) explain that:

> The value of an intangible asset such as a customer database cannot be considered separately from the organizational processes that will transform it and other assets – both tangible and intangible – into

customer and financial outcomes. The value does not reside in any individual intangible asset. It arises from the entire set of assets and the strategy that links them together.

Kaplan and Norton (2004b) note that creating value from intangibles differs from managing physical and financial assets in four important ways:

1. Value creation is indirect ... Improvements in intangible assets affect financial outcomes through chains of cause-and-effect relationships.
2. Value is contextual ... The value of an intangible asset depends on its alignment with the strategy.
3. Value is potential. The cost of investing in an intangible asset represents a poor estimate of its value to the organization. Intangible assets ... have potential value but not market value ... if the internal processes are not directed at the customer value proposition or financial improvements, then the potential value of employee capabilities, and intangible assets in general, will not be realized.
4. Assets are bundled ... Maximum value is created when all the organization's intangible assets are aligned with each other, with the organization's tangible assets, and with the strategy.

Rather than trying to 'fix' accounting, this perspective realizes that financial accounting does not attempt to convey the market value of a company on its balance sheet. All it does is to value a company's assets in accordance with financial reporting standards. International Accounting Standards (IAS 38) specify that a company can only recognize an asset if it is identifiable and controlled. Control means that an organization has the ability to gain future economic benefits from an asset and to restrict the access of others to these benefits. If an asset meets these requirements then it should normally be amortized over the best estimate of useful life up to a maximum of 20 years. However, companies do not own an individual's human capital so it cannot be controlled. It therefore lacks the essential characteristics of an asset. In fact, the standards specifically prohibit capitalizing internally generated goodwill, brands, publishing titles, customer lists and similar items including staff training costs. Outlays on intangibles therefore need to be recognized as expenses when they are incurred. The important point is that the accounting standards do not exclude intangibles from a balance sheet because they are too difficult to include. The real reason is that they do not really belong there. As Boston Consulting Group (Barber and Strack, 2005) explain:

> The fact that companies don't own their employees, as they do their capital assets, is why methods for valuing 'human capital' on balance sheets are so tortuous.

Keeping intangibles off the balance sheet means that the information on it is still relatively comparable. But it also needs to be recognized that the total value of the balance sheet will not reflect the market value of the company and that some of the things that are not on the balance sheet will be more important than what is included. This takes us back to the points I made about reliability and validity in Chapter 1.

In this perspective, financial reporting still needs to be improved to meet the new, broader information needs of its users, but by developing and improving non-financial forms of reporting. Rather than changing the information that is included in the financial accounts, the need is to share more knowledge, to describe qualitatively what an organization is doing, and the sorts of intangibles it is creating, in order to provide earnings in the future. This is what Becker *et al.* (2001) are referring to when they encourage HR to take a different approach to measurement:

> The bottom line is this: If current accounting methods can't give HR professionals the measurement tools they need, then they will have to develop their own ways of demonstrating their contribution to firm performance ... Investors have made it clear that they value intangible assets. It's up to HR to develop a new measurement system that creates real value for the firm and secures human resources' legitimate place as a strategic partner.

Evaluating Intangible Capability

Levels of Value

I have already described how the value of intangibles is contextual and dependent upon alignment with an organization's strategy. This means that the only way of valuing intangibles financially is to do so indirectly. Even indirect valuation is difficult if the aim is to allocate a financial measure to a particular intangible. Scorecards provide a better approach because they do not try to establish a hard link between intangible value and a financial metric, but describe a potential relationship between these elements.

If we want to compare two programmes to develop different intangibles a scorecard helps understand the potential financial impact of each programme. One option then is to take decisions about people management based upon an understanding of the financial impact that is planned to, or it is hoped will, result. However, financial valuation can only ever provide an estimate of potential and it is never going to be definite how much financial value will result. For example, referring to Kaplan and Norton's balanced scorecard (see Chapter 6), the Conference Board (Gates, 2003) notes the difficulty in linking people measures with financial ones:

> Although learning and growth measures tend to be early leading indicators of company performance, they often do not reveal an immediate, direct impact on final outcome measures like revenue. Consequently, when linking strategy to people measures, it is important to keep in mind the relative distance between people measures and intermediate and final outcome measures. When respondents from companies using the Balanced Scorecard are asked to name the other quadrant people measures link to best, they choose either the customer or the internal processes quadrant, but never the financial quadrant.

In addition, we cannot wait until a financial value actually exists at which point it can be measured more accurately because by this time the intangible will have lost its value of being a lead indicator of future business performance. Kim Warren (2000) explains the point:

> Soft factors – intangible resources and capabilities – are powerful drivers of growth and decline in the tangible resources that determine performance at any moment. Thus there is no possibility of understanding performance over time unless these too are evaluated and dealt with rigorously.

Therefore, as well as needing to understand the potential financial return of intangibles by using a scorecard, we also need a way to measure the intangible itself, in whatever unit is appropriate. So, for example, capability could be measured on a 1–5 scale based on some form of assessment, engagement on a different scale based upon an overall response to an employee survey, turnover as a percentage, sickness absence as a certain number of days and so on. However, some intangibles like trust and creativity are less easy to measure quantitatively in any units.

In addition, it is useful to have a common way of describing two different intangibles in the same terms. Having this comparability enables the intangible value of increased engagement to be compared with the value of increased capability. The best way of comparing these intangibles is to describe the way they inform the strategy and their impact on it, probably in a qualitative form. As Kaplan and Norton (2004a) explain:

> It becomes clear that measuring the value of intangible assets is really about estimating how closely aligned those assets are to the company's strategy. If the company has a sound strategy and if the intangible assets are aligned with that strategy, then the assets will create value for the organization.

There are actually three ways that tangible assets and intangibles can provide value in alignment with the strategy. Each of these impacts on the business and generates financial results in different ways. The three levels are value for money, added value and created value:

- *Value for money*. Value for money refers to basic, largely tangible value that may represent increased efficiency; incremental improvements in effectiveness; meeting compliance requirements or other basic standards. It is useful value but is not necessarily about meeting business objectives or providing customer satisfaction. It has a direct impact on financial outcomes but this is fairly insubstantial and is mostly limited to reducing costs.
- *Added value*. Added value represents capabilities required to meet business needs. These capabilities can relate to major improvements in efficiency but are more likely to be about increased effectiveness leading to growth, change and development. Added value typically has an indirect impact on financial results by acting through improvements in operational processes, customer satisfaction and so on.
- *Created value*. Created value represents capabilities that offer the potential to sustain and transform the way the business works and to create new opportunities for competitive advantage. The principle of created value is that continuous improvements are no longer enough. Created value capabilities are needed to surprise competitors and change the nature of the competition. Like the capabilities in

resource-based strategy, created value intangibles must be valuable, rare or unique, sustainable over time and not easily imitated.

Created value can be hard to develop and even harder to maintain. The pace of change in the economy together with increasing competitor activity can mean that, left alone, resources and capabilities slip down to a lower level of value. This tends to mean that what is created value today will be only added value this time next year and value for money five years after that.

Creating Intangible Value at Skandia UK

Skandia Group is a leading financial services firm that provides a range of innovative solutions for pensions, investments and financial protection and has operations in over 20 countries. In the UK, Skandia employs 2000 people and is the fastest growing life company measured by both new sales and asset accumulation. At the time of writing, the group was in the process of being acquired by Old Mutual.

Inspired by Karl-Erik Sveiby's work in knowledge management (1997), Leif Edvinsson, Corporate Director for Intellectual Capital at Skandia AFS in Sweden, developed an approach to managing intellectual capital based upon a model called 'Navigator'. This model was used to replace traditional financial budgeting with what the company described as a real-time planning process. It was also used to raise employee commitment by cascading the company's vision into more concrete factors that could be linked to individuals' own objectives. The Navigator provided a balanced, overall picture of value creation along five areas of focus by reviewing the past (financial focus), the present (customer focus, process focus and human focus) and the future (renewal and development focus).

Edvinsson's main interest was knowledge, and he wanted to provide the company's own investors with as much information as possible. So in 1995 Skandia published a supplement to its worldwide financial report, 'Visualizing intellectual capital at Skandia', that provided information on about 40 different factors which investors said were important to them. Edvinsson claimed that the company's ability to measure and report on its intangibles reduced its cost of capital by 1 per cent. Skandia hoped that its reports would also encourage other companies

127

to report on their intangibles – believing that this would help Skandia invest its own funds more effectively. Skandia published its intellectual capital supplement twice a year until broader problems started to affect the brand of its Swedish firm, making it more difficult to boast about the company's intangibles.

I talked to the Group HR Director for Skandia UK, Mark O'Connell.

Author: 'What are Skandia in the UK doing to manage intellectual capital today?'

O'Connell: 'Our business is predicated on people, it's all about people. As you know, we're just being acquired in a hostile takeover and £100 million of the £3.5 billion that is being spent to buy us is going on goodwill. So we need to get the most value from our people that we can. Of course we need to look at how we can make efficiencies after all, 70 per cent of our total costs are people costs. But if we can show how we can harness this asset, of course that's going to add more value, it's going to have more impact and sustain us for longer.

We use a similar tool to Navigator called Prism. The three sides of the prism represent our shareholders, customers and people. It's a vehicle to help us express our strategy in each of these three terms. Like a real prism, depending on where you stand when you shine light through it you get a different perspective, you see slightly different colours but it's all part of the same. It ensures we see people as a basic element in what we're trying to do, that the people perspective is part of all of our strategy discussions.

We believe and present ourselves to be an innovative financial services provider. We always look at the market differently to our competitors. Ten years ago we made an important strategic decision not to sell direct, but only through financial advisers which meant that we would move to business-to-business sales. Since we weren't going to be selling directly and would be relying on a wholly independent person to sell our products, it meant that these products needed to be at least better than average. The change implied a significant strategic risk and the rest of the market didn't really understand what we were doing.

As a result, although our HR processes don't look any different to anywhere else, they're different in how we use them. Our employees need to understand our unique perspective on the customer and to demonstrate what we call 'the Skandia way', demonstrating our values of creativity, passion, commitment, courage and contribution. Interestingly, we've not tried to explain what we mean by these values in words, we tend to demonstrate them in pictures instead. This has worked for us very well – everyone knows what we mean, what being passionate is about. If someone puts forward a proposal but they don't believe in it, it's very unlikely to be accepted. Someone would say, 'Let's take this off the table as I'm not seeing any passion'.

We've put a lot of work into ensuring we recruit the right people. We quite often say when we turn people down that they're not the 'Skandia type of people'. We don't pay top dollar so it's important that potential recruits are committed to what we're doing. So I spend at least half an hour with new head hunters talking about the culture of this business and explaining that we won't recruit anyone if they give us a short list of very competent candidates but where the chemistry, interplay, the right decision-making style is not there.

Our training and development tends to be very specific as we are very attentive to where the business is going. We don't have long lists of training courses you can request to go on. And we spend time on succession planning and talent management. We segment our people and look at their performance and potential. We have identified people who have very high performance and are therefore very important to the business. But they may not be the leaders of tomorrow, there may be people in the business who are more junior to them but who have more potential. So we'll engage with the business to help them plan what they're going to do about this.

The level of commitment in the business is very high. This impacts on retention and the average length of service now is 15 years. It's not about being old-fashioned, our Chief Executive has 17 years' experience at Skandia and he's only 43. But this brings us a level of maturity, of understanding of the business, that helps us to continue to do things differently and do this well.'

Skandia's staffing model is also linked to their particular position in the market. The company has now got one of the smallest but highest paying sales forces in the industry, which is just in technical sales. Because of Skandia's reliance on a non-employed sales force, the company has had to become involved in developing these non-employees (while being careful not to provide an indirect benefit that could be deemed an inducement). HR's credibility in the business is demonstrated in its involvement in this external development.

Author: 'Can you give me an example of this development?'

O'Connell: 'A key need was that the financial advisers should be as competent as they could be and we've put a lot of effort into training these people who are not our employees. They need to know why our products are complicated to be able to explain them simply. HR is involved in this to ensure what we communicate externally we communicate internally as well. And we have commissioned and provided access to our training provision. For example, in Hong Kong, the government under Chinese rule decided to introduce an accreditation for financial advisers. Our Regional Director there commissioned two of my team to build and deliver a training course. A day and a half was spent purely on the products but another day and a half was spent on time management and presentation skills, and helping the self-employed advisers manage themselves effectively.

Author: 'And has the capability of your employees and non-employed advisers provided the business with any specific opportunities?'

It's difficult to say we've done anything different because of the capability we have. We employ good people and we let them get on and do their jobs. But we do a lot of blue sky thinking and generate a lot of ideas. For example, our salespeople might come back from a sales call and say they didn't sell anything because of some factor about the product, so we'll feed this back into the ideas factory. Or marketing will ask our salespeople: 'If we do this to a product will it fly?' And there's a lot of cross-functional dialogue, so a salesperson may take someone from IT along with them to meet a customer to help them fix a problem with their use of the extranet. So in this way, our success is all about the people we have got.

That doesn't mean we don't need to change. If you take the sigmoid curve, we need to recognize that all businesses go through this sort of change. We're the fastest growing life and pensions company in the UK and one of the few financial services firms that have had no regulatory sanctions; we've never been in breach. In three years' time the business will be fundamentally different. In this environment, we only know one way of managing the business and that's full on.'

Author: 'Given Accounting for People and the debate about the OFR, what are your views on the role of measurement, both in general terms and at Skandia?'

O'Connell: 'I think it's very sad that people view HCM in this way, that they have latched onto the data angle, that they think having the same sort of data as Finance will some how get HR better recognized. Even now, you read things that suggest that responding to the OFR or some other regulation will make HR more important. How can being driven by regulation to record HR activity for shareholders make the value of HR increase? Just because you can report it doesn't mean that it has more impact. This has got to be the wrong answer!

Measurement does have its place. For example, I know that our absence rates are less than 3 per cent and I know how these compare to the national benchmark for the sector. We're redesigning and realigning our incentive plan at the moment, and I need to be able to have hard numbers for this when discussing it at the company level – I need to be able to express the impact of the policy in this way. This type of thing shows that I am managing my function effectively. And showing I can do this gives me the right to comment on what's happening in the other functions and across the business too.'

Author: 'And what about more strategic aspects of people management – your values for example. How do you measure their impact?'

O'Connell: 'Well, we have a 90-question on-line staff survey and we do all the normal statistical analysis on this. But we don't have any formal measures around our values. Our values are mostly about behaviours. People will say, 'I don't think you're being passionate about that'. It's subjective. I don't think you can say someone is or is not passionate in a hard and definite way. Everyone is passionate about something so it's about finding the right hooks to engage them. I don't think it helps to try and pin it down or put a number on it – people know it when they see it. Reporting on it is about saying we think we made this happen and that this may lead to whatever it might be.'

Author: 'What about your role and that of the HR team – how does HR support the business to deliver on its strategy?'

O'Connell: 'Having an impact on the business is the *raison d'être* of HR and the HR strategy. We have to understand the business strategy at quite a simple level and translate the people perspective of it. The business strategy is the big tapestry and we need to ask ourselves what is our piece underneath it? It's what we call our 'core translation'. How can we communicate the strategy in a way that people can relate to? What are the employee messages that link through to the strategy?

At the executive level I spend more time on the business strategy than on HR strategy. For example I'm working on plans for the acquisition, what I need to do to prepare the HR community, so that we all understand what we need to do before the organization works out what's hit it. The organization is just waiting for this juggernaut coming at us and our value added is planning for it so that when the executive is ready, we can say, 'this is what's going to happen'. We can give them the tools and information flows to understand it and communicate it to their teams.'

Summary of Intangible Value

Reader: *'There are a lot of new ideas in here!'*

Author: 'Well, there's some, but like much of the rest of the book, most of these ideas are already out there, I've just grouped them together in a new way. There are three main exceptions to this. The first of these is the customer value chain. Again, the pieces are all there, but I don't know of anyone else who has connected the service value chain and customer capital in this way. But this is only included in this book to support some of the other ideas on intangibles. It doesn't really form a core model within the book.

The second new piece which is a much more pivotal model within HCM is the HCM value chain. Again, in one way there's nothing new here. A lot of people are talking about the importance of HCM. But there's still not much action. I think all the organizations that go around saying, 'people are our most important asset' need to understand that this statement has to have some consequences. They need to understand that there is a process that leverages these assets, that this is a key business process, and that it puts HR in the driving seat. Of course it's also possible to think that people only provide value through Porter's value chain but this means that people are really only resources and have the same level of value as buildings and machinery.

The third area is the three levels of value. More than any-thing, the need to differentiate between creating value, which is the activity required to produce created value, compared to the other levels of value, is the central message of the book. It is the concept of creating and created value that is the key differentiator between HRM and HCM.'

Reader: *'So does creating value always rely on intangibles?'*

Author: 'No, not always. I think intangibles account for a large pro-portion of created value, but there are other ways to create value too and these are described in Chapter 5. I also think it's interesting that, without considering intangibles, the Boston Consulting Group (BCG) come to similar conclusions about the importance of people and people management in their review of people businesses (companies in which people costs account for between 40 and 70 per cent of total spend-ing and are larger costs than capital, R&D and suppliers):

> It goes without saying that managing people is a key task for any company. But in a people business, this task becomes central to success. Because employees represent both the major cost and the major driver of value creation, people management moves that lead to even small changes in operational performance can have a major impact on returns … Given the high financial stakes, people management needs to be a core operational process and not solely a support function run by the human resources department. (Barber and Strack, 2005)

BCG also explain that people businesses need to use differ-ent performance measures. For example, these companies should focus on measures like employee rather than capital productivity.'

References

Armstrong, M. and Baron, A. (2002). *Strategic HRM: The key to improved business performance.* Chartered Institute of Personnel and Development.
Barber, L., Hayday, S. and Bevan, S. (1999). *From People to Profits: the HR link in the service-profit chain.* Institute for Employment Studies, Report 355.

Barber, F. and Strack, R. (2005). 'The surprising economics of a people business', *Harvard Business Review*, June, 81–90.

Bartlett, C.A. and Ghoshal, S. (2002). 'Building competitive advantage through people', *MIT Sloan Management Review*, Winter, 34–41.

Bates, S. (2003). 'The metrics maze', *HR Magazine*, December, 50–55.

Becker, B.E., Huselid, M.A. and Ulrich, D. (2001). *The HR Scorecard*. Harvard Business School Press.

Ernst & Young Center for Business Innovation (1997). *Measures that Matter*. Ernst & Young.

Finn, R. and Ingham, J. (2004). 'United Kingdom mulls HR metrics', *HR Magazine*, April, 27.

Flamholtz, E.G. (1985). *Human Resource Accounting: Advances in Concepts, Methods, and Applications*, 2nd Edn. Jossey-Bass Publishers.

Gates, S. (2003). *Linking People Measures to Strategy*. The Conference Board. Report Number: R-1342-03-RR. December.

Heskett, J.L., Jones, T.O., Loveman, G.W., Sasser, W.E. Jr. and Schlesinger, L.A. (1994). 'Putting the service-profit chain to work', *Harvard Business Review*, March–April, 164–73.

Heskett, J.L., Sasser, W.E. Jr. and Schlesinger, L.A. (1997). *The Service Profit Chain: How Leading Companies Link Profit and Growth to Loyalty, Satisfaction, and Value*. Harvard Business School Press.

Heskett, J.L., Sasser, W.E. Jr. and Schlesinger, L.A. (2003). *The Value Profit Chain: Treat Employees like Customers and Customers like Employees*. The Free Press.

Huselid, M.A. and Becker, B.E. (1995). *The Strategic Impact of High Performance Work Systems*. Rutgers University.

Kaplan, R.S. and Norton, D.P. (2000). 'Having trouble with your strategy? Then map it', *Harvard Business Review*, September–October, 63–72.

Kaplan, R.S. and Norton, D.P. (2004a). 'Measuring the strategic readiness of intangible assets', *Harvard Business Review*, February, 52–63.

Kaplan, R.S. and Norton, D.P. (2004b) *Strategy Maps: Converting Intangible Assets into Tangible Outcomes*. Harvard Business School Press.

Kearns, P. (2004). *One Stop Guide: Human Capital Management*. Personnel Today Management Resources.

Kirn, S.R., Rucci, A.J., Huselid, M.A. and Becker, B.E. (1999). 'Strategic human resource management at Sears', *Human Resource Management*, **38**(4), Winter, 329–35.

Lev, B. (2001). *Intangibles: Management, Measurement and Reporting.* Brookings Institution Press.

Lev, B. (2004). 'Sharpening the intangibles edge', *Harvard Business Review*, June, 109–116.

Mayo, A. (2001). *The Human Value of the Enterprise: Valuing People As Assets – Monitoring, Measuring, Managing.* Nicholas Brealey Publishing.

Nahapiet, J. and Ghoshal, S. (1998). 'Social capital, intellectual capital, and the organizational advantage'. *Academy of Management Review*, **23**, 242–66.

Purcell, J., Hutchinson, S., Kinnie, N., Rayton, B. and Swart, J. (2002). *Sustaining Success in Difficult Times: Research summary.* Chartered Institute of Personnel and Development.

Purcell, J., Kinnie, N., Hutchinson, S., Rayton, B. and Swart, J. (2003). *Understanding the People and Performance Link: Unlocking the black box.* Chartered Institute of Personnel and Development.

Reichheld, F.F. (1996a). *The Quest for Loyalty: Creating Value through Partnership.* Harvard Business School Press.

Reichheld, F.F. (1996b). *The Loyalty Effect: The Hidden Force Behind Growth, Profits and Lasting Value.* Harvard Business School Press.

Reichheld, F.F. and Sasser, W.E. Jr. (1990). 'Zero defections: quality comes to services', *Harvard Business Review,* September–October, 105–11.

Rucci, A.J., Kirn, S.P. and Quinn, R.T. (1998). 'The employee–customer-profit chain at Sears', *Harvard Business Review*, January–February, 82–97.

Scarborough, H. and Elias, J. (2002). *Evaluating Human Capital.* Chartered Institute of Personnel and Development.

Schlesinger, L.A. and Heskett, J.L. (1991). 'The service-driven service company', *Harvard Business Review*, September–October, 71–81.

Stacey, R.D. (2000). *Strategic Management and Organizational Dynamics: The Challenge of Complexity.* 3rd Edn. Pearson Education.

Stewart, T.A. (1997). *Intellectual Capital: The New Wealth of Organizations.* Doubleday.

Sveiby, K.E. (1997). *The New Organizational Wealth: Managing & Measuring Knowledge-Based Assets.* Berrett-Koehler Publishers.

Tobin, J. (1969). 'A general equilibrium approach to monetary theory.' *Journal of Money, Credit and Banking,* **1**(1), 15–29.

Ulrich, D. and Smallwood. N. (2004). 'Capitalizing on capabilities', *Harvard Business Review*, June, 119–127.

Youngman, R. (2003). 'Understanding and measuring intangibles: a journey of learning', *Spectra*, Autumn, 38–40.

Warren, K. (2000). 'The softer side of strategy dynamics'. *Business Strategy Review*, **11**(1), 45–58.

Work Foundation. (2005). *Cracking the Performance Code. How Firms Succeed.* The Work Foundation.

5

Creating Value in People Management

Introduction

Reader: *'It sounds as if this will be quite a key chapter?'*

Author: 'Yes, I think Chapter 5 marks a turning point in the book. It links together everything we have covered so far and forces us closer to defining HCM. Talent management is used as an example to illustrate how HCM is fundamentally different from HR.'

Reader: *'And are we talking theory here or are there organizations which are managing talent and human capital in the way that you describe?'*

Author: 'There are some organizations that are doing this. The case studies provide some examples of organizations which are using some aspects of the processes I describe. I also spoke to other companies which were doing even more. Unfortunately, these companies did not want their competitors to know about what they were doing. So I'm not able to write about these.'

Levels of People Management Strategy Development

James Walker (1992), founder of the HR Planning Society, identifies three main methods for developing people management strategy: a separate process; an aligned process and an integrated process. In this chapter, I will review these three levels and also link them to the evolution of the HR function: from Personnel to HR, and now on to HCM.

A Separate Process (Personnel)

This level of people management strategy is associated with the self-standing Personnel function of the 1980s. At this level, top management sets the overall business strategy and then Personnel develops a distinct people management plan to support it. This plan ensures that business priorities are implemented through a set of basic people management practices supporting the generic employee life cycle.

In some cases, the people plan has no real link to the business plan. For example, it might deal with improving the speed or efficiency of recruitment without considering changes in the business's recruitment needs. In other cases, the people plan is developed after the business plan so that the people implications of the business objectives can be examined. For example, like the causal chain case study from Chapter 2, a company might decide to start up some new operations. At this level of planning, the Personnel function would be told to develop a people management plan for the recruitment of 2000 people. This is a significant action for the business but all Personnel needs to do is extend the existing recruitment processes to the new recruitment needs. The function needs to ensure the appropriate people are recruited but it is in no way responsible for the effectiveness of the new operations or the people working in them.

The outputs of the separate people plan are generally fairly incremental, value for money improvements in mainly tangible human and organizational resources. These tangible outputs can have relatively clear financial impacts but these are normally limited to relatively small reductions in costs.

Bartlett and Ghoshal (2002) describe the role of the Personnel function in this environment:

> In the 1980's era of competitive-strategy analysis, their function was typically supportive and administrative. Once line managers had

translated top management's strategic objectives into specific operational priorities, the role of HR staff was to ensure that recruitment, training, benefits administration and the like supported the well-defined strategic and operational agenda.

Being divorced from the business tends to result in Personnel having dysfunctional relationships with line managers and processes that are not fit for purpose. A Personnel function operating at this level is also always at risk of being outsourced. An external supplier is almost certainly able to provide these value for money activities better and cheaper than the organization's Personnel function by making them their source of added or created value.

This separation from the business can also mean that Personnel has to cope with a business strategy that has not been well thought through from a people management perspective. This is the reason why, following their joint publication on re-engineering (1993), both Hammer (1997) and Champy (1995) reflected separately that lack of attention to people is one of the main causes for the failure of many re-engineering projects.

A Personnel Approach to Talent Management

Talent management gained very quick acceptance following publication of McKinsey and Gibson's War for Talent report (Chambers *et al.*, 1998) and as yet it shows no sign of losing popularity. One reason for this endurance is the significance of McKinsey's findings, including that firms with better talent provide a 22 per cent higher total return to shareholders.

However, this conclusion does not explain the fact that the term 'talent management' is actually used to cover a very wide spectrum of approaches. So a more fundamental reason for the term's broad usage may be the positive implications of the word 'talent'. In fact, many organizations have just renamed their employees 'talent' and nothing much else has changed. This approach works all right as long as everyone provides more or less the same level of performance and can be engaged in more or less the same sort of way. For example, Watson Wyatt (Pfau and Kay, 2002) recommend that organizations should:

'Focus on the basics. People are more alike than different.' It seems counter-intuitive when researchers use detailed data to identify the unique factors that make people tick, but we suggest that companies stop looking so hard for differentiating factors. Over and over again we have seen organizations spending phenomenal amounts of money figuring out what their target employees (say, female Generation Xers) want, and then putting special programs in place to attract them. In our view, this is a serious misallocation of resources. Because what those female GenXers want the most from the workplace is exactly what everyone else wants the most: pay for performance, opportunity, strong leadership, fairness. It is very difficult for companies to get those big things right, so they should place their resources where they do the most good.

Engagement of talent is based on the development and communication of an employee value proposition (EVP) that at least partly articulates the psychological contract, the value exchange, or the deal between the employer and employee. The EVP also forms the basis for an employer brand that the organization can use to market itself to potential employees. The creation of an 'extreme' EVP is one of the seven talent imperatives identified by McKinsey and Gibson (Chambers *et al.*, 1998):

> You can win the war for talent, but first you must elevate talent management to a burning corporate priority. Then, to attract and retain the people you need, you must create and perpetually refine an employee value proposition: senior management's answer to why a smart, energetic, ambitious individual would want to come and work with you rather than with the team next door.

The firm explains that an EVP needs to address four areas: great company, great leaders, great job and attractive compensation. The EVP also needs to be consistently demonstrated in all of an organization's talent management processes. However, in the same way that the term 'talent' is used to refer to 'people', the term 'talent management' can be used to refer to all or part of an organization's approach to people management. So some organizations apply the term talent management or talent acquisition to their recruitment or resourcing processes, often to imply they are taking a supply chain perspective to the sourcing of their people. Many 'talent managers' in organizations are in fact recruiters. Other organizations see talent management as the development of 'talents' or potential and place it within their approach to leadership development.

Any of these approaches can indicate adding or creating value if an organization is trying to compete on, for example, its ability to recruit more talented people (see the Ernst & Young case study) or to get more

141

from its people by really helping them to achieve their full potential (see the Microsoft case study in Chapter 7). But most of the time this sort of 'talent management' reflects a fairly basic, value for money and Personnel-level attempt to recruit good people and provide them with a fairly typical amount of personal development.

An Aligned Process (HRM)

At the aligned level, people management strategy is developed alongside the business strategy, helping the business achieve its objectives through the capabilities of people and the processes required to produce this capability. The two strategies are discussed and presented together but are developed through distinct although linked processes. However, there is at least 'some likelihood that they will influence each other and be adopted as a cohesive, or at least an adhesive, whole' (Walker, 1992).

Supporting the business in this way tends to require the use of particular bundles of best practices appropriate to the business plan and implementing these practices in a way that is aligned with, but not yet integrated into the fabric of the organization. The practices do not provide a direct impact on the business but act in combination with other intangible and tangible factors, and through complex systems of cause and effect relationships. It is virtually impossible to isolate the effects of any individual people management practices.

An appropriate update on the resourcing requirement might mean HR proposing to delay starting up some of the new operations until the new people have been hired and fully trained, but offering other ways to meet the same ends. For example, they might suggest using economies of scale to invest in a better approach to induction in order to achieve the same revenue growth, potentially at a better level of profitability. But the recruitment activity does not result in financial benefits on its own. The recruitment enables the new operations and it is these that provide the financial results.

Kaplan and Norton (2004) provide another example that explains how training can lead indirectly to improvements in sales and margins:

> Employee training in total quality management (TQM) and six sigma techniques can directly improve process quality. Such improvement can then be expected to lead to improved customer satisfaction, which, in

turn, should increase customer loyalty. Ultimately, customer loyalty leads to improved sales and margins from long-term customer relationships.

The outputs of these processes are intangible or tangible resources and capabilities (the right people in the right place at the right time with the right competencies and attitudes) that are aligned with a particular competitive positioning or strategic intent.

At this level, HR's role is about being given the business plan, figuring out what needs to be done in people management terms and then delivering this. On an ongoing basis, it is about asking clients what they want. In responding to both sets of inputs, HR assumes that the rest of the business knows what it needs. However, because the people management strategy is aligned with the business strategy, the HR function has broader responsibilities than at the Personnel level. These responsibilities include the organization's people management processes, the capability of the people and a shared responsibility for the business results. Because of this responsibility, the function is often seen as a business partner that shares comparable boardroom status to other disciplines.

Bartlett and Ghoshal (2002) add:

> In the 1990s, human-resources managers increasingly were included in the strategic conversation, often to help define and develop the company's core competencies – and almost always to align the organizational design and management skills to support those strategic assets.

An HR function adds more value than an outsourcing company could do because it has a better understanding of the business and its needs. One of the ways that HR has improved its understanding of the business has been by developing more effective partnerships with line managers. But this has also tended to result in an increasing separation from individual employees. Out of the two schools of HRM discussed in Chapter 2, this has led to a heavy focus on the hard rather than the soft approach and to questions over HR's employee champion or employee advocate role. In many organizations, a separate organization development function has emerged to take forward the softer aspects of people management. In other organizations, the employee advocate role has been delegated to line managers, but not always that effectively. This has led us to the point where people are increasingly recognized as an organization's main source of sustainable competitive advantage, but where people are still not managed in a way that would demonstrate that this is understood.

An HRM Approach to Talent Management

In contrast to the perspective described earlier where everyone is talent, a more strategic approach to talent management is likely to see talent as people in specific segments of the workforce. These key people have the particular skills, knowledge and experience that provide the rare, difficult to imitate, intangible value that underpins resource-based strategy.

Although some companies dislike the inequality inherent in segmenting their workforce, there are good reasons for doing this. Firstly, this is exactly what they do with investors of other forms of capital. Companies do not treat all of their financial investors the same – they focus on those that make the greatest and longest-term contribution. In fact, some large companies have tried to cut down the number of small investors to save costs. Neither do companies treat all of their customers the same, again they focus on the most loyal and the highest spenders.

Secondly, an organization's most important people are often also the most likely to look elsewhere. Talent will always be in high demand, and many talent groups will be attracted by the prospect of short periods of employment with a large number of employers. This is why Peter Cappelli (2000) promotes a 'market-driven retention strategy' which is focused on specific talent pools:

> You can't counter the pull of the market; you can't shield your people from attractive opportunities and aggressive recruiters. The old goal of HR management – to minimize overall employee turnover – needs to be replaced by a new goal: to influence who leaves and when. If managing employee retention in the past was akin to tending a dam that keeps a reservoir in place, today is more like managing a river. The object is not to prevent water from flowing out but to control its direction and its speed.

This need to segment people is also supported by research evidence. One study found that even in simple jobs, there was a 19 per cent difference in value added discretionary performance between average and superior performers. In complex jobs the difference was 48 per cent and in high-ticket industrial sales the difference was as great as 120 per cent (Hunter *et al.*, 1990).

In any case, talent management, implemented effectively, does not have to be seen as divisive by those people not identified as talent. This does not mean they are 'talentless' and talent management should not stop organizations developing skills, 'talents' and potential in all of their employees. After all, as Delong and Vijayaraghavan (2003) explain, discussing the competent, steady performers they call B players, these 'supporting actors of the corporate world' are still the main drivers of overall organizational performance. However, using the rather emotive terms 'talent' and 'talent management' often does not help. Instead of this, I believe that organizations should set up different groups for different purposes (graduate fast-track, key client managers, leaders to watch, and so on) and ensure there are clear criteria, entry and exit mechanisms for each of these groups.

So how should organizations identify the right sorts of talent? Wendy Hirsh at the Institute for Employment Studies notes that pools must fit with business needs (Warren, 2006):

> Business fit is the issue for me: having a clear idea of the different talent pools of people required for different sorts of business need. Talent can be a plural thing, but not a wishy-washy thing. A lot of organizations do need to identify a pool of people who will be able to do senior roles, but there are also your most talented specialist people and the need to identify talent lower down for people to make the transition to middle-level roles. It is about thinking about the critical talent pools you need to identify for roles in the business.

As examples of this fit, a company developing globally might define talent as people with diverse experience in several countries. A company that is becoming increasingly diversified might refer to talent as people with particular skills that form part of its core competencies and help to consolidate its different companies and brands.

Cappelli (2000) discusses United Parcel Service (UPS) which considers its drivers to be its most important talent. The company had suffered high turnover of drivers and discovered that the reason for this was that drivers disliked the tedious job of loading trucks. When UPS gave this task to another group of staff, driver turnover dropped dramatically. This example illustrates the fact that talent does not have to refer to an organization's leadership team or even a graduate management population.

In fact, an organization's talent pools can be any combination of key people and other people who may be matched against key roles. For example:

Key people
- The current leadership team.
- Other senior people with specific capabilities, networks and relationships which would be difficult or time-consuming to replace.
- Individuals with generic skills which are scarce in the employment market and would also therefore be difficult to replace.
- High performers who make a particularly significant contribution to the organization.
- High potentials, which could include employees and especially graduates in early career grades, or at positions just below the leadership team.

Key roles
- Roles in which investment provides the greatest return – which Boudreau and Ramstad (2004) define as 'pivotal roles'.
- Roles that are particularly central to business strategy – which Kaplan and Norton (2004) call 'strategic job families'.

The HRM approach to talent management recognizes that different talent pools have varying engagement needs. This contrasts with Watson Wyatt's findings but is supported by Penna's research which has found, for example, that knowledge workers have different engagement drivers from production workers. The main driver of engagement for people who have a direct role in manufacturing a product or delivering a service tends to be their relationship with their line manager (measured by questions in a staff survey like: 'my manager deals with poor performance fairly'). Secondary drivers include employees' life at work ('I have control over my work/home balance'), the organization's values ('the organization shows commitment to ethical business decisions and conduct') and senior leadership ('I am able to give my input to our leaders'). Knowledge workers usually have a low amount of direct management and the manager is just one element of several factors which are all important in gaining their engagement. The order of factors tends to be life at work first, followed by senior leadership, organizational values and then the knowledge worker's relationship with their manager.

Supporting these findings, research by Purcell and colleagues (2002) found that knowledge workers are engaged by factors linked to their careers, training and job challenge while clerical and manual workers were engaged by involvement and teamworking. Similarly, RBS has found that managerial staff are most affected by work–life balance and clerical staff by their relationships with customers supported by the quality of the brands. BT has also done some interesting work in this area. The company has identified separate engagement profiles for groups of individuals sharing similar lifestyle needs (for example, homeworker, mid-life parent, enthusiastic line manager and so on). Each of these groups has distinct engagement needs which can be used by line managers to engage people in these groups in different ways.

These different engagement needs mean that a key requirement in this perspective is for an organization to develop and deliver against a different EVP for each of its talent pools.

An Integrated Process (HCM)

Walker (1992) explains that, at the top level of strategy development, people management is integrated into the business strategy along with other functional strategies. The discussion within business and people strategy development is not about people management processes but business issues that people management can support. In fact, at this point the HCM strategy and the business strategy become so aligned and integrated that they are no longer distinct.

Given the prime importance of people and the transformational potential of the HCM value chain, I would also suggest that to make the integrated process suitable for HCM the links between the business and HCM strategy need to be truly two-way. Business strategy will lead most of the time, but in some areas and at least for some of the time business strategy should be influenced and driven by the people management strategy.

To have this sort of impact the people management strategy needs to focus on finding ways to delight customers, investors and existing or prospective employees (as investors of human capital) based upon the capability or potential capability of people in the organization. This is about creating capability the organization will need in the future rather than just the capability that it needs today. It is about driving and accelerating business strategy by developing capabilities in agility and flexibility, and creativity and innovation.

This level of people management strategy is an example of resource-based strategy but it also much more than this. People are not just part of a valuable resource or core competency, they are the resource, they really are the most important asset. Jim Collins demonstrates the point in his book, *Good to Great* (© 2001 Jim Collins):

> The executives who ignited the transformations from good to great did not first figure out where to drive the bus and then get people to take it there. No, they *first* got the right people on the bus (and the wrong people off the bus) and *then* figured out where to drive it. They said, in essence, 'Look, I don't really know where we should take this bus. But I know this much: If we get the right people on the bus, the right people in the right seats, and the wrong people off the bus, then we'll figure out how to take it someplace great.' … if you have the wrong people, it doesn't matter whether you discover the right direction; you *still* won't have a great company. Great vision without great people is irrelevant.

I talked to Peter Reilly, a director of the IES, who made a similar point about the importance of people and HCM:

> To me, HCM is about more than having good HR policies and good line manager practices. It's about putting these elements on the same footing as the other factors that inform financial performance. Only a few companies treat people this way, like Google, which gives all its staff one day a week to spend on innovation. In general, this still isn't what's happening. Businesses are continuing to treat their people as expendable resources. So when push comes to shove, employees are seen as a cost, not an asset. The key test for me is whether – when an organization faces a downturn, and they don't need the same number of staff doing what they've been doing – is the management of that organization thinking about what else these people could usefully do? That's the way it is in Japan where they're more interested in core competencies. They would ask, what is the capability of this organization, and what can we do with this capability? This type of thinking may apply to those people who are sufficiently prized, the Chelsea football club model, where an organization finds very talented people and thinks of a way to fit them in. But very few organizations are applying this thinking more broadly.

But HCM does not have to be about the development of intangible capability. HCM recognizes that much of what we do in people management, even at the level of created value, is designed to have a direct impact on people's performance and on business activities and results, without any intangibles being involved. For example, HCM can refer to the HR function producing truly wonderful business solutions through its knowledge of people's and the organization's capability, something the business just had not thought would be possible. It can also refer to taking advantage of exceptional opportunities that are not in the business plan but come along once in a blue moon. Sull (2005) calls these 'golden opportunities' and explains:

> *Golden opportunities* are the infrequent occasions when a firm can create significant value disproportionate to the resources invested, in a short period of time. Many variables influence the nature and timing of an opportunity; these include technology evolution, customers' evolving needs, government policy, changes in the capital markets, and rivals' priorities. Golden opportunities arise when several windows of opportunity open simultaneously. Golden opportunities are rare. They pass quickly. And generally they emerge because of exogenous factors – that is, variables outside the company's control.

An example within HCM might be taking advantage of the opportunity to acquire an important team from a competitor.

This level of people management strategy results in significant business and financial impact but it does not directly produce these results. The HCM value chain produces the capability and potential for sustainability and transformation of the business. This capability is converted to business results through other value chains in the business. It is down to the rest of the business (influenced by HCM) to make the best use of the capability that HCM has generated. This explains why many successful firms do not have particularly sophisticated people management architectures, and some of the leading companies in HCM are not the most profitable. HCM can tip the balance in favour of business success but it cannot assure it.

An HCM version of the recruitment example discussed for the two previous levels now becomes a situation in which HR would say something like: 'There are still substantial opportunities in the market if we can recruit the right sort of people to deliver our offer in the way we require. We need to develop our employer brand to attract a particular type of people. Doing this will enable us to grow by at least another 2500 people this year.'

At this level, the HR function is a strategic player in the business. Its focus is on nurturing, managing, and extracting the maximum possible performance from the organization's people. So Bartlett and Ghoshal (2002) explain that in the 2000s:

> Now, as companies move into the war for talent and as individuals with specialized knowledge, skills and expertise are recognized as the scarce strategic resource, HR professionals must become key players in the design, development and delivery of a company's strategy.

HCM strategy at Deutsche Bank

Deutsche Bank is developing the capability of its people in order to make it possible to manage them in an integrated way across the diverse banking group. I talked to Elizabeth Warren, Managing Director, People and Culture.

Author: 'What does HCM mean for you?'

Warren: 'Human capital management is about the acquisition, development and retention of the very best talent we can get. We're an intellectual capital-based organization. You could argue that we've got lots of financial capital so we're a capital-based organization. But if you look at where our profits come from, our true profits, it's large global markets, our sales and trading businesses. It's in derivatives and our entrepreneurial, new product areas. We're totally reliant on our creativity and intellectual capital to develop these. Our intellectual capital leverages our financial capital. Of course you need the financial capital too – to fund the intellectual capital. But if that's all you focus on then you get forced into commoditized areas where margins are very low. So our success depends on fully utilizing the talent we have available.

We've been trying to build the right behaviours to create a performance culture, and an integrated culture across the different acquisitions, all very different businesses. For example, the retail and investment bank are chalk and cheese. The investment bank is very Anglo-Saxon and the retail bank very German and continental European. Previously we had very product-driven talent programmes and nothing that could be called an employer brand. People were not talking very positively about Deutsche Bank, the way they would talk about the organization that employed them before the acquisitions. And we had done very little to publicize ourselves, or to engage our staff.'

Author: 'I've always found that engagement is an interesting concept in financial services – what does it look like here?'

Warren: 'Real engagement can be a problem at an investment bank. We bring in bright, able people and pay them a lot. But just doing this has a high risk associated with it. We wanted to make them feel proud and good about the bank, as well as being committed to whatever the individual is doing. We wanted to create an organization they could be genuinely proud of. We've got a huge heritage and there's an incredible amount of philanthropy going on.

People said, 'what are you talking about?, they're money motivated, they're bought and this isn't what they're looking for'. I disagreed. I think all people have similar, broad needs. They may be money motivated but pay is about a need to prove themselves, an indicator of self-worth, it's not a means in itself. If you treat them as if they're just money grabbing people who don't care about others, and some organizations do, you're not going to get the best out of them. I believe everyone has a higher goal. We're not here just to make a profit; we don't exist just to create shareholder value. Of course, we need to do this too, but there needs to be something beyond this.'

Author: 'And what else have you been doing to implement HCM?'

Warren: 'We've built an integrated HCM strategy, bringing together L&D; diversity; talent resourcing; performance management; talent development; leadership development and our leadership standards. All these programmes are now global and cross-divisional. And we linked reward to our HCM strategy too. This has helped us create a single employer brand and we've linked this to our external brand and to our HCM strategy. Doing this has given us one integrated approach. Our HCM strategy hangs together better, we can communicate it cohesively, and we've become less wary of communicating it. Previously, our processes varied across the business specific and national groups. These were bound to be sub-optimized because they were not integrated and not adequately focused on the end result. Having them integrated allows us to focus on how our processes, in their totality, optimize our talent, rather than worrying about developing the latest, state of the art processes within each separate area.

We created joint ventures – with our corporate and culture management; our communications, PR and marketing teams; our business management teams; our art foundations. We combined initiatives that were often very trivial at one level. For example, in London we sponsor the Royal Academy, National Gallery and the Tate but we've not done much with this. So we introduced an Art Card that everyone could use for free entry for themselves and their partner. Financially, it was peanuts for our guys, but it made quite an impression. We've got a huge art collection here so we organized tours of the office. Staff said that before this they would have used these rooms and seen the art but never thought about it.

We've achieved a lot but it's not got as far as it needs to go. We have often had to operate tactically and wait while support has built at the top level. We've focused on identifying champions and using them to help us. But we've had remarkable success in persuading the business to come together as they have.'

Author: 'And what's the role of measurement in HCM?'

Warren: 'I think measurement is important. But it's not measurement for measurement's sake. It's about helping you to see where you are and where you're progressing to. Measurement is only worth doing if you're going to change something or what's the point of measuring? It's a validation of other activity, not a goal in itself. We've used Saratoga too and got some value out of this. It gives you some comfort to know you're not in a dire bottom-quarter positioning. But you get huge amounts of data and the level of feedback from it is very limited – it doesn't tell you much more than talking to your counterparts in other organizations anyway. And it's like statistics and damn lies sometimes with these measurements; you can always twist the results. So I'd much rather focus attention on developing solutions rather than measuring them.'

An HCM Approach to Talent Management

Various surveys show that senior executives understand the strategic importance of talent but many of the same surveys suggest that these executives are underwhelmed with the value created by their talent management programmes. For example, when Hay Group with *Human Resources* magazine (Carrington, 2004) asked over 400 senior HR practitioners about their talent management practices they found that:

- Sixty-six per cent of respondents said talent management is their senior leaders' number one priority or one of their high priorities.
- However, only 48 per cent of respondents said that talent management was on the boardroom table more than once or twice a year.
- Only 46 per cent of respondents said that senior leaders follow existing talent management processes.
- Only 19 per cent thought all their senior leaders would agree that talent management processes add business value.

Hay concluded that:

Business leaders know that talent management is strategically important but HR has failed to make the most of its big opportunity ... The vast majority of firms see it as a series of interventions. 67% say it's about developing people; 63% say it's making the right recruitment and promotion decisions and 48% say it's succession planning. (Carrington, 2004)

Survey findings like this show that there is a disconnection between talent management's importance, and the attention that is paid to current talent management programmes. This gap is caused through the use of value for money or adding value programmes that treat talent very much the same as everyone else in an organization. There will be some incremental additions – a little bit more development, some coaching, a few more career moves, but the basic career dynamic remains the same. As Bartlett and Ghoshal (2002) explain:

> They are tackling a strategic task with old, functional tools, and they are trying to bring about major systemic change with incremental, programmatic solutions.

I think for many organizations the greatest opportunity to create value in talent management is to identify a group of people working within a pivotal role or strategic job family whose own human capital forms a major input to an organization's intangible capability. In addition, there should be a close link between the organization's business activities and what the individuals in this group want to do; their values; the organization's main locations and where the people want to live; their languages and so on.

Chosen carefully, the individuals in this group should be the people most likely to make the greatest and the longest-term investment of their own human capital. This means that these people should be the natural long-term partners of an organization and the organization should be these individuals' employer of choice. Note that I do not use this term in the rather superficial way it is often used. Being an employer of choice could, and I think should, be about becoming the only organization where the people in this group feel they truly belong. Of course, these talented people are not only ever going to work for this one organization but there might be a basis for a new type of relationship with them. (Although note that some research suggests that having seen what Cappelli's market-driven workforce has done to their parents, many GenXers and GenYers would be happy to stay with one employer – they just do not believe it would be possible to do so.) I have previously described this relationship as a career partnership (Ingham, 2006) and now extend the point to refer to the people who have this relationship as career partners, and the group as a partner group.

An HRM approach to talent management suggests that an organization should employ people who fit within its various talent pools for as long as possible. The organization knows these people will leave in a few years time and it tries to guard against them doing this as much as it can. This often seems to involve keeping people identified as talent as busy as possible, so that they do not have time to apply for other jobs! An HCM perspective to talent management and career partnership also recognizes that these individuals are going to want to leave at some point, if only to gain more variety in their careers. However, rather than fighting for a few more months or years of service before these people leave, the organization looks longer term and effectively says, 'Look, we know you are not going to work for us for the next ten years. But we'd very much like it if you would work for us for ten years during the next twenty. We'd like you to partner with us during this time. During some of this period you will be employed by us and at other times you won't. But we're going to keep a special relationship going with you throughout.'

The focus of this approach is on maximizing the lifetime value (not the length of a single employment contract) of people in the partner group. An analogy using customer rather than human capital is relationship marketing's focus on maximizing a customer's lifetime spend (rather than the revenue from an individual transaction).

An organization needs to focus on engaging all its career partners, not just those partners that are in employment at any one point in time. This means that organizations actually have to maintain two partner groups: an internal group and an external one. The external group consists of people who have previously worked in the organization's internal partner group, or have been invited to join the external partner group for later employment when the time is right for both parties.

In this way, an organization's relationship with its career partners changes from being a single transaction to an ongoing cycle, as shown in Figure 5.1.

Managing the External Relationship then Recruiting or Re-recruiting Partners when the Time is Right. The organization needs to manage carefully its relationship with its career partners while they are not employed: keeping in contact with them; engaging them; checking that they are being looked after and possibly influencing the development they are receiving from their current employers.

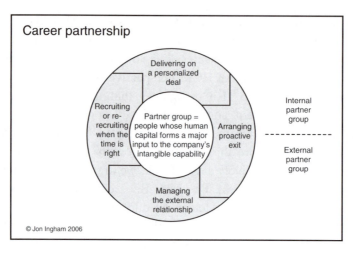

Figure 5.1 Career partnership

The organization also needs to recruit the best possible talent into the external partner group (or potentially directly into the internal partner group). An HRM approach to recruitment involves reactively searching for talent to fill a particular role when a vacancy occurs. Doing this allows an organization to recruit good talent but it cannot guarantee the best talent – these people are not likely to be available during the time-frame in which the organization is recruiting. An HCM perspective develops recruitment into an ongoing and proactive process that aims to find the very best people whenever they are available. Recruiting the best people sets up a positive feedback loop in which, because the organization employs great people, it is seen as an employer of choice by other people with similar qualities, and this helps the organization recruit more great people. In Collins's terms, people get on the bus because of the other people who are already on it (Collins, 2001).

Once the organization has identified people who might have the same attributes as those in the partner groups, these people can be assessed, probably informally, although the stronger the employment brand the more formal and competitive the assessment can be made. The assessment can also be used to benchmark people in the partner groups against the external talent that is available. This means that the organization is able to resource internally with knowledge of all options and to plan succession externally as well as internally, transforming the level and quality of talent that can be made available.

If the people who have been assessed show that they do have the required attributes, they can be invited to join the external partner group and then be recruited into the organization when the time is right for both parties.

An example of this type of proactive pre-recruitment activity is Ernst & Young's approach.

Head Farming at Ernst & Young. Ernst & Young's services operate in relatively specialized, discrete areas. This has enabled Ernst & Young (E&Y) to focus on getting to know the key talent in their specific talent pools, not just to meet specific recruitment needs, but also so that they have a great source of talent to tap when the time is right.

This shift in thinking has occurred since setting up a new HR model in 2003. Along with creating new business partner teams and a central service centre, this has meant that all E&Y's recruitment specialists have been brought together in one place. The new group set up a preferred supplier list of recruitment agencies and bought BrassRing's web-based recruitment system to help them manage the relationship between hiring managers, the recruiters and external agencies. E&Y have also developed a sophisticated recruitment offer that involves more direct hiring. But this change has involved much more than just bringing headhunting in-house. The team's focus has become much more proactive, and farming is now a better analogy than hunting.

I spoke to Mohan Yogendron, who led recruitment services for E&Y's Transactional Advisory Services which has expanded out of the firm's Corporate Finance offer over the last few years.

Author: 'Can you tell me a bit more about what head farming involves?'

Yogendron: 'Our direct recruitment work has grown significantly, both to support net growth in the business and the increased responsibility we've taken on. There were 29 of us recruiting 700 people a year and there's now about 70 (with 20 to 30 of these focusing on graduates) recruiting 3000 people a year. Sixty per cent of these new people are direct recruits – from referrals, direct calls and so on. All the recruiters have individual targets of the percentage of hires they should aim to make from direct sources. Our other key metric is cost per hire, and inevitably as recruitment markets gets tighter this goes up.

In Transaction Advisory Services, and even more so in Tax, the community is very well defined. We do a lot of networking to find out who the relevant people are. And every week we work off our data on new joiners in E&Y. The relevant recruiter will talk to each new employee from target or competitor firms. We'll ask about who they know, who we should be approaching and so on – if it's relevant, of course. Increasingly we find that we may already know everyone in their firms. Of course we stay clear of this when new joiners are under restrictive covenant constraints.

We've grown an in-house research capability of two to three people, each with a recruitment agency background. And we have an effective and interactive approach with the external researchers we're working with. Research costs are quite low so we'll quite often commission research just to map out a market – but usually with some specific hiring in mind. We prefer to do this if we're going to need to recruit within the next six months and it's always easiest to research around a known need. But it's often useful to have the research information to hand. So for example, we had a need to recruit some forensics people for our Global Investigations service. We had only recently done some general research so the core data was still there. We just said that we've already got the data, we can reactivate it.

Once we've mapped out the contacts, we'll decide who is going to make a call – whether it's someone from our team, an agency or whether we ask the head of the business team to do it – and we'll say, by the way, here's the briefing. We're all very strong on etiquette – we can't lie and if someone asks, we'll say where we're from. We don't allow people to pretend they're from some other organization or anything like that. It's one reason we may use an external researcher – they've got more scope to say genuinely that they're calling on behalf of a client. But it helps that we can say we're EY. It's not obviously a recruitment call. If pushed, we can just leave a message for someone at a competitor firm as it's usually conceivable that we may be contacting them around a client assignment in which they are also involved.

One good example of this approach was some work we did for a team within our deal-related services who were developing a new capability. We used external researchers to map out the community, to map out who is where, and to add in information from talking to the clients of these services on who they rate in the market. Eventually we realized there was one name we came across most often and we talked to him – and hired him to lead this activity for the firm.'

Author: 'And what if they're not interested at that time, what happens to them then?'

Yogendron: 'If the time's not right for someone, we'll just arrange to stay in touch and we've been organizing some recruitment-oriented 'Staying in Touch' events. We did one at the Design Museum for all those people from all the roles we've handled that we thought could be right for us but for whatever reason didn't get the job. Either they came close but someone else got it, or they turned us down or we turned them down at the final stage. We've done drinks and jazz and we've had Will Carling presenting on rugby at an event called 'Try EY'. The invites for these events don't use any recruitment related words. We just say, 'We've been in touch; we'd like to check in with you.'

Our Audit recruitment team did something similar with one of the professional accountancy bodies where people could easily go along and say they simply went to an Institute event. We're sensitive to the possibility that people might bump into their colleagues. So we keep the conversation flowing and make sure everyone has met with the right people.'

Delivering on a Personalized Deal. An HCM perspective recognizes that we all have different, individual engagement needs. This view is supported by Delong and Vijayaraghavan (2003), who describe four common misconceptions about employees:

> Everybody is the same; Everybody wants the same thing out of work; Everybody wants to be promoted; Everybody wants to be a manager.

If you do not believe people have different engagement needs, try asking the people you work with what gets them up in the morning. You will generally be provided with a wide variety of needs. I think this diversity is only going to increase. People who see themselves as investors of their own human capital are going to be increasingly interested in what they are getting in return for their investment and how this meets their own individual needs. For example, Gratton and Ghoshal (2003) suggest:

> Managing personal human capital as if it was a business is about having absolute clarity of where to best allocate scarce resources (personal human capital) for short and long-term leverage. It is about choosing among equally attractive options which may yield different benefits. Increasingly, the 'volunteer' employee will want to make an informed choice of allocation by accessing deep information about the potential of different work options for building their intellectual, emotional and social capitals.

Organizations are increasingly going to have to personalize their support. This is the 'individualization' that Tim Miller referred to in his Foreword and the basis for the move from mass production through mass customization and now on to mass personalization that was discussed in Chapter 4. It is also the basis for Ghoshal and Bartlett's vision of an individualized corporation (1998):

> At the heart of the emerging concept of the Individualized Corporation is a fundamentally different belief that companies can and must capitalize on the idiosyncrasies – and even the eccentricities – of people by recognizing, developing and applying their unique capabilities. It takes skill and sensitivity to see the potential in a struggling new recruit, and courage and patience to let him or her develop the unique capabilities he or she brings. But in the end, the personal and organizational rewards can be huge.

To engage career partners individually in this way organizations need to clarify the individual's needs and articulate these, together with the organization's requirements of the individual, in a tailored version of the organization's EVP. The performance management process can then be extended into a two-way 'deal' management process in which delivery against the personalized EVP is the 'parallel agenda', on a par with the business agenda as a topic of conversation between the organization and its career partner.

Arranging a Proactive Exit. Organizations typically use rather reactive approaches to retain their staff. In HRM, companies are generally at least proactive in discussing opportunities within their organizations, but there is still a tendency to pretend the outside world does not exist. So the unwritten rules in many organizations state that if an employee identified as talent and their line manager see a marvellous job for the employee advertised elsewhere neither person can mention the fact that they have seen this. Only once the employee has resigned does the organization take action. At this point, they will use exit interviews as an attempt to re-recruit the employee. If this fails, they will maintain ongoing contact with the ex-employee for six months or more following their departure, in case the career move proves to be unsuccessful. If this does not work, they will invite the ex-employee to join their alumni network hopefully to encourage them to rejoin the organization again at a later date.

These options are often introduced reactively in response to particular business needs. For example, when Cisco was forced to cut staff in 2001, it gave people the option of a year's secondment to a non-profit organization with the option to return. People on secondment received a reduced salary but continued to have access to some of Cisco's benefits including their in-house training programmes.

A more proactive, HCM-level approach to retention recognizes that the best development opportunities can sometimes be found elsewhere. In this approach, organizations encourage their career partners to review their long-term career development needs and how these needs can best be met – internally or externally. At the appropriate point, organizations may even want to proactively encourage their partners to leave, in order to rejoin as even more valuable talent at a later date. Implementing this approach would fundamentally alter the talent career dynamic and make it absolutely clear which organizations were operating as true employers of choice. It would also enable organizations to make the most of their career partners and these partners to make the most of their careers.

Externships at Bain & Company. Bain & Company, the global business consultancy, actively encourages its employees to take six-month 'externships' and longer-term sabbaticals through a retention programme designed to help maximize the lifetime contributions of Bain's staff members. So if an individual wants to take a career break, Bain lets them.

Bain employees participate in externships in various fields, including venture capital, government and not-for-profit organizations. Staff members also have the opportunity to work for Bain's Private Equity Group, which focuses on leveraged buyout cases, or for the Bridgespan Group, Bain's innovative non-profit firm dedicated to bringing strategic capability to the charitable sector. At any time, approximately 15 per cent of Bridgespan's staff are 'externs' from Bain. Each individual is encouraged to secure the opportunity of his or her choice, with the help of Bain partners.

In 2005, more than 35 Bain employees participated in externship programmes, giving them the chance to explore other employment opportunities without negatively affecting their Bain career trajectory. The firm structures externships as leaves of absence from the firm. Externs commit to returning to Bain after the externship ends. In order to facilitate externships with not-for-profit organizations, Bain provides stipends to externs who work for non-profits and earn less than 50 per cent of their base salary. These stipends range from $500 to $2000, depending on the extern's level at Bain.

Bain staff benefit from externships by broadening their professional development and receiving hands-on experience in an industry in which they are interested. Bain increases its ability to retain promising employees. In addition, because externships are arranged to expand employees' skills and experience, staff who have participated in one will have enhanced their value to Bain when they return. This reflects Bain's commitment to developing its employees – one factor that helped make Bain the number-one ranked employer in the UK according to the FT's Best Workplaces 2006 survey.

Bain's clients also benefit from the externship programme since some externs work with Bain clients directly. This dynamic reinforces the long-term relationships that the consultancy seeks to cultivate in addition to giving Bain employees line management experience. And Bridgespan gets an ongoing input of fresh insights and ideas.

Summary

Reader: *'You've linked Walker's three levels with Personnel, HRM and HCM. And you've linked three different forms of talent management to these levels too. To what extent does an integrated approach to strategy development plus a partnership approach to talent management form a definition of HCM?'*

Author: 'Walker's three approaches to people management strategy development are a fairly key part of HCM, but then so are the other attributes we've discussed so far, even if I've not formally linked these to HCM. Table 5.1 links the five attributes of people management strategy that we have now discussed with Personnel, HRM and HCM.

Note that I think these three levels build on each other. HCM is Walker's integrated process which uses best fit activities to create value and relies on knowledge to make sense of complexity. However, HCM includes the attributes of HRM as well. HRM is Walker's aligned process which uses best practice activities to add value and calls on information to make sense of dynamic systems. And HRM includes the attributes of Personnel as well. Personnel is Walker's separate process which uses basic practices to provide value for money and relies on data to make sense of causal systems.

HRM and Personnel are essential parts of HCM. You need to be able to walk before you can run and HR needs to be able to deliver transactional activities seamlessly before the function can be seen as a credible source of added and created value.

There is also a very natural fit with the different types of talent management we've reviewed, but they're examples rather than requirements. So a bit like Motorola's use of DMAIC, I think that career partnership is an example of the

Table 5.1: Attributes of Personnel, HRM and HCM

	Personnel	*Human Resource Management = Personnel plus*	*Human Capital Management = HRM plus*
People management strategy development (this chapter)	A separate process focused on activity (e.g. talent management for everyone)	An aligned process focused on activity and capability (e.g. development of talent pools) to meet business objectives	An integrated process focused on intangible capability (e.g. career partnership), that provides the potential to sustain and transform the business
People management practices (Chapter 3)	Basic practice	Best practice	Best fit
Outputs of people management (Chapter 4)	Value for money	Added value	Created value
Assumptions about business (Chapter 2) environment	Causal chains	Dynamic systems	Complex processes
Appropriate form of information (Chapter 1)	Data	Information	Knowledge

creating value approach. I'm not suggesting it as a best practice approach that all organizations should use.

In addition, looking back at what I've written, I think it's probably no accident that all the case studies in Chapter 5 have turned out to come from professional and financial services. I think in these sorts of organizations there's a more obvious opportunity to concentrate on developing the supply of human capital as well as meeting whatever demands for products or services the organization can create. However, I can see that in retail, for example, a career partnership approach might be less relevant, and a value for money approach that treats everyone the same might fit their situation best.

One of the other examples of creating value HCM approaches I quite often use, particularly where I'm developing HR teams, is creating organization capital through business process design. It's a good example for a number of reasons: it's a key area of organization design that many companies forget about; often no other functions have responsibility for it; and it calls on many of the skills that HR professionals already have. However, it's also an area that provides HR with a wonderful opportunity to mark out their new role. Often the first time an HR business partner offers to support a business client to redesign their business processes, they get told to go away and come back once the manager has done the redesign, and they know how many redundancies they need. It gives HR a great opportunity to respond back that no, this is not what they mean. They have a methodology and particular skills to help facilitate the development of better processes. It gives them an opportunity to point out that there is a separate administration centre that handles the redundancies – this is not their job.'

References

Bartlett, C.A. and Ghoshal, S. (2002). 'Building competitive advantage through people' *MIT Sloan Management Review*, Winter, (43)2, 34–41.

Boudreau, J.W. and Ramstad, P.M. (2004). '"Talentship": a decision science for HR', *Strategic HR Review*. **3**(2), January–February, 28–31.

Cappelli, P. (2000). 'A market-driven approach to employee retention', *Harvard Business Review*, January–February, 103–11.

Carrington, L. (2004). 'A waste of talent', *Human Resources*. October, 26–33.

Chambers, E.G., Foulon, F., Handfield-Jones, H., Hankin, S.M. and Michaels E.G. III (1998). 'The war for talent', *The McKinsey Quarterly*, **3,** 44–57.

Champy, J. (1995). *Reengineering Management: The Mandate for New Leadership*. Harper Business.

Collins, J. (2001). *Good to Great*. Random House Business Books.

Delong, T.J. and Vijayaraghavan, V. (2003). 'Let's hear it for B players', *Harvard Business Review*, June, 96–102.

Ghoshal, S. and Bartlett, C.A. (1998). *The Individualized Corporation: A Fundamentally New Approach to Management*. Heinemann.

Gratton, L. and Ghoshal, S. (2003). 'Managing personal human capital: New ethos for the "Volunteer" employee', *European Management Journal*, **21**(1), February, 1–10.

Hammer, M. (1997). *Beyond Re-engineering: How the Process-Centered Organization Is Changing Our Work and Our Lives*. Harper Business.

Hammer, M. and Champy, J. (1993). *Reengineering the Corporation: A Manifesto for Business Revolution*. Harper Business.

Hunter, J.E., Schmidt, F.L.S. and Judiesch, M.K. (1990). 'Individual differences in output variability as a function of job complexity', *Journal of Applied Psychology*, **75,** 28–40.

Ingham, J. (2006). 'Closing the talent management gap', *Strategic HR Review*. March–April, 20–23.

Kaplan, R.S. and Norton, D.P. (2004). 'Measuring the strategic readiness of intangible assets', *Harper Business Review*, February 52–63.

Pfau, B.N.and Kay, I.T. (2002). *The Human Capital Edge: 21 People Management Practices Your Company Must Implement (or Avoid) to Maximize Shareholder Value*. McGraw-Hill.

Purcell, J., Kinnie, N., Hutchinson, S., Rayton, B. and Swart, J. (2002). *Understanding the People and Performance Link: Unlocking the Black Box*. Chartered Institute of Personnel and Development.

Sull, D.N. (2005). 'Strategy as Active Waiting', *Harvard Business Review*. September, 120–9.

Walker, J.W. (1992). *Human Resource Strategy*. McGraw-Hill.

Warren, C. (2006). 'Curtain call', *People Management*, 23 March, 25–9.

6

Managing and Measuring Human Capital

Introduction

Reader: 'What is this chapter about?'

Author: 'Chapters 2 to 5 of this book have focused on building an understanding of human capital management rather than measurement, but we do also need a way of measuring human capital and HCM as part of an effective approach to management. I presented options for the financial valuation of human capital in Chapter 4 and concluded that organizations should financially value their success, not their people. I also explained why scorecards provide a sound basis for the valuation of human capital and evaluation of HCM. This chapter picks up on the use of scorecards and provides a framework to support the management and measurement of HCM strategy.

  The rest of the book is then about using this framework to develop, measure, manage and report on HCM. From this point on, the book becomes less theoretical, more practical and includes more case studies too.'

Reader: 'And what are the key models in this chapter?'

Author: 'There are two models, or actually there are three. The first two we have already referred to in passing. The first is the HCM value triangle. In Chapters 4 and 5 I referred to created value, added value and value for money as measures of output. In this chapter I want to widen these out to the broader concepts of creating value, adding value and producing value for money. These descriptions refer to the activity of HCM and also the activity of business management.

The second model is the HCM value chain that again we touched on in Chapters 4 and 5. In Chapter 4 I indicated that this value chain is the reason that human capital is so important and in Chapter 5 we reviewed what the value chain looks like at each level of value. At the Personnel and HRM levels of people management strategy, the HCM value chain is really only part of Porter's and the customer value chains, producing the human resources that are required to meet business needs. At the HCM level, it has a more important role as a self-standing value chain that produces the intangible capability discussed in Chapter 4.

I think this discussion shows that the value chain and the value triangle are interlinked. I can't talk about the value triangle without referring to the steps in the value chain. And I can't talk about the value chain without referring to how it changes at different levels of value. So the third model simply puts the value triangle and value chain together to produce an HCM value matrix. This provides the framework I will use to describe the management and measurement of HCM throughout the rest of the book ...'

Kaplan and Norton's Balanced Scorecard and Strategy Map

The balanced scorecard was developed by Kaplan and Norton (1992) to provide a basket of performance indicators balancing traditional but lagging financial measures with three other non-financial perspectives: customer, business processes and learning and growth. This last perspective focuses on what Kaplan and Norton believe are the three main categories of intangible capabilities: human, organization and information capital. A slightly different version of the scorecard is provided for the public and not-for-profit sectors in which ultimate success is measured by an organization's performance in achieving its mission, rather than just financial results, and the customer perspective is split between customer-stakeholders, and those other stakeholders, whether donors or taxpayers, who provide funding.

Kaplan and Norton compare the use of the scorecard to the variety of measurements needed to fly a plane:

> Think of the balanced scorecard as the dials and indicators in an airplane cockpit. For the complex task of navigating and flying an airplane, pilots need detailed information about many aspects of the flight. They need information on fuel, air speed, altitude, bearing, destination, and other indicators that summarize the current and predicted environment. Reliance on one instrument can be fatal. Similarly, the complexity of managing an organization today requires that managers be able to view performance in several areas simultaneously. (Kaplan and Norton, 1992)

The realization that the balanced measures of the scorecard need to be grounded in an organization's strategic objectives led Kaplan and Norton to develop the strategy map. This is a diagram which uses arrows to indicate cause and effect relationships between objectives in each of the scorecard's four perspectives. The diagram can also be used to illustrate the time-based dynamics of a strategy.

The strategy map extends what was a measurement tool into a 'strategic management system' that helps ensure the measures in the scorecard support one other. Kaplan and Norton (2004) describe this shift from focusing on measures in the scorecard to describing an organization's strategic objectives using strategy maps, stating:

> Once the executives agreed to the word statements of what they wanted to accomplish – how they wanted to describe success – the selection of the measurements became much simpler. And in an interesting twist, the selection of measures became somewhat less consequential. After all, when agreement existed about the objective to be achieved, even if the initial measurements for the objective turned out to be less than perfect, the executives could easily modify the measurements for subsequent periods, without having to redo their discussion about strategy.

The objectives would likely remain the same even as the measurements of the objectives evolved with experience and new data sources.

However, neither the balanced scorecard nor the business strategy map captures much detail within people management strategy. Norton (2001a) reports that executives typically have a good understanding of priorities in the financial and process quadrants, improving understanding around customers but:

> The worst grades are reserved for their understanding of strategies for developing human capital. There is little consensus, little creativity, and no real framework for thinking about the subject. Worse yet, we have seen little improvement in this.

A Framework for Managing and Measuring Human Capital

I think the need is to provide a framework for managing and measuring human capital that extends on the information included within the learning and growth perspective of the balanced scorecard. This framework may take the form of a scorecard but in order for it to provide a 'strategic management system', the framework needs to be based upon a strategy map for people management. I believe that the HCM value chain that was described in Chapter 4 provides a basis for this strategy map. However, before I present this solution, I want to look at some of the other people management models that exist.

Existing Scorecard Models
The HR Scorecard (Using Perspectives from the Balanced Scorecard)

Most attempts at including more information on people management in a scorecard have been focused on developing a scorecard for the HR function using the same four perspectives as the balanced scorecard. But whereas the customer and financial perspectives of the balanced scorecard provide clear deliverables for the business, the same is not found with the use of the HR scorecard for the HR function.

A good example of this scorecard is the 'prescriptive measurement framework' developed by Norton's consultancy, the Balanced Scorecard Collaborative. Working with 20 leading organizations, Norton (2001b) found that each had a different view about which components of people management are important:

> Most identified 'leadership' as an important component of their strategies, but several did not. Most organizations identified 'motivation' as a key driver, but their definitions of motivation were wide-ranging and inconsistent ... While we understand that every organization is different, and that their strategies must reflect these differences, we did not expect every organization to have completely different objectives and measures.

I am not sure why Norton was so surprised. Given everything we have covered about the need for best fit and differentiation in HCM and the need for its integration with business strategy, I think it would be strange if different companies' measures were the same. I also find it odd that, given Kaplan and Norton's understanding that intangibles need to be valued in the context of a business strategy (described in Chapter 4), they then suggest enforcing a common and prescriptive approach with which to measure them. My view is supported by McKinsey whose health metrics resemble Kaplan and Norton's non-financial measures. McKinsey consultants, Dobbs and Koller (2005) explain that 'we differ in believing that companies should develop their own metrics tailored to their particular industries and strategies'.

Developing a strategy map for the HR organization, Norton (2001c) explains that, 'since HR is a support organization, its financial objectives are a subset of the broader enterprise strategy'. He suggests that the appropriate measures for the financial perspective of the scorecard are HR effectiveness and HR efficiency. These are minor goals compared to HR's potential impact on the overall financial objectives of the organization, like overall revenue growth and profitability. In addition, promoting a financial measure like HR efficiency takes people management back to an operational focus independent of business strategy.

Norton (2001b) suggests basing the customer perspective of the HR scorecard on five relatively common 'dimensions of human capital': strategic skills/competencies; leadership; culture and strategic awareness; strategic alignment; and strategic integration and learning. However, although some of the measures within these five dimensions are outputs of HCM such as leadership gap and key employee retention, others are activity measures like the percentage of incentives.

This confused picture is replicated in published case studies of organizations using HR scorecards. For example, Walker and

MacDonald (2001) describe the development of one of the first HR scorecards at GTE (now Verizon). They provide an example of a team that used the scorecard to lower cost-per-hire and time-to-fill but which achieved this by targeting candidates that turned out to be harder to train and keep. The net result was actually to reduce unit performance. This problem was a direct consequence of using measures that did not have the reinforcing alignment that comes from being part of a strategy map.

I think Norton, GTE and others who have developed HR scorecards have made things difficult for themselves because, rather than using a strategy map for people management as the basis for their scorecard, they have tried to retrofit their measures to the four perspectives of the balanced scorecard and I do not think this has worked.

The HR and Workforce Scorecards (Using High-Performance Work Systems Theory)

An alternative approach to the HR scorecard has been developed by Becker, Huselid, Ulrich and Beatty and is described in their books on the HR and workforce scorecards. In the second of these books, Huselid *et al.* (2005) explain that the balanced scorecard's four perspectives do not work for people management processes:

> These categories work well when applied to an entire firm. They don't perform well, however, when applied to elements of the workforce. We have seen many HR professionals who have tried to apply these four 'boxes' to HR functions and/or the workforce, and they have been consistently frustrated by the outcomes. The problem is that the categories, which were intended to be used to describe how *all* of the elements of firm success contribute to the bottom line, don't work well when we are interested in highlighting the contribution of a single element – for example, the workforce.

Instead, the professors propose a double scorecard system that is based on Huselid's research into high-performance work systems (HPWS) that was described in Chapter 3:

- The HR scorecard includes measures for the high-performance work system; HR system alignment; HR deliverables; and HR efficiency (Becker *et al.*, 2001).

- The workforce scorecard includes measures for workforce mindset and culture; workforce competencies; leadership and workforce behaviours; and workforce success (Huselid *et al.*, 2005).

Paul Kearns's response to these complicated and unintuitive models was rather blunt but also quite accurate:

> The Scorecard risks inflicting a complicated solution on a relatively simple problem. He writes off the case study material as unintelligible to anyone without a degree in astro-HR and, ultimately, unconvincing. 'It is academics going beserk trying to analyze things to the nth degree,' he says. (Hall, 2001)

Talentship

John Boudreau from the University of Southern California and Pete Ramstad from consultancy, PDI, outline a much better management and measurement framework they call 'HC BRidge®', supported by a strategic approach to people management they call 'talentship'.

HC BRidge® provides a value map 'to articulate the logical connections between investments, changes in the nature or deployment of workforce talents, and sustainable strategic success' (Boudreau and Ramstad, 2004). It involves three stages: efficiency, effectiveness and impact:

- Efficiency is the area closest to what HR is currently doing with measurement and answers the question, 'How much are we spending and on what?' This is where most of today's HR measurements lie.
- Effectiveness calls for questions such as 'Do our investments in programs and practices enhance employees' capability, opportunity and motivation to contribute?' Effectiveness measures (such as employee performance and attitudes) are commonly collected but not organized to reflect connections between investments and employee outcomes, nor that different initiatives are all aimed at common ends. Effectiveness measures should let you know if the staffing practices are working in concert with the compensation practices and so on.
- Assessing the impact of talent reflects questions like, 'What difference does it make to have high performers rather than average performers in this role?' Impact measures (such as profit margin and new product success) are often located outside the HR function.

(Boudreau and Ramstad, 2004)

I do not like this terminology as I think 'efficiency' and 'effectiveness' have more to do with value for money and added value than they do with the steps in an HCM strategy map, but the model at least works better than the HR scorecard frameworks reviewed previously.

However, I am much less keen on the concept of talentship which Boudreau and Ramstad (2002) define as a decision science. This is an agreed-upon and rigorous set of methods that provides:

> A logical, reliable and consistent – but flexible – framework that enhances decisions about a key resource, wherever those decisions are made. A decision science does not rigidly prescribe what to do, but rather provides a logical system to identify and analyze key decision issues.

Boudreau and Ramstad explain that the consequence of not having a decision science is that 'talent decisions will be made using non-logical decision frameworks', for example by following politics, fads and fashions. Although I agree that it can be dangerous to follow fashionable management theories (it certainly reduces the scope for best fit), I disagree that logic is the sole basis for creating a new strategic role for HR. Given the degree of complexity in business that was described in Chapter 1, I believe it is these very 'non-logical decision frameworks', for example, using people's creativity, that provides the key to HCM (see Chapter 7).

I also believe that Boudreau and Ramstad have made a mistake in embedding their concept of talent, 'pivotal roles', within talentship. Although, as I discussed in Chapter 5, I believe talent management has a very natural connection to HCM, I think it is inappropriate to hard-wire talent pools into the framework. Talent management has a very natural fit with HCM but is not the only approach to HCM and may not be the right one in many situations.

However, my greatest challenge to Boudreau and Ramstad's approach relates to their strategic ambition for people management. Boudreau and Ramstad compare HR to finance professionals who, given the same business challenge, will 'approach it with similar logic, and develop a reasonably similar analysis of the issue' (2002). This standardization in approach would certainly assist in moving from Personnel to HR, but would do nothing to help the HR function advance to the level of creating value in HCM. Neither talentship nor

HC BRidge® have an equivalent to the value triangle. It is combining this with the HCM value chain that creates the framework I am going to propose.

Building the HCM Value Matrix
The HCM Value Triangle

The value triangle (Figure 6.1) is a model that I have been using fairly extensively over the last four or five years. It describes the level of value associated with business and people management activities (described in Chapter 5), and the outputs of these processes (described in Chapter 4).

There are no hard distinctions between the three levels and whether something is above or below the dividing line between the levels does not really matter. What is important is that organizations think about how they can continuously increase their level of alignment and value in the intangibles they are developing.

Value for money and creating value are not quite the same as Porter's cost leadership and differentiation but the two constructs do have similarities. The value triangle implies, in contrast to Porter who saw the poles as trade-offs, that companies should be thinking about a paradox in which they need to deliver a differentiated service at low cost. Jim Collins and Jerry Porras (2002) call Porter's perspective 'the tyranny of either/or' and point to the experience of many successful companies that focus on 'and/also' and assume they can 'have it all'.

HCM value triangle

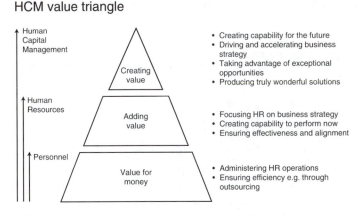

Figure 6.1 The HCM value triangle. © Penna / Jon Ingham 2006

Professors Kim and Mauborgne (1997) also refer to created value when they write about companies that achieve superior and sustainable performance by delivering products or services with an outstanding set of attributes while keeping costs and prices down by under-delivering on features not critical to customer satisfaction. Doing this requires innovative strategies to create what the authors refer to as 'blue ocean' – a space that is right for growth – compared to the 'red ocean' – in which companies fight head-to-head over a shrinking profit pool (Kim and Mauborgne, 2005).

The HCM Value Chain

The HCM value chain (Figure 6.2) describes the people management activities that take place within the learning and growth perspective of the balanced scorecard. In Chapter 5, I described how some of the steps in the value chain change at different levels in the value triangle. At lower levels of value, the value chain represents the delivery of capability to inform Porter's and the customer value chains. At the creating value level, it represents the transformation of individual skills into organizational capability that was described in Chapter 4.

The HCM value chain describes a transformation in which a number of inputs, including the existing capability of people in the organization, progress through a series of activities based on the organization's people management practices to provide tangible and intangible resources and capabilities. These then produce impacts in the rest of the

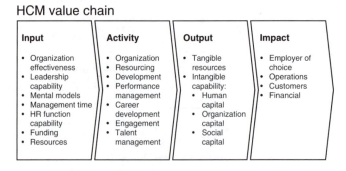

Figure 6.2 The HCM value chain. © Jon Ingham 2006

business which show up in the business process, customer and financial perspectives of the balanced scorecard. The value chain actually forms one part of an integrated value chain with the strategy map of the balanced scorecard, where 'output' in the HCM value chain leads on to 'business processes' in the balanced scorecard. This integration is the reason for the CIPD's description of human capital as a 'bridging concept – defining the link between HR practices and business performance in terms of assets rather than business processes' (Scarborough and Elias, 2002).

Figure 6.3 describes how the two value chains are linked.

The split between the two value chains marks the interface between the people management system and the business system. This split is the reason why most balanced scorecards fail to make clear linkages between the objectives and measures in the learning and growth perspective and the other perspectives. (You often see arrows drawn from financial to customer and customer to business process but not from business process to learning and growth. At this level, scorecard designers recognize that people management objectives and measures do not always have one-to-one relationships with business objectives and measures. In fact the greater the strategic value, the harder it is to draw these links. This is a result of the effect described in Chapter 5 in which the higher the level of value, the less direct the relationships appear.)

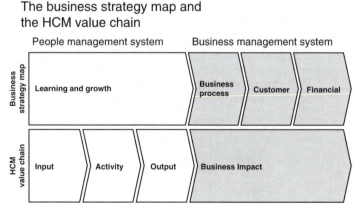

Figure 6.3 The business strategy map and the HCM value chain.
© Jon Ingham 2006

HCM value chains also tends to break at this point – between the output and the impact perspectives (see especially, discussions on BBC's evaluation framework in Chapter 8 and BT's HCM value chain in Chapter 10).

The value chain provides a mix of lead and lag measures where inputs are generally lead measures and business impacts are generally lag measures and activities and outputs can be either lead or lag depending on where one stands along the value chain. Lead and lag is not the same as before or after an event. For example, training days is an after the event measure but can be a lead indicator of human capital capability and business performance.

The HCM Value Matrix

Figure 6.4 demonstrates how the value chain and value triangle are combined to form the value matrix. The matrix shows that at the value for money level, the discrete steps in the value chain are linked together by unidirectional causal relationships. At the adding value level, the steps are less discrete and relationships are more complex and often circular. At the creating value level, the steps are interlinked by complex relationships.

The matrix ranges from largely intangible at the top left to largely tangible at the bottom right. Intangible top left to tangible bottom right.

HCM value matrix

	Input	Activity	Output	Impact
Creating value – tends to be expressed as knowledge	Integrated approach, complex processes	Best fit people management practices	Intangible capability	Reinventing and regenerating
Adding value – tends to be expressed as information	Aligned approach, dynamic systems	Best people management practices	Intangible and tangible resources	Re-engineering /continuous improvement
Value for money – expressed as data	Separate approach, causal chains	Basic people management practices	Tangible resources	Restructuring and downsizing

Figure 6.4 The HCM value matrix. © Jon Ingham 2006

Input. At the value for money level, this step in the value chain refers mainly to tangible inputs such as budgets, management time and the effectiveness of the HR function. At created value, it is mainly intangible, relating to the capability of the organization, the leadership team, management and the workforce as a whole.

Activity. Chapter 3 reviewed this step and concluded that the three levels of value were associated with basic, best and best fit practices. Best fit practices create intangible capability which seems to be one of the major reasons why moving from best practice to best fit increases the impact of people management on business results. Best fit approaches help ensure that the intangibles which are developed can inform and drive business success. Best practice approaches may result in the development of various intangibles, but if these are not aligned with business strategy they will not be things the business can utilize, and no extra value will result.

Output. The output step focuses on both tangible and intangible deliverables. Tangible outputs include numbers of employees, their observable behaviours and readily assessable knowledge and skills. Intangible outputs refer to the creation of human, organizational and social capital and include people's capability, engagement and opportunity to contribute.

It is increasingly these intangibles which are the real drivers of business success, with financial results a consequence of this human capital rather than a true measure of the value that the business has created.

This interface between the business and people management systems is marked best in non-business situations. One example was the point at which NASA mission control handed control of the Eagle over to Neil Armstrong and Buzz Aldrin when a few hundred feet above the moon's surface so that they could manoeuvre the craft over a boulder field. It is an interesting example because measurements were important. Armstrong needed to know his speed, pitch and particularly his fuel as this was running very low. But what the crew down on to the moon's surface was Armstrong's quick thinking and capability. Of course, in most business situations, HCM does not look quite like this. Both the people management and business management systems arc operated in parallel not in series and there is ongoing movement between the two.

Impact. This step focuses on the business (non-people management) perspectives of the balanced scorecard. Hamel and Prahalad (1994) describe three types of business strategy that correspond to the three levels of value:

- value for money: 'Restructuring the portfolio and downsizing headcount';
- adding value: 'Re-engineering processes and continuous improvement';
- creating value: 'Reinventing industries and regenerating strategies'.

Hamel and Prahalad are also thinking about created value when they write about 'products that customers need but have not yet even imagined'.

The Return on Investment in Human Capital

Return on investment (ROI) is not included as a separate step but can be included in the impact column of the HCM value matrix. However, I do not believe that ROI is a necessary or natural measure of HCM. It is certainly not a 'holy grail'. To understand why, we need to look at the three levels of value.

At the separate level of Personnel strategy, where the focus is on value for money, tangible outputs; calculating ROI can make some sense. Investments have a monetary value and outputs can have a direct impact on financial outcomes, although this is mostly limited to reducing costs. So ROI can be a fairly easy calculation to make but it is not likely to be a very important one as the actual return is never going to be that great.

At the aligned level that focuses on adding value, ROI will be much more difficult to calculate as people management activity does not usually result in a financial impact on its own. For example, a major sales training programme will typically be implemented alongside changes in the sales organization or the introduction of new sales technology. A more appropriate ROI calculation uses the whole investment required by a business strategy and the overall benefits that result, rather than just focusing on the people management piece of this.

It is even more difficult to calculate ROI at the integrated level of creating value. People management acts and impacts on the business very indirectly and is linked to overall improvement and transformation in the business, not to current and specific business objectives. Measurement is also made more difficult by the likelihood that current activities will only have a financial impact in subsequent years.

This difficulty is increasingly understood. For example, recommending better recognition of intangibles in the accounting system, Lev proposes that companies should report on the intangible itself (in this case, the human capital) and the return on a company's investment in intangibles. Lev's belief in ROI may be influenced by the fact that he focuses on research and development which produces fairly tangible intangible results. However, Lev (2004) also acknowledges that:

> Calculating ROI is trickier in other areas, where the relationship between intangibles investments and their outcomes is more complex ... Even where there is an apparent link between, say, employee training and productivity, it isn't always possible to confirm a causal relationship between the investment and the positive result, given the variety of factors – information technology and so on – that affect employee productivity.

Lev goes on to explain that if it is not possible to report on ROI the actual investment in an intangible will often do instead:

> Even where returns on investments in intangibles can't be calculated with precision, companies can at least track and disclose the investments themselves. Breaking out a company's expenditures in training, brand enhancement, information technology and the likes from general cost figures would let managers and investors see how those investments change over time and how they compare with those made at related companies.

Lev's conclusion emphasizes the need for the input step in the HCM value chain. However, it is important to realize that measuring input is not simply the best that can be done given the difficulty in calculating ROI; it is actually the most appropriate form of measurement. As we have already discussed, human capital not financial capital is the constraining resource in most businesses. In addition, the HCM value chain describes a more important and fundamental transformation than the production of margin from financial capital which is all ROI measures. As I have already stated in Chapter 4, this is why BCG (Barber and Strack, 2005) recommend the use of performance measures that focus on human rather than financial capital. What we really need is an equivalent to ROI that focuses on people and the transformation in capability that forms the HCM value chain. This is the difference between the human capital that people invest in the organization and the capability that is the basis for investment by financial investors.

One attempt at measuring this transformation is Saratoga's Human Capital ROI, a ratio of expenditure on pay and benefits to an adjusted profit figure. It has similarities to economic value added (EVA) but with a focus on human rather than financial capital. Although this sometimes helps to get people's attention, it is a very complicated metric that disguises meaning rather than adds insight. For example, Howard Winkler (2005), HR Strategy Director at Southern Company notes:

> In one draft of our KPIs, we used a much-vaunted measure, Human Capital ROI ... While sometimes considered the gold standard in productivity measures, I quickly found that I couldn't explain the brilliance of the measures within the attention span of the executive I was talking to. Valuable? Yes. Useable? No. Another metrics on the trash heap of unused measures.

I think that 'return on people' needs to be seen as a qualitative measure, an agenda for discussion, that cannot be distilled down into a single financial metric, without being severely compromised.

However, I think even this qualitative return on people measure has limited value. Strategic decisions in HCM are about creating a particular type of organization focused on specific and differentiated intangible capabilities. These decisions are not about providing a return on investment, in whatever way it is defined. This is why RBS, even with its sophisticated HCM model described in Chapter 2, has not been able to calculate an ROI for its multi-million pound business school. Instead, it has declared this an 'investment in a belief'. Quoted in *Personnel Today* (Millar, 2006), HR Director Neil Roden explained that:

> The lack of success companies have had in tracking the ROI on leadership training – despite trying for the past 30 years – had led the bank's chief executive, Sir Fred Goodwin, to go back to basics with the business school.
>
> 'He reverted back to asking: "Do we think that if people are trained it will make a difference? Will improving our leaders make a difference?",' Roden explained. 'It is a symbol of commitment and a statement of intent to make us the UK's number one employer.'

A lot of what is written about ROI is not actually very useful. For example, a CFO/Mercer report (CFO Research, 2003) found that only 16 per cent of executives have more than a moderate understanding of their return on labour costs. I presume people are supposed to infer that such a low percentage is a bad thing. However, I would ask whether a deep understanding of this return is actually something that companies can have, and what would they do differently if they did? Suppose they have a return of, say, 20 per cent? So what? Would these companies reduce their employee base and invest in something else instead? I think this is too simplistic. Making decisions based on an ROI may work for comparing acquisitions, expansions to new markets or new technology. Staffing should be a result of the business strategy and opportunities to create value, not a calculation that is not really appropriate and is in any case based on so many assumptions it cannot ever provide a reliable result.

Using the HCM Value Matrix

The value matrix can be used as a tool to support the strategic HCM planning cycle (that needs to be an integrated part of the business planning cycle). The next five chapters will describe the strategy development, measurement, benchmarking, implementation and reporting stages of this cycle. In a complex environment, these are not necessarily sequential activities but measurement will normally follow, not precede, the development of strategy. Measurement supports the review of the strategy; it is not the main basis for the strategy.

Aligned but tailored value matrices should be developed for each area of the business that needs a different approach to strategy development or measurement. In addition, different HCM value matrices need to be developed to support different elements of an HCM strategy.

HCM can consist of lots of small, tailored activities like the arts promotion at Deutsche Bank or the loyalty dinner at Standard Chartered. However, most commonly, it tends to take place through major strategic programmes. In fact, a good sign of an environment orienting itself towards creating value is its progression from service delivery to project and then programme management:

- *Service delivery.* Traditional Personnel departments focus on the delivery of services rather than the management of projects. Their focus is on how they can best respond to operational and strategic challenges confronting them at a particular time.

- *Project management.* A project management mindset involves managing a substantial proportion of HR's workload as projects rather than services. However, many organizations run far too many poorly resourced and managed projects, few of which ever deliver what they are set up to do.
- *Programme management.* This approach involves focusing on a maximum of three or four key programmes that each focus on the development of a particular intangible capability, or another means of creating value. These HCM programmes should be seen as strategic and important undertakings from a business viewpoint as well as from a people management or HR function perspective. Each programme may involve a number of aligned projects.

The need to focus on a few, key priorities (which is also seen in various other strategy models, for example Michael Porter's activity systems) ensures strategic alignment and enables effective management, resourcing and communication. Lynda Gratton (2000) also explains this need to focus on a few critical themes which become the basis for HCM programmes:

> The principle here is to identify those three, four or possibly five themes which could really make a difference and with which people can identify and believe in. We need to create a message which is simple but compelling, and has sufficient clarity and focus to remain intact as it moves through layers of communication and interpretation.

Some of the typical attributes of an HCM programme are:

- Being mission critical. HCM programmes focus on sustaining and transforming the business, not just meeting the needs of the business plan.
- Being seen as a business project not just an HR project, so there is clear ownership, leadership and participation from the business.
- Being relatively expensive, broad-ranging and enduring. Programmes need to be a key area of focus for quite some time and are often branded to increase recognition and engagement.

- Being based on a set of aligned, bundled and well-executed people management practices that will provide systemic change and the potential for ongoing business success.
- Using an appropriate measurement framework which does not need to include the calculation of a return on investment.
- Having a tangible and significant impact on the business.
- Recognizing complexity and the fact that there is always room for improvement, so there is an emphasis on learning and improvement throughout the programme.

The value matrix also provides the basis to develop an HCM scorecard and dashboard. A scorecard contains measures rather than objectives. Most valuable scorecards also include a degree of narrative explanation and interpretation to provide usable information rather than just raw data. For example, scorecards can be developed upon a traffic-light reporting system that indicates performance against strategic objectives. Red typically indicates that performance is substantially below target, amber that performance is close to target and green that performance is on target. A further symbol, for example an arrow pointing up, down or across, can indicate whether changes in performance are heading in the right direction. An HCM scorecard can be used in presentations to various stakeholders (see Chapter 11) and as a management tool within the HR function.

A dashboard takes some of the most important indicators from the scorecard to provide a high-level, real-time and usually graphic monitoring tool focused on the most important areas of HCM strategy. It typically includes a variety of gauges and instruments. Some gauges may provide measures of real-time data, for example, the latest levels of engagement obtained from a pulse or real-time survey (see Chapter 8). Other instruments might keep a cumulative track of progress, for example, numbers of training courses, or might illustrate variances, where performance is above or below target. The dashboard may also include warning lights to indicate problems that may be brewing. Different dashboards can be created for the various teams within HR. So for example, a recruitment team dashboard might monitor current levels of applications, numbers of critical new roles filled and outstanding, and spend against the recruitment budget.

Managing and Measuring HCM at Oxfam

I talked to Andrew Thompson who was previously International HR Director for Oxfam, where he was responsible for leading 600 HR business partners around the world. He is currently working as HR Business Partner at Scottish Re.

Author: 'What does HCM mean for you?'

Thompson: 'HCM is about the patterns and drivers of business performance you should be seeing in the workforce. However, I think HCM needs to go beyond making the best out of the capability you've got. It should be more equivalent to zero-based budgeting with financial capital. So it's not just about your current workforce creating new ideas but about creating the workforce that would give you the best possible potential. What could you do if you imagined you had no staff? What should your workforce look like this year? How could you create a workforce that would attract the sort of people who are going to surprise you? I think this takes you towards looking for qualities in your workforce like learning and creativity – abilities that might take you in any number of directions.

I think there are three broad approaches to implementing strategy. The first is to look at your people and ask whether you can do a certain job with them, and if not, devise an agenda to develop this fit. The second is a craftsman-based approach, asking what are the tools and what can I build with them? This is your point about influencing business strategy because of the capability you've got. The third generation approach is to fill the workshop with tools I can do anything with. This is about having the adaptive, creative, dynamic workforce that will be required in the future.

Chaos theory is very relevant to this. You need to think about things like the shadow organization. HCM falls down if you model the organization incorrectly, if you conceive of the organization and the way that work gets done too simplistically, too traditionally. HR defines a lot of the language used by the organization, so the organization will be constrained if HR has used language that is out of date, for example using a basic systems approach.

Given the need for adaptability, I think benchmarking is almost useless. I get passionately cross about this focus on benchmarking. It just reinforces what everyone says about HR not understanding the business. I think HR's shot itself in the foot about this.'

Author: 'So if HCM is about creating agility, what is the role of measurement? How would you suggest organizations should measure agility?'

Thompson: 'Would it surprise you if I said that at Oxfam, talking about turnover was almost irrelevant? It just wasn't a measure that was aligned to the design of the business, to what really mattered. You can have low turnover across a global organization as a whole and still have complete instability – if, in reality, staff are moving too quickly to their next job.

Turnover is about stability, but what sort of stability is it that really matters? You don't want to manage people leaving as a whole. If the business is predicated on projects and the projects change by a third every year, and looking by geography the nature of projects also changes by a significant percentage, you don't want to keep all the same people as they won't all adapt to this level of change. You want some, you want a core that can adapt, who are interested in building up an Oxfam CV, and that will be the project leaders of the future. This is the group you want to retain to ensure you are developing skills you can apply to the next project. So it's about managing turnover in a range. If it's too low, you can't have got the right staff for new projects.

More importantly, what drives most value, as well as people's competence, is their relationships and the knowledge you can circulate around the world. Turnover doesn't tell you the rate this is moving around. So the measure we came up with was tenure in posts. We wanted to ensure that people in our most important roles with client contact stayed in these roles for two to three to four years and sometimes even longer. I think it illustrates that you don't have to use measures just because there are common measures to be had and because benchmarks have been published and you think you should use them.

I think you also need to remember that yes, developing agility is about understanding how agile you are as an organization, but it's also about enabling agility. The measurement is only important if it helps you to do something differently.'

Author: 'So what was your experience at Oxfam? What approach did you take in your HCM strategy to develop this agility, adaptability and creativity?'

Thompson: 'Agility is largely about how you redesign jobs. For example, HR likes people to adopt common job titles. But it's easy to develop a stylized view of how complicated an organization can be and common job titles can lead people to think that there is common job content too. I think job titles and job descriptions are too crude a measure – and they're a big block to agility. It's a problem when you realize that succession planning, career development, internal selection, even learning and development – they all tend to be driven off job titles. For example, at Oxfam we had a role of Project Officer. But what this means is very different in different parts of the world. In Mexico it's about working with third parties to co-ordinate funding. In Bangladesh, it's being a community mobilizer. In some places the projects are so small; Project Officers have five or six other functions – being an advocate; a media person; and expert in written English and so on.

I trained Oxfam's HR staff to do job analysis by function. We identified the smallest unit of work you can't split into two jobs except by volume and then identified the functions that formed each of our jobs – that consisted at most of four or five functions. We also linked this to the phase of operation on a project – whether their experience suited phase one or two, setting up the project, or the implementation phases that are more about following instructions. Now we know who has had what functional experience, and at what project stage. We surveyed all staff that were capable of being redeployed to support a humanitarian crisis but we could only accept people who had experience in phase one or possibly phase two. We knew that if they had this experience they could safely be put in.

I think this sort of approach is needed in any organization over a hundred people, basically as soon as it's grown bigger than the typical entrepreneurial organization where everyone mucks in. It's certainly still needed in the voluntary sector. People tend to think that funding goes almost directly to relieve suffering. But in fact the value of voluntary organizations is in the skills that they employ to manage funding. Oxfam focused on relieving poverty not giving out handouts. It needs to change the conditions people live in, not to improve their access to money. This means that voluntary organizations need to drive the value of their workforces, they need to measure this, communicate it. If they don't understand how their organization works, they'll never be able to communicate their value to donors. You can't measure what you can't explain and you'll end up measuring and managing people as admin costs.'

Author: 'Anything else you would like to mention before we finish?'

Thompson: 'Another thing I think is rather scary is what does HR do when there are no meaningful measures for HR to get involved in ... what happens if the rest of the business doesn't really understand what is important? If they don't have the clarity of a strategy map? How does HR get the business focused on it? I don't think HR can do its job if there's no focused business plan, the business hasn't specified what's important, so you can't line up marketing and so on, and certainly can't line up HR and IT which are further down the value chain.

I think it's about getting everyone at the table and agreeing why we need to do this, to do that. What is the test that everyone should be able to apply to each activity? Can everyone in the room agree on what really matters in this business? This gives you a set of common things you can all be passionate about and describes the business at a deeper level than just the financials. Once you've got this basic idea you've got the beginnings of a strategy map, a cause and effect diagram you can use to rate the value of each activity that's contributing to the end effect.

I think HR needs to challenge the business on this point. HR needs to ensure the business focuses on what's important, that it's able to tell a story and use the strategy map or something like it to explain this. The strategy map also gives HR an opportunity to chip in and start to challenge itself to explain whether it's planning and working on the right initiatives. HR can use this to draw a cause and effect diagram for HR, perhaps with a few feedback loops to take account of the degree of complexity we discussed before. I also think it's important to talk about outcomes not activities. I refused to let my team talk about recruitment, diversity, career planning and so on – they're just activities. I only allowed them to talk about deliverables. Once you have agreed on the deliverables you can develop the activities and show how these fit in a cause and effect chain.

I'm passionate about wanting to only engage the business in this way – I could give myself an easy life by leaving my boss to define my role, and only look at the basic factors of the organization. But it would always be at the back of his mind – why is my HR Director doing this? I'd much rather get out of this box and ask afresh for each organization, what should HR be doing here?'

Managing and Measuring HCM at Standard Chartered

Standard Chartered bank specializes in consumer and wholesale banking. It employs more than 44 000 people in 56 countries and has operations in Asia, the Middle East, Africa and Latin America. I talked to Tim Miller, Director, People, Property and Assurance and Debbie Whitaker, Group Head, Human Capital Management.

Author: 'How do you ensure human capital management aligns with your business strategy?'

Miller: 'Every year we submit a strategic paper to the Board outlining our approach to HCM and showing how we're going to refresh it and what's going to be our focus for that year. For example, one of our key business strategies is 'Outserve' – about how we provide better service than the competition.'

Author: 'And what is HCM's input to Outserve – what does Standard Chartered do differently in people management to help you outserve the competition?'

Miller: 'We have a resource-based view of the firm, so you don't notice which piece is HCM. It's contingent, configurational; we do it automatically. You could argue that everything we do is configured to meet our business needs. And a lot of the difference is in the how not the what. It's why sharing data on what we're doing is actually quite harmless. It does make a lot of HR colleagues very nervous – they'll ask what if someone picks it up and reproduces it. But why would they do that, what would it really give them?

We use Gallup's Q12 to inform management activity. The top team are really interested in the insights it gives us – what it's saying, what it means given our strategy

191

and growth. And it's been fundamental to the change in culture of the bank. But its impact is the way it's helped us understand ourselves. For example, we recognized that some of our longest serving people were the most highly engaged. This is in direct contrast to Gallup's experience with other clients – that peoples' engagement declines gradually the longer they're employed. I think the fact that people become more engaged the longer they stay with us is an indication of the positive environment we've created. And we've used this insight to influence behaviours in the organization.

So, for example, we have two themed weeks every year, and our Chief Executive suggested we have a loyalty week. So we focused for a whole week on our most loyal customers and employees. We organized dinners for our longest serving staff. We recognized the longest employee working partnerships within the Bank. It's not a very elaborate example and in many ways it bucks the trend in other organizations where long service isn't seen as very sexy any more, but it was right for us. And it came from the data.'

Author: 'And what's been the role of measurement in HCM?'

Whitaker: 'We measure what we need to based upon our strategy. We ensure our key people enablers are lined up behind our strategy and then we look at what clusters of data inform how well we are building our people capability. This gives us our metrics. I don't believe in reporting just on the data you've got available – what I call flat reporting because it's one-dimensional. We put together information covering a number of different dimensions and it gives us richer and deeper insights. It gives us enormous and rich possibilities for interpreting and assessing what's going on.'

Miller: 'We want to complete a triangle of data points that help us manage the business. Human capital is about the people point of data. This is about whether people do what we intend them to do to build our people capability in a way that will deliver our strategy. It provides information we can give managers and will respond to the questions good managers want to ask. We have developed a quarterly human capital scorecard which covers these insights in depth. For example, how fast are we moving our best people around? What sort of retention do we have, particularly during employees' early years? This helps us understand whether our selection process is right, whether our induction is right. Or in terms of reward and performance – are we rewarding our better performers and higher potential staff disproportionally compared to average performers? Managers have finite resources so we need to use these resources effectively, and ensure we are discriminating in our judgements.

The second point is customer data. We capture intricate amounts of data that helps us understand the voice of the customer. And the third point is a slate of financial measures – all the usual suspects. In parallel with this, we're upgrading our management financial accounting processes. Our human capital work has created massive demand for better data from Finance so we can measure all of the things we need to – so that we can understand the impact of what we do to build engagement in terms of business performance. For example, we measure the effect of a proprietary selection tool we use to select Personal Financial Consultants who sit in the branches and sell higher value equity products. We can correlate performance on the selection tool with their revenue generation, which is dramatically better than others. We can track the tool's success accurately.

Then we also want to understand how these data points link together. If we are able to look at engagement and understand how our customers respond and then link this to business performance this is a phenomenally important triumvirate.'

Whitaker: 'We understand the impact of highly engaged employees. We can see the differences across branches of the bank — how engagement improves performance in terms of profit growth, employee retention, customer satisfaction and so on. We've also looked at what is going on within branches that makes people engaged. We've run some interpretative, qualitative research looking at why things are happening in a number of different markets. This has involved looking at the bottom and top performing branches, having interviews and focus groups with managers, and with employees, providing a dual perspective.

We've identified certain behaviours that mean some managers engage staff more readily than others. And we've incorporated this learning into individual management development programmes, development more generally, and our approach to corporate communication. This insight has fundamentally influenced the way the Chief Executive and our top team communicate with the bank and what they say. For example, we've discovered that we're very story driven. Our best managers use a lot of metaphors, analogies and stories to bring to life our values and our strategy. So a teller in a branch in Ghana can appreciate their contribution as part of a bigger picture.'

Miller: 'But leadership and management development programmes are no substitute for talented managers. So we're overhauling our selection process to give us more talented managers. We're looking for the patterns of feelings, thinking and behaviour that are linked to success in jobs and roles. This isn't about competencies, skills and abilities. We want the right talent for the job and then we'll leverage the hell out of it.'

Author: 'So what's your scorecard like — does it have quadrants, a range of metrics, that sort of thing?'

Whitaker: [showing me their scorecard — about 30–40 pages, with lots of colour graphics and obviously a lot of information on each page]: 'No, I don't believe in scorecards with a couple of metrics in a one-pager. I think you need much more than this. If you asked our business to pick just one metric, they'd say 'attrition' which is OK apart from you miss out on a lot of important dimensions. Also I don't think you get enough information from what I call a flat or static metric. Our scorecard contains more intelligent narratives; we call them 'analytics', which shows trend and rate of change. 'Attrition' is probably our dullest analytic. But even this shows different subsets of information, like the percentage of leavers who are high performers or with different periods of tenure. So with this, we can focus on key issues like turnover within the first 12 months of service. Take this analytic on succession planning – you could have a simple ratio reported at different grades, or something like this, which shows how talent flows through the organization. It's just got a lot more information in it.

Or this one on diversity [shown in Figure 6.5]. You can see that the female representation at senior management level in Hong Kong is 29 per cent. That's higher than the average for the rest of the bank. But it doesn't just show what current representation looks like, which let's face it, doesn't tell you much. The beauty is you can also see the trend data – if it's improving, or if it's going backwards, whether you're losing women and whether you're appointing enough to overcome any issues. So here female representation at senior management level fell by 6 per cent last year, which looks like it's down to a disproportionately higher attrition rate amongst female senior managers than males – 12 per cent. So potentially we're going backwards. But look at our appointment rate – 46 per cent of all senior appointments and promotions were women. So what does it tell us? Well, we look like we're doing a good job at getting women in, but we've got a higher attrition rate than for men which we need to watch.

In fact we've done some organizational modelling on female senior managers – a quarter of all our future appointments to senior management roles would need to

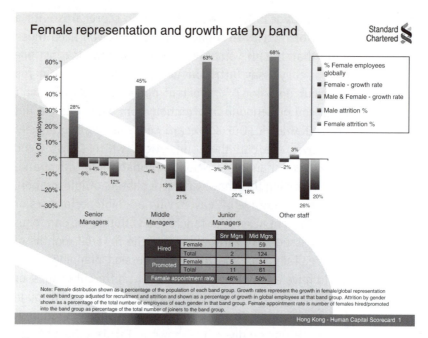

Figure 6.5 Standard Chartered HCM scorecard (Hong Kong) 2006–7

be female to get to where we want to be by end 2008. These analytics give you the sort of information you need to understand what's really going on. It's too easy to get hung up on one metric if that's all you've got to go on, if you're not looking at a rich picture like this.'

Author: 'And what do you do with this information, how are you dealing with diversity in response to this measurement information you've got?'

Whitaker: 'I just need to put diversity in context to start. We're a very diverse organization; it's one of our strengths in terms of what we value. It's about getting our hands on the best talent in the market, whatever their ethnicity, particularly somewhere like China where there are no ready-made bankers to recruit. So we do need to leverage our diversity more. Over the last 12 months we've established some key principles and developed a simple application framework with four key areas. The first, not surprisingly, is metrics. To understand where we are, how we're trending, agreeing some directional success measures. What we didn't want was to set targets. Targets can drive the wrong behaviours. People in financial services like their bonuses and if you target them on getting one more Chinese person, say, they're going to do it. We're a meritocracy and we don't want to interfere with this.

The second area is diagnostics. There are very different issues in each country – in the UAE it'll be Emiratization and gender representation. In Africa there'll be issues around tribal differences. So we've appointed a Diversity Champion in every country to look at the enablers, what gets in the way, and what we need to do differently to enhance our diversity and inclusive practices. It's often the subtle nuances that count.

The third area is education and awareness, bank-wide. Ensuring diversity isn't seen as a separate bolt-on but how we do business. Fourth is about addressing some big ticket people policies that will have the biggest impact. A fundamental overhaul of our end-to-end selection process, externally and internally, to ensure we get more diverse talent onto our shortlists. And a global framework for flexible working – minimum standards to give 'permission' and encouragement across our network that can be applied in local contexts.'

Author: 'You mentioned the power of tools like Gallup's to help you understand engagement issues at Standard Chartered – what about using benchmarking tools like this to understand how you compare to other organizations? What role does benchmarking play in your measurement approaches?'

Whitaker: 'We've got a number of concerns about external benchmarking. Firstly, benchmarks tend to operate at a macro level and mostly assume organizations are homogeneous when they're not! Also, aggregate data tends to be meaningless. So it's very superficial. Secondly, they can hide a multitude of sins. There's often a difference between what people claim to be in the data and what's really there. I think benchmarking firms do try to apply rigour but companies' data is not always that good. And they try to present themselves in the best light. Thirdly, I'm interested in how we're doing against our own strategy levers rather than against Jo Bloggs anyway. Benchmarking doesn't say anything about how we're doing on building our own capability to deliver our strategy. If we do it, we'll do it at the micro level – to understand patterns of data across our call centres and how these apply to call centres in other organizations. It's largely a waste of time at the macro level – it's just 'gee whiz' data.'

Miller: 'What we will do is participate in surveys on things like talent management with organizations like the Corporate Leadership Council where they'll feed back on the four or five things the best firms are doing. But this is more on the qualitative side, on the hows. Benchmarks of the absolutes, on the whats, are almost irrelevant. When I joined I was asked to compare our turnover rates to one of our competitors. I said I haven't got a view – we're both banks and that's where the similarities end!'

Author: 'And what about reporting – does your scorecard provide a framework for external reporting?'

Miller: 'Yes, we think reporting on HCM is increasingly important. Over the last few years we've included increasing amounts of information in our Annual Report and Review. We need to educate investors on the right measures to look at. Organizations that do report well will create pressure on investors and other companies. They'll see that Standard Chartered believes HCM reporting is important and that our reports are helpful and meaningful, so they'll start to do it too. HR professionals have a key role in providing the supply side and this will give the demand side a big kick.'

Author: 'Thank you. Just before we finish, can we go back to the recruitment and development of talented managers that you mentioned before. Can you explain more about their role?'

Miller: 'I think most of the research into HR and performance conducted by Huselid and others looking at which practices are important, which ingredients lead to higher engagement and link to performance, misses out a whole range of areas including vision, values, corporate responsibility, the work environment and so on. All these are at least as important as more traditional HR practices. And they are all about what managers are doing rather than about HR.'

Author: 'Well OK, although you could argue that these areas are part of a strategic HR function's remit too.'

Miller: 'Yes, but they're not, HR people aren't doing these things – just look at the CIPD curriculum – there's nothing about these areas in it. And even if HR's involved, it's the manager who makes it work. If you look at engagement within one country, you've got the same national culture and people practices – the same performance management and so on, but a wide variety, a broad distribution of results. So there's something else happening than just people practices – and this is about the way that managers are applying them.

We've conducted real longitudinal research over a number of years, taking upper quartile and lower quartile performers and tracking their engagement scores against our values, costs, diversity and so on. In our most engaged teams, 50 per cent of people strongly agree that they are fairly recognized and rewarded. In our least engaged it's very low. But the teams have the same bonus system, the same type of reward. If employees have different perceptions of whether they're fairly rewarded this isn't about their reward. Something's going on that's very different.

199

For example, better managers will tell someone they've got a salary increase and link it to their performance, and explain how they can do better. Lower performing managers, exaggerating to make a point, will just leave someone's salary letter on their desks. And if you're a manager and you want to drive business performance you've got to adapt a whole range of things to your local environment and your team – not just HR practices. It's the manager that holds up a local umbrella of reality for their staff.

Within HR, we want to find out what makes this difference and then operationalize it. This provides a contextualization for HR – a different strategy, objectives, a wider canvas. It helps HR focus on what it spends its time doing and not spending time on things that detract from this. Ulrich suggests that HR should be spending 17 per cent of its time on being an employee champion – it's utter rubbish. This is the fundamental role of the manager – to manage the relationship between them and their staff. If HR gets in the way it diminishes the role of the manager and wastes HR's time.'

Author: 'Although I don't think this is quite what Ulrich is suggesting – he's not saying that HR should spend time with employees, but they need to be employee advocates, to understand what factors would motivate them, to be their sponsors.'

Miller: 'But why do they need to do this? The argument's intellectually flawed. The biggest advocates of staff should be the managers. There will be the occasional case where managers discriminate or employees are short-changed but these will be one-offs. And yes, HR needs to provide a sense of arbitration, but it's *de minimis*. HR's job is to make the heads of the organization more effective and help them make their managers more effective. But we need to stay out of doing it for them – if we surrogate for poor managers then we've got a big problem.'

Summary

Reader: 'What do you hope that people have got out of this chapter?'

Author: 'Unlike the last few chapters, I've not attempted to provide any new input. Most of the chapter has focused on justifying the use of the HCM value matrix which is based on the value triangle and value matrix that were both introduced earlier on. I wanted to spend a whole chapter focusing on the value matrix because it forms the basis for the rest of the book, certainly for Chapters 7 to 11 which provide the processes that support HCM strategy development and execution.'

Reader: 'And I think your reasoning is clear, but what I'm interested in is why you are so interested in cause and effect based strategy maps when you do not believe causal chains exist in most areas of HCM?'

Author: 'Yes, it's a good challenge. Scorecards are anchored in a systems view of organizations. In fact, Norton (2000) states that:

> Balanced Scorecards, and the strategy maps on which they are based, reflect the philosophy of the systems approach. The view of strategy as a linked set of actions and outcomes which take place over time describe the system. The double-loop management process on which the Strategy-Focused Organization is based is derived from the principles of cybernetics (feedback and control), which are fundamental to systems.

So there is an argument for believing that scorecards are not fit for purpose in a complex environment. And, in fact, there is evidence that given this complexity, organizations do struggle to use scorecards well. For example, PwC (DiPiazza and Eccles, 2002) found that although 69 per cent of executives reported that they had 'attempted to demonstrate empirical cause-and-effect relationship between different categories of value drivers and both value creation and future financial results', less than one-third of these had been successful. However, the fact that the actions and outcomes identified in a scorecard do not turn out to have cause and effect relationships is not necessarily a problem. In a complex environment, the greatest benefit of the scorecard, and the HCM value matrix, is in supporting learning about the relationships between these actions and their outcomes.

Organizations should still try to use the value matrix to show expected correlations and the main direction of causality, although some of these may indicate a two-way or even a reverse flow. For example, engagement, which can be included as an output in the value chain, can cause satisfaction with people management processes, which will generally be included as an objective or measure of activity. Organizations need to understand that expected correlations may not turn out to exist and to see any variance between target and actual performance as an opportunity to understand more about how their organizations work.

The value matrix provides an agenda for worthwhile conversations about how to improve relationships between actions and outcomes. It helps to get business leaders, HR and line managers talking and learning about HCM strategy. In this way, the value matrix provides a language for thinking more deeply about people management and determining what is really meant by terms that can otherwise be rather vague. In a complex environment, it's not really a tool for management control.'

References

Barber, F. and Strack, R. (2005). 'The surprising economics of a people business', *Harvard Business Review*, June, 81–90.

Becker, E.B., Huselid, M.A. and Ulrich, D. (2001). *The HR Scorecard: Linking People, Strategy and Performance*. Harvard Business School Press.

Boudreau, J.W. and Ramstad, P.M. (2002). 'From "Professional Business Partner" to "Strategic Talent Leader": "What's Next" for Human Resource Management?', CAHRS, Working Paper 02–10.

Boudreau, J.W. and Ramstad, P.M. (2004). '"Talentship": a decision science for HR', *Strategic HR Review*, **3**(2), January–February, 28–31.

CFO Research Services (2003). *Human Capital Management: The CFO's Perspective*. CFO Publishing Corp. in collaboration with Mercer Human Resource Consulting.

Collins, J. and Porras, J. (2002). *Built to Last: Successful Habits of Visionary Companies*. Collins.

DiPiazza, S.A. Jr. and Eccles, R.G. (2002). *Building Public Trust: the Future of Corporate Reporting*. John Wiley & Sons.

Dobbs, R. and Koller, T. (2005). 'Measuring long-term performance', *The McKinsey Quarterly*, 2005 special edition: Value and performance.

Gratton, L. (2000). *Living Strategy: putting people at the heart of corporate purpose*. Pearson Education.

Hall, L. (2001). 'The HR Scorecard 10-minute guide', *Personnel Today*, 11 September, 29.

Hamel, G. and Prahalad, C.K. (1994). *Competing for the Future*. Harvard Business School Press.

Huselid, M.A., Becker, B.E. and Beatty, R.W. (2005). *The Workforce Scorecard*. Harvard Business School Press.

Kaplan, R.S. and Norton, D.P. (1992). The Balanced Scorecard – Measures that Drive Performance, *Harvard Business Review,* January–February, 71–79.

Kaplan, R.S. and Norton, D.P. (2004). Strategy Maps: Converting Intangible Assets into Tangible Outcomes. Harvard Business Review, 71–9.

Kim, W.C. and Mauborgne, R. (1997). 'Value innovation: The strategic logic of high growth', *Harvard Business Review*, January–February, 101–112.

Kim, W.C. and Mauborgne, R. (2005). *Blue Ocean Strategy: How to Create Uncontested Market Space and Make the Competition Irrelevant*. Harvard Business School Press.

Lev, B. (2004). 'Sharpening the intangibles edge', *Harvard Business Review*, June, 109–116.

Millar, M. (2006). 'RBS invests in belief that staff development will bring returns'. *Personnel Today,* 2 May, 4.

Norton, D.P. (2000). 'Is management finally ready for the "systems approach"?' *Balanced Scorecard Report*, 15 September, 3–4.

Norton, D.P. (2001a). Foreword, in *The HR Scorecard* (Ulrich, D.) Harvard Business School Press.

Norton, D.P. (2001b). 'Measuring the contribution of human capital', *Balanced Scorecard Report*, July–August.

Norton, D.P. (2001c). 'Managing the development of human capital', *Balanced Scorecard Report*, September–October.

Scarborough, H. and Elias, J. (2002). *Evaluating Human Capital*. Chartered Institute of Personnel and Development.

Walker, G. and MacDonald, J.R. (2001). 'Designing and implementing an HR scorecard', *Human Resource Management*, Winter, **40**(4), 365–77.

Winkler, H. (2005). 'Developing KPIs at Southern Company', *Strategic HR Review*, **4**(4), May–June, 28–31.

Part 2

The Strategic HCM Planning Cycle

7

HCM Strategy Development

Introduction

Reader: *'I take it we're moving into the first stage of the strategic HCM planning cycle. What are we going to cover?'*

Author: 'This chapter focuses on how HCM strategy, and in particular, creating value HCM strategy, can be developed. The chapter emphasizes the need for strategic alignment and provides a case study from Microsoft which demonstrates alignment and best fit. The chapter also highlights the need for creativity in strategy development and provides some tools and techniques for this. But probably the most important point in the chapter is the use of the HCM value matrix to show, I think really for the first time, why and how it is that business strategy can be led by people's capability. I know a lot of people talk about putting people before strategy. A good example is Jim Collins's call to get the right people on the bus. But it's one thing to say that people management drives strategy, and quite another to illustrate diagrammatically why it's the case ...'

Identifying the Focus for HCM Strategy Development

The first stage in the strategic HCM planning cycle is the identification of a set of strategic objectives to describe an HCM programme. The HCM value matrix is a useful tool to support objective-setting for two reasons. Firstly, the matrix provides a template for capturing and communicating lead and lag objectives. Secondly, and more importantly, the matrix helps focus objective-setting on the right steps in the HCM value chain. As Figure 7.1 shows, the primary focus or starting point for strategy development (represented by the circles) changes according to the level of value being considered (the box labelled number '2' for value for money, box '8' for adding value and box '11' for creating value).

In Chapter 5, we identified that at the value for money level, people management strategy is developed through a process that is separate from the development of the business strategy. The HCM value matrix helps articulate that this separate strategy development process is also inside-out. The primary focus of attention and effort is within the HR function and on the current state. More specifically, focus is on the activity step in the HCM value chain (labelled as box 2 in Figure 7.1), which provides objectives for the organization's people management practices. A lesser focus is applied to the input step (box 1), which includes objectives about the HR function itself. For some changes to the organization's practices there may also be measurable outputs (box 3) or even clear impacts on the business (box 4) but these are consequences of, not the drivers for, the activity.

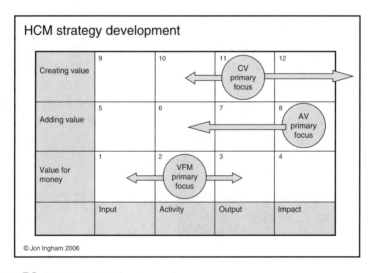

Figure 7.1 HCM strategy development

Adding-value strategy development is externally-oriented or outside-in. It is also forward-looking, focusing on achieving the impact objectives in the annual business plan (box 8), by aligning people management activities (box 6), and to a lesser extent, the organization's human resources (box 7) with these business objectives. As Figure 7.2 illustrates, business impacts are caused by bundles of HR activities and these HR activities can contribute towards a number of business impacts. The nodal points within these multiple relationships (shown by the ovals) indicate the human and organizational outputs that result from these HR activities and lead on to the business impacts. The work required at these nodal points can be prioritized depending on the extent of the relationship between activities and impacts, as illustrated by the size of the ovals in Figure 7.2. This degree of interrelationship between activities, outputs and impacts is the reason why organizations need to take a systemic approach to HRM strategy.

Creating value strategy has a real external focus in which external means outside of the business as well as outside the HR function. The focus now is on an organization's customers, shareholders and other stakeholders, including those people the organization identifies as talent. The focus also needs to be on the future state, looking at what needs to be different and then working backwards from this future position.

This concern for external customers and meeting shareholder expectations is supported by an internal focus on people's potential capability

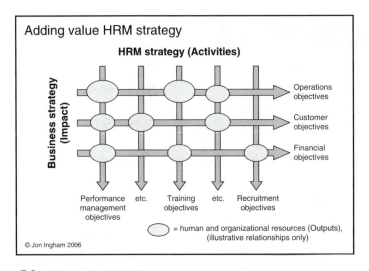

Figure 7.2 Adding value (HRM) strategy

as outputs (box 11) of the HCM value chain. This means that creating value HCM strategy requires more focus on the human capital and intangible capability that will be required in the future than on the operational and financial results that are typically the focus of HR and business plans. This conclusion flies in the face of the generally prevailing mindset that HR needs to get closer and closer to the business. In fact, this mindset is so strong that my original report on this (Finn and Ingham, 2004) showed the primary focus for creating value to be business impact (box 12).

Something similar is proposed by Kaplan and Norton. Although they typically approach strategy as competitive positioning, which means completing the customer and then the internal business perspectives in the balanced scorecard, they also understand that:

> Companies deploying a strategy based on core competencies or unique capabilities may wish to start their strategic planning process by identifying those critical competencies and capabilities for their internal business process perspective, and then, for the customer perspective, selecting customer and market segments where these competencies and capabilities are most critical for delivering customer value. (Kaplan and Norton, 1996)

The creating value approach to HCM planning follows this principle but moves strategy development even further back into the learning and growth perspective of the balanced scorecard, and the output step in the HCM value chain.

Completing the Matrix

An HCM strategy or programme plan can be articulated and communicated by specifying objectives in the appropriate boxes in the HCM value matrix. The starting point for completing the matrix is the identification of a few 'primary objectives', or 'primaries', in whichever box is the primary area of focus.

Once these primaries have been identified, the matrix can be used to identify a selection of other key objectives to inform and support the primaries. Boxes to the left of the primaries can be used to identify objectives that need to be met further up the value chain. So a value for money activity, for example ensuring compliance with legislation (box 2), may need something to happen in the HR function as an input (box 1) to this activity. For example, HR might need to automate operations to help collect data for compliance audit purposes. An adding value business requirement, for example reducing customer price sensitivity (box 8), may need to be supported by a particular output, for example increasing employee comfort with selling value (box 7), or an activity based upon a set of best practices, for example shadowing of sales champions (box 6). Boxes to the right of the primaries can be used to identify things that may be expected to happen further down the value chain. For example, a created value output, such as improving employee advocacy (box 11), may be expected to result in a particular transformational change in the business, for instance attracting new types of customers (box 12). These linked objectives are indicated by arrows extending from the primary areas of focus in Figure 7.1. But there may be other boxes that can be usefully completed as well.

In particular, cascading objectives from the primaries may also lead to boxes at different levels of value being completed. The usual direction of movement is towards the top left. So, for example, a particular added value output (box 7) might be developed, possibly as a by-product, by a creating value, best fit activity (box 10). It is less likely, although far from impossible, that this link would work from bottom left to top right, in which an adding value, best practice activity (box 6) would result in a creating value capability (box 11).

There may also be boxes where, for various reasons, it is not appropriate to identify any objectives or measures. This is fine, especially as it is useful to keep the number of objectives to a minimum.

In completing the matrix, three other factors are important. Firstly, organizations need to ensure alignment between the objectives within a strategy or programme plan. Secondly, if attempting to create value, they need to use creativity to help develop strategies that can transform the business. And thirdly, they need to use measurements appropriately. The use of measurement has already been covered in Chapter 1. The need for alignment and the use of creativity are described below.

Ensuring Alignment to Create Value

HCM strategy creates value when best fit practices are used to develop intangible capability that is uniquely tailored to a particular organization's needs. This is also about differentiation. As Huselid *et al.* (2005) explain:

> A central theme in this new perspective is the need for greater *differentiation* – of employees, of jobs, and of the way that firms manage workforce performance – based on the firm's competitive strategy and operational goals. Successful strategies and competitive advantage nearly always rely on some form of differentiation in the marketplace; yet traditional workforce strategies are remarkably undifferentiated both within and across firms. That is, we often see firms with very different organizational strategies adopting highly similar workforce strategies. And as a result, one of the firm's most important strategic assets, the workforce, becomes one of its most underperforming assets.

Part of being clear about what an HCM strategy is designed to do is being clear about what it is not intended to do. Porter's explanation of why business strategy requires trade-offs applies to people management strategy as well (Porter, 1996):

> Trade-offs arise for three reasons. The first is inconsistencies in image or reputation. A company known for delivering one kind of value may lack credibility and confuse customers – or even undermine its reputation – if it delivers another kind of value or attempts to deliver two inconsistent things at the same time…. Second, and more important, trade-offs arise from activities themselves. Different positions (with their tailored activities) require different product configurations, different equipment, different employee behavior, different skills and different management systems…. Finally, trade-offs arise from limits on internal coordination and control. By clearly choosing to compete in one way and not another, senior management makes organizational priorities clear.

Trade-offs in HCM strategy occur for similar reasons. Porter's first point translates into a need for consistency in an employer brand. It is difficult to communicate an offer to an organization's partner group or its talent pools if the organization's offer is not clear. Secondly, we have seen that best practice bundling and best fit configurations require coherent sets of people management practices. As an example, it is difficult to combine equality and collaboration with meritocracy and forced ranking. Porter's third and final point applies just as it is written. Trade-offs allow organizations to focus on what is really important, and support the programme management-focused approach to HCM that was discussed in Chapter 6.

If an organization has developed a clear alignment, supported by trade-offs, then each of its value matrices should tell a clear story about what it is trying to achieve. Microsoft's experience provides a good illustration of this.

Strategic Alignment at Microsoft

Microsoft is one of those organizations people either love or hate. Not just because of its software or its alleged monopolistic practices, but because of the sort of organization it is. An article in *Fortune* compared the company to a 'raucous, runaway Mensa meeting' (Schlender, 2004) and an article in the *Financial Times* noted that:

> Chris Bartlett, a professor at Harvard Business Schools, calls it an 'intellectual pissing contest' – hire the brightest and the best, then let them fight it out for dominance. (Waters, 2003)

However, Microsoft is clearly doing something right and came first in the *Sunday Times* Best 100 Companies to Work For survey in 2003. The same year, I presented at a CIPD platform on HCM along with Steve Harvey, Senior Director of People and Culture at Microsoft UK. Most of the information in this case study dates back to 2003, since when Harvey has left and Microsoft's people management strategy has changed.

Harvey explained how Microsoft's business and people management strategies were very closely aligned with each other and with the sort of people Microsoft employed. The company had developed an EVP which was very finely-tuned to the sort of people the company wanted to employ and it worked hard to ensure that this proposition was delivered consistently well.

However, some attributes of this EVP will switch many people off. In fact this is exactly what these attributes had been designed to do. Microsoft had made trade-offs. By appealing to a particular group of people so well it meant the firm would not appeal to other people who might otherwise have considered themselves prospective employees.

So, for example, work–life balance had not been a high priority, at least not in the way that most organizations understand it. Microsoft worked hard to recruit highly talented people who would love working for Microsoft. Because the company employed very driven people, gave them work they enjoyed and that they were able to get a lot out of, people tended to work long hours. People knew that they would need to

213

dedicate themselves to the company and understood the great jobs, development and environment they would receive in return. It was a clear deal that employees could commit to for as long as it worked for them to do so. Harvey expressed the deal saying that, 'we want people who balance work–life over their life'.

Microsoft's people management practices provide a great example of best fit. The company's EVP had been developed to suit the firm's specific needs, rather than by relying on best practice as is more usually the case. Many of these practices would not work elsewhere and any organization that wants to learn from Microsoft should focus on achieving the firm's level of alignment and performance, not (unless the organization has a similar business strategy and employs similar people) on copying the way that this level of performance has been achieved.

Microsoft's HCM Strategy

To attract, develop and retain very bright, talented people, Microsoft was trying to 'create an environment where great people can do their best work and be on a path to realize their potential'. Harvey described his vision for the organization as an environment where:

> Microsoft is the UK IT employer of choice, where people have the opportunity to do what they do best every day. When a head-hunter calls, our people answer: 'Why would I want to work anywhere else?' and even if they tried to leave their families would stop them.

Harvey articulated the alignment between the firm's business and HCM strategies using a value chain based upon the Gallup Path (Buckingham and Coffman, 2001). This value chain suggested that if great people were put in great jobs and were led by great managers and leaders, then satisfied customers, growth, results and rewards would naturally follow. Harvey's comments on the integration of Microsoft's people and business strategy were reported in *Personnel Today* (Kent, 2003):

> Harvey consciously avoids the compartmentalization of people management from the rest of the business – a fact borne out by his own job title.
>
> 'The whole philosophy is around creating a long-term strategy,' he says. 'It's not just an HR strategy, it's not purely about people, it's about the overall strategy of the company.' Harvey doesn't drive this strategy,

it is created by the board of directors and realized through the work of every manager.

It is difficult to discuss specific HR initiatives or policies because the organization is constantly responding to the demands of its own customers and sector, rather the addressing general employment practice.

Microsoft also used measures to support its HCM activities. For example, senior managers were held responsible for succession planning by identifying potential replacements from high potential or promotable people within the organization, or from elsewhere. The effectiveness of this approach was tracked at country level through the coverage of senior managers and direct reports for which successors would be ready within twelve months. Countries were tracked towards increasing this coverage to 80 per cent. Measures tended to focus at this strategic level rather than the basics like sickness and absence as these were no longer seen as highly relevant.

Activities

Great Hires and Re-hires. Microsoft wanted to recruit people who were the 'brightest and the best': people with a passion for technology, a passion for helping customers achieve great things with software and who were adaptable enough to meet the changing demands of the business and industry. The acquisition and retention of talent was such an important part of Microsoft's strategy that recruitment, engagement and development were seen as key business processes.

Globally, Microsoft employed a couple of hundred people to keep an eye on the world's most talented young software engineers including every graduate from related disciplines in the USA, China, India, Brazil and Russia. In the same way as in Ernst & Young, these people's jobs were not to recruit this talent, but to attract them to join when the time was right. Microsoft also used current employees to recruit new ones, with a high proportion of hires coming through referrals.

Microsoft kept staffing levels at an absolute minimum by using industry partners to take up slack created by changes in demand. However, even by controlling headcount and with this sophistication of recruitment, Microsoft could not recruit all the high quality people it required – Harvey commented that they had taken on only 14 people from out of 13 000 applications received in the previous year. The company reinforced the importance of recruiting talent by organizing a party to celebrate the arrival of each new recruit (surely a more value adding activity than splashing out when they eventually leave).

Microsoft offered a broad range of development, although most of this was provided by frequent increases in responsibility rather than through long lists of training courses. Most development was targeted on Microsoft's star performers – people rated 'A+' – and their future talent pools. This focus on top performers was balanced by a robust focus on poor performers who would be given clear objectives with regular reviews to put things right. All this was supported by Microsoft's 'great managers' who were trained to do the right things in developing weaker performers or helping them to move elsewhere.

Great Job. Ensuring Microsoft had the best talent was not just about recruitment and development. The company also focused on engaging and retaining people for as long as they could. This was about really looking after their people, and not just in financial terms, as the company paid less than some competitors in the sector. For Harvey, it was about 'allowing people to do what they do best every day' on the basis that 'when people really enjoy what they do, the ideas begin to flow'.

HR best practice says that you find people to fit the role, not design roles around people. Microsoft would do the opposite – they recruited great people and would then find them roles where they could play to their strengths. This required a thorough, in-depth knowledge of the talent they employed. Microsoft used Gallup's survey tool Q12 to gauge employees' belief, on a scale from one to five, that they had a chance to do their best work every day. When starting out on this process, Microsoft discovered that only a low proportion of staff believed they were doing what they were best at every day, while in the HR department the figure was even lower. Harvey thought that a very high result was probably unrealistic, but wanted to move towards a much higher level.

Using Gallup's Strength Finder, staff would take a 45 minute assessment based on a set of emotive questions to identify their top five strengths from a potential list of 34. Microsoft then tried to match people with the most suitable jobs where their skills could be put to best use. This helped the company help its people to meet their full potential and ensured that staff remained engaged in the business. For example, having analysed the profiles from the HR team and implemented some simple changes, the proportion of the HR team who believed they were using their key strengths improved substantially, along with their morale.

The strength-finder process was supported by effective performance management with clear objective-setting and differentiation of people based on both performance and potential. Promotions could take place at any time of year as determined by an employee's performance rather than their job grade. This supported Microsoft's philosophy of encouraging everyone to play to their strengths and not moving for promotion's sake.

Ensuring the right fit also involved empowering and educating employees to take control of their working lives through inputs on personal development, for example Covey's seven habits (Covey, 1999). Microsoft's Personal Excellence programme explained more about the 'deal' and made the point that if people wanted to spend time with their family or take up golf they needed to be honest with themselves and the company about what sort of job they could do in the organization.

Great Managers and Great Leaders. In Microsoft terms, great managers would create great people. They were coaches who were committed to bringing out the best in people by developing their natural talents. Great leaders were people who could break through barriers to create the sort of business Microsoft needed in the future. What great managers and leaders were not were just great technicians who had been promoted into line management roles on the basis of their technical rather than their managerial capabilities.

The company did find it difficult to recruit and develop the quality of managers and leaders that it needed. It tried to recruit people who had the potential to develop into these roles and conducted leadership interviews to gauge skills and potential. When suitable people were identified, they were provided with structured courses, coaching and mentoring to support their development.

Great Company. Microsoft believed that to engage employees they needed to provide an appropriate physical environment and to support people's intellectual and emotional well-being. At Microsoft UK's offices, the physical environment included 'great workspaces' supported by Microsoft's latest technology and state of the art office accommodation with plenty of facilities, situated in landscaped grounds. Emotional well-being was supported by a well-being centre, an employee assistance programme, fit for life training, health screening, alternative medicines, a motivation and morale budget, and a lifestyle management programme to help its senior managers. Intellectual well-being was supported by an open, trusting environment 'where ideas can flourish', supported by training in personal excellence and the use of technology to take people out of routine work.

Outputs. Microsoft's annual employee turnover was well below the national industry average and only a small part of this was unmanaged. Table 7.1 presents some of the results from Microsoft's 2003 employee survey which had a 93 per cent response rate, kept

Table 7.1: Microsoft's employee survey results 2003 (Microsoft UK Organizational Health Index)

Questions	Percentage favourable
1. People at Microsoft have a passion for the work	97
2. I clearly understand Microsoft's vision	92
3. Microsoft attracts and retains smart people	90
4. I am encouraged to work co-operatively with people in other groups	90
5. My manager demonstrates respect for diversity	90
6. I like the kind of work I do	90
7. I have the authority to carry out my responsibilities	90
8. I have confidence that Microsoft will continue to be the world's leading software company	89
9. The people in my work group cooperate to get things done	89
10. I can see a clear link between my work and my work group's objectives	89

high by the company's proven track record in acting on employees' responses.

Using Creativity to Create Value

In a complex environment, organizations need to make transformational rather than incremental improvements in their products, services and the way they operate and manage their businesses. This is an ongoing need as what is created value today becomes a commodity tomorrow, and what is creating value becomes a standard procedure and is outsourced and offshored.

Hamel and Prahalad (1994) illustrate the danger of slippage in value by using an example of competition from Japanese companies towards the end of the last century:

> It is entirely possible for a company to downsize and reengineer without ever confronting the need to regenerate its core strategy, without ever being forced to rethink the boundaries of its industry, without ever having to imagine what customers might want in ten years' time, and without ever having to fundamentally redefine its 'served market'. Yet without such a fundamental reassessment, a company will be overtaken on the road to the future. Defending today's leadership is no substitute for creating tomorrow's leadership.
>
> In the 1970s and 1980s quality, as measured by defects per vehicle, was undoubtedly a core competence for Japanese car companies. Superior reliability was an important value element for customers and a genuine differentiator for Japanese car producers. It took more than a decade for Western car companies to close the quality gap with their Japanese competitors, but by the mid-1990s quality, in terms of initial defects per vehicle, has become a prerequisite for every car maker. There is a dynamic at work here that is common to other industries. Over long periods of time, what was once a core competence may become a base-line capability.

Talking about the need for radical thinking and approaches, Richard Pascale presents an analogy from athletics in which the height required to win the Olympics high jump has increased in small and ongoing increments interspersed with more substantial leaps forwards (or in this case, upwards) in performance. This is shown in Figure 7.3. I have superimposed three sigmoid curves alongside the results, illustrating how each new technique resulted in what were initially small improvements, which then grew and subsequently levelled off at a new height.

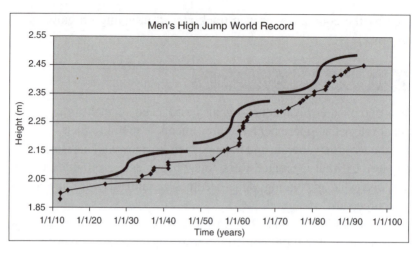

Figure 7.3 Men's high jump world record.
Source: wikipedia (http://en.wikipedia.org/wiki/High_jump) Licensed under the GNU Free Documentation License

Each of the breakthrough changes in performance were the result of someone successfully introducing a new technique. The first breakthrough came in 1912 with the development of the Western Roll that quickly replaced the existing Scissors approach. The next breakthrough followed the introduction of the Straddle in 1956. The most recent change came in 1968 when Dick Fosbury created the Fosbury Flop, jumping backwards over the bar. Fosbury's breakthrough was partly about better use of technology, in this case, laying foam under the bar, so that he could jump over backwards without sustaining a serious injury. But it also relied on improvements in human capital – Fosbury was a former gymnast who introduced a set of new capabilities to the sport.

The ongoing, incremental improvements that have followed on from each breakthrough have been down to changes in people's mental models about what it may be possible to jump. Another analogy, also from athletics, that may provide an even better example of the power of new mental models is the breakthrough of the four-minute mile, achieved by Roger Bannister in 1954. Breaking this barrier had previously seemed impossible, but once Bannister had shown that humans could run this fast his record was beaten in less than 50 days. Within the next three years, a total of 16 other runners also ran a sub-four-minute mile.

Finding ways to achieve breakthrough changes in performance and resetting people's mindsets about what may be possible requires the use of creativity at least as much as it requires more data and better information. After all, when people think like they have always thought, they tend to get what they have always got.

Creative thinking can supply ideas and insights that linear, logical thinking cannot provide. It opens up new opportunities that lay outside existing mindsets and points the way towards to the next sigmoid curve. Building upon research that has shown considerable independence between the brain's left and right hemispheres, this type of thinking is associated with the right side of the brain. The need for right-brained thinking is supported by Luc de Brabandere (2005), partner at BCG who states, 'The left "here and now" side of the business brain is alive and well – the right side needs to be awakened and given room to roam.'

Some of the characteristics of the left and right sides of the brain are:

Left brain	Right brain
rational, logical	intuitive, imaginative
linear, sequential	multiple, simultaneous, holistic
parts and details	wholes and relationships
analysis (breaking apart)	between parts
verbal, numerical	synthesis (putting together)
directed	visual, spatial
	spontaneous

Hayashi (2001), writing as a senior editor at the *Harvard Business Review*, has commented on the difficulty senior executives have in explaining the process of intuitive and imaginative thinking:

> To describe that vague feeling of knowing something without knowing exactly how or why, they used words like 'professional judgment,' 'intuition,' 'gut instinct,' 'inner voice,' and 'hunch,' but they couldn't describe the process much beyond that.

Hayashi suggests that the higher someone progresses up the organization, the more important this type of thinking becomes. He quotes Ralph Larsen, former CEO of Johnson & Johnson, as explaining:

> Very often, people will do a brilliant job up through the middle management levels, where it's very heavily quantitative in terms of the

decision-making. But then they reach senior management, where the problems get more complex and ambiguous, and we discover that their judgment or intuition is not what it should be. And when that happens, it's a problem; it's a *big* problem.

I would argue that complexity and ambiguity are particularly significant in HCM and therefore that judgement and intuition are also particularly important within this field. In fact, much of this book has been concerned with rebalancing existing debate on HCM from an excessively left-brained focus. Similarly, much of my work in HCM has involved working with managers and particularly HR professionals to help them extend their range of thinking to include more room for imagination and intuition.

However, the rest of the organization and particularly its managers need to be creative too. The aim has got to be to create what Richard Florida, author of *The Rise of the Creative Class*, and Jim Goodnight, CEO of software company SAS, refer to as 'creative capital ... an arsenal of creative thinkers whose ideas can be turned into valuable products and services' (Florida and Goodnight, 2005). This often requires an organization to become more receptive to a different style of working. For example, organizations should not rely too much on measurement and data. As well as distracting people from what they need to do, and reducing their discretion in how they do it, this can mean that using intuition becomes increasingly unacceptable. People need to be able to put up their hands and say, 'all the data may say we should do it, but it just doesn't feel right'.

Organizations need to ensure that they employ people who have principles and ideals that are aligned with their organization's values. Where this is not the case, it is very difficult for people to trust their instinct. And organizations need to create enough slack in people's roles so that they still have time to think. As Gratton (in Gratton *et al.,* 1999) notes:

> The ability to respond quickly to changing needs and to build long-term capability depends in part on the ability of managers to visualize and create mental pictures of the future, to move from a fire-fighting mode to one where they have the potential to think in the longer-term.

People also need the right capabilities, a set of skills, tools and techniques to enable them to be creative.

Techniques for Encouraging Creativity

I have found that various approaches to creative thinking help develop creative capital and can also be used more specifically to help generate creating value HCM strategies. For example, I often open strategic planning sessions (or even less formal conversations about the future) with problems like the nine dots puzzle, shown in Figure 7.4. Can you draw four straight lines that go through all nine dots without taking your pen or pencil off the paper?

The problem is solved by thinking outside of the box (extending the lines beyond the dots). If you are really creative, you can also solve the puzzle using three or even one straight lines (for example by folding or tearing the paper, or imagining a line going round the world three times). After this initial brainteaser, I might use a couple of further creative thinking exercise followed by the use of one or more of the following techniques to generate ideas for potential intangible capabilities, and the programmes which will develop these capabilities.

The principle behind most creative thinking techniques is that we cannot consciously force the right brain to operate. We have to distract the left brain and give the right brain enough space to allow intuition to develop. One set of techniques use a rather left-brained approach to right-brained thinking. These techniques include brainstorming which can be used to generate a large number of ideas. As with other creative thinking approaches, one essential rule in brainstorming is to avoid criticism to ensure that apparently absurd ideas which can contain the keys

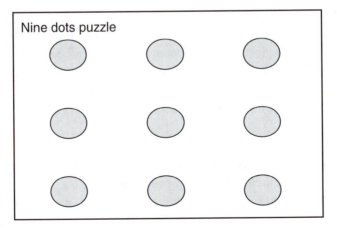

Figure 7.4 The nine dots puzzle

to new perspectives are not dismissed. Brainstorming helps move people out of habitual thinking patterns and encourages new thinking. But this technique still revolves around words, and can end up producing long lists of logical analysis (data) rather than flows of intuition (knowledge). The technique has also been heavily overused and as such is unlikely to create an appropriately positive response from many groups of people.

A better technique is mind mapping, developed by Tony Buzan (2002). Recognizing that we think in a radiant and expansive manner, this approach creates a visual network of thoughts, ideas and associations. Mind maps are developed around a particular subject that is presented as a colourful and stimulating central image. A number of branches which indicate key themes are identified by a word or picture and radiate from this central image. Smaller branches radiate from higher level branches to indicate topics of lesser importance. A group mind map can be developed by using a two-stage process involving individual brainstorming or mind mapping followed by an exchange of a ideas and the creation of 'multiple-mind mind map'.

Another useful technique is six thinking hats, developed by Edward de Bono (1999). In this approach, people are asked to put on one of six real or metaphorical hats to ensure different thinking styles are all included within a decision-making process. The six hats with their corresponding thinking styles are:

1. White hat: facts, figures and information.
2. Red hat: intuition, feelings and emotions.
3. Black hat (logical negative): judgement and caution.
4. Yellow hat (logical positive): potential results and benefits.
5. Green hat: creativity, alternatives, proposals, provocations and changes.
6. Blue hat: overview or process control.

The hats can be used in parallel where each person in a group of six people would wear a different hat, or in series, where the group wears first one hat and then another as it proceeds through a number of decision-making stages. The hats can also be useful in helping people understand other people's thinking styles and the way these preferences can be managed to ensure effective decision-making.

More interesting and potentially transformational but more risky techniques involve the use of visualization and metaphor. These approaches free up the right brain by tackling a problem in a different sort of way. However, an HR function which is considering using these techniques to facilitate the development of an HCM strategy, or for another purpose, needs to consider carefully whether they are appropriate. This will depend in part on the perceived value provided by HR.

An HR function moving from a traditional Personnel focus to an HRM, adding value approach should not use these techniques. A Personnel function does not generally have enough credibility within the business to take risks. In any case, a Personnel function needs to emphasize its business credentials to progress forward (moving from box 2 to box 8). These functions should stick with brainstorming or even rely on data and logic until they have developed the credibility they need. However, I think proposing something like visualization would be totally appropriate and very helpful to an HR function moving from HRM to creating value HCM. Here the function already has credibility in the business and using unconventional techniques helps demonstrate that the HR function has something special to offer based upon its knowledge of people's capability (moving from box 8 to box 11).

The two approaches that are explained here can be used to support groups in thinking about HCM strategy. However, the techniques also work for individuals as well as a group and can be used in any area of life. Both methods require an initial issue, problem or question that a group wants to explore. The Mind Gym (2005) supports the need to have an objective for creative thinking, explaining that: 'Aimless creativity is usually just that. Some sense of purpose greatly increases the odds of coming up with something that is not only original but also worthwhile.' To provide examples in using the two techniques, we will look at the question, 'how can we find the best talent?'

Visualization

Visualization recreates the state of relaxed attention halfway between full concentration and deep sleep that accounts for many people's common experience of having their best ideas in the bath or while driving a car.

Facilitation involves bringing a group together somewhere quiet and asking people to relax by breathing deeply, closing their eyes and stopping conscious thinking. The facilitator will probably need to explain that it is not about pushing thoughts away but letting them drift into the mind and slowly out again. Most people also find it useful to focus on the rhythm of their breathing. When everyone has relaxed, they can be asked to visualize an image in response to the question the group has defined. For example, they might see recruiters sitting in team meetings at competitors', a sponsored award dinner for the best people in their sector; something happening at a key university, a non-recruitment recruitment advert – or possibly much more creative scenes than this. Images may be still or they may involvement movement.

People may need to be quite patient and not try to force an image to come forward. When an image does appear, they should accept the image without trying to judge or analyse it. People will often find it helpful to draw images as they arise rather than keeping the mind occupied trying to remember them. It is also useful for people to think about the sounds, touch, taste and smell that go alongside the picture they are seeing. People can be asked to explore the emotions that these senses are creating in them.

People should be given some personal time to interpret the images before sharing them. They should also be encouraged to use their intuition rather than rational analysis to provide more explanation on the pictures they have seen. After a while, people can be invited to discuss the images with the others in the group.

Metaphor/Analogy

A metaphor is a comparison between two unlike things. It can be used to disguise a relatively conventional problem as something else in the hope that this may create new associations and possibilities. This is useful if a group has got stuck or people need to be encouraged to break out of an existing mindset. A good example of this use of metaphor is Gareth Morgan's images of organizations. Morgan (1996) identifies eight archetypical organizational metaphors including machines (causal chains), brains (dynamic systems) and organisms (complex processes). Morgan (1997) also provides a process, Imaginization, for developing new images to support new ways of organizing. However, metaphor can also be used to deal with an unfamiliar problem by relating it back to something more understandable.

In general terms, the process that a facilitator can use after agreeing on an initial issue or question is as follows. Firstly, the group should be asked to brainstorm potential metaphors to work with. For example, finding talent could be compared to drilling for oil or looking for treasure. People should use their intuition to choose which metaphor they then want to work with. The facilitator should then ask people to list as many characteristics of the chosen metaphor as they can. For example, drilling for oil involves finding good sites, specialists teams, complex technology, patient investors, and so on. For each characteristic, the group should identify what parallels there are, or there could be, to the initial issue or question. For example, finding good sites for drilling for oil involves understanding the topography. Comparing this back to the initial issue might mean marking out the sorts of places that could be possible sources of talent.

An analogy represents the same problem in a different context. Working with analogy involves the same process as metaphor but because the comparison is more direct it usually makes sense to ask people how they would solve the analogy and then transfer the solution back to the problem. For example finding talent could be compared to meeting a wife/husband/partner. Solving the analogy might involve organizing some dinner parties. Applying this solution back to the initial issue might mean holding some network events like Ernst & Young's 'Staying in Touch' events described in Chapter 5.

People Strategy Lab

In HCM, strategy is emergent, but it is still possible to influence the way that strategy emerges by getting the right sort of conversations going and intervening in them appropriately. Doing this cannot ensure that the outcomes of these conversations will be realized, but it will influence the organization's dynamic decision-making processes to increase the likelihood that people value will be created.

One useful approach is a large-scale facilitated event in which highly energized collaboration can take place. This sort of temporary community is no substitute for more effective organizational dynamics back in the workplace and it does attempt to structure self-organization which is rather self-contradictory. But as long as the event is seen as part of a broader approach, for example by being supported by other conversations before and after the event, it can form a very useful part of the strategic HCM planning cycle.

However, none of the existing large-scale facilitation methodologies quite work for this purpose. The following outline is based on some elements of *Future Search* (Weisbord and Janoff, 2000), *Real-Time Strategic Change* (Jacobs, 1997) and other approaches (Bunker and Alban, 1996). This is the process that seems to me to best meet the generic need to develop HCM strategy, although it always needs to be tailored to a particular client's needs and I have never run an event in quite this form.

The event consists of a large group planning meeting that brings together a diverse group of stakeholders who are concerned with the way people provide value to an organization. I do not personally believe that the absolute number of people at the event is that significant, but it might typically include 50 to 200 people depending on the size of organization. Participants should include the CEO; at least one other Board representative; most of the leadership team; HR, Finance, IT and other functions; line managers; core talent representatives; other talent pools especially young people to balance what is likely to be a fairly senior group; other people who do not usually get to be involved in this sort of forum such as the secretaries and cleaners; customers and key shareholders; preferred suppliers of people management services; outsourcing partners and thought leaders connected with the organization. HR professionals are facilitators of the process, not owners of all of the results.

First Day: Understanding

The objective on the first day is to build a common database where everyone has had the same sort of information and has had the chance to discuss and question this information with people from other stakeholder groups. As much as possible, data should focus on the future. Anticipated customer and labour market trends are likely to be more useful than analysis of historic trends within the organization. Information should also balance metrics and benchmarks with anecdotes and stories. These can be gathered from across the organization before the event, and may be presented as video diaries and in other emotionally rich forms. External speakers may also be used. Information should include strategies of the business and its competitors; existing people and organizational capability; the external customer, investor and talent marketplaces; and broader people issues including demographic trends and cultural changes.

Second day: Creating

The objective of the second day is to think creatively about future possibilities. It is useful to start with some creative thinking exercises. The main part of the day can consist of an Open-Space forum (Owen, 1997) in which people are able to suggest the areas they want to work on to meet the challenges discussed on the first day. The only constraint on these groups is that they have to help in imagining the capabilities the organization will need about five to ten years into the future. Groups can generate ideas and examples about their chosen future, and the barriers and enablers that may be encountered in the journey of getting there. Groups may wish to use some of the creativity techniques I have reviewed and facilitators, hats and so one should be available to support them.

At the end of the day, people come back together to share the ideas that have been generated. After small group discussions, people prioritize the ideas, using post-its to note down what they agree and disagree with, and what questions they still have. Senior managers take these notes away for some evening work and come back the next day ready to present their conclusions about the way they want to take the organization forward.

Third day: Programme Planning

At the start of the third day, managers present their conclusions, answer questions and respond to areas of disagreement. The final list of strategic themes/intangible capabilities/programmes is agreed and measures are identified for the outputs and impacts of these programmes.

People then get into groups to work on the areas they are most interested in. Each group is tasked with creating a multi-mind mind map in which the central theme focuses on the capability of the people and the organization. Some of the branches will relate to the impacts of these outputs, that is what the organization will be able to do differently as a result of these capabilities, and other branches will relate to the actions that the organization needs to execute to develop these capabilities. Measures for activities and inputs also need to be identified.

The final stage in the process is preparing each of the programmes for communication. Each mind map needs to be unpacked into an HCM value matrix (hopefully focusing on the creating value level) and visual and compelling communications prepared to cascade the strategy to the rest of the organization.

Summary

Reader: *'You mentioned that HR shouldn't take responsibility for the activities of the people strategy lab – why is this and what is HR's role in HCM strategy development?'*

Author: 'The HR function obviously does have a key role in strategy development and in the people strategy lab. I just think that the power of a large-scale facilitated event comes from harnessing the energy and contribution of all the people who are there. Very often, these people want to take forward ownership of programmes and activities after the event. HCM relies on responsibility for people management being distributed across the organization and HR needs to ensure that its natural desire to own people strategy doesn't interfere with this. So I just think the HR's more important role is acting as a facilitator of this process, not the owner of whatever comes out of it.

More broadly, HR needs to ensure people are thinking about people management strategy on an ongoing basis. And that they are continuing to think creatively too. Plus HR can use its skills as facilitators to help the business and other functions develop creating value strategies in their areas as well. More generally, HR plays a particularly important role in enabling creativity by providing resources and developing processes for creativity, by ensuring that ideas and suggestions are recognized and rewarded and by creating space for innovators and intrapreneurs.'

References

Buckingham, M. and Coffman, C. (2001). *First, Break all the Rules*. Simon & Schuster.

Bunker, B.B. and Alban, B.T. (1996). *Large Group Interventions: Engaging the Whole System for Rapid Change*. Jossey-Bass.

Buzan, T. (2002). *How to Mind Map*. HarperCollins.

Covey, R.S. (1999). *Seven Habits of Highly Effective People*. Simon & Schuster.

De Bono, E. (1999). *Six Thinking Hats*. Back Bay Books.

De Brabandere, L. (2005). *The Forgotten Half of Change – Achieving Greater Creativity through Changes in Perception*. Kaplan Business.

Finn, R. and Ingham, J. (2004). *Taking Measures: Harnessing People Measures to Drive Business Performance*. Penna Board Partnership.

Florida, R. and Goodnight, J. (2005). 'Managing for creativity', *Harvard Business Review*. July–August, 124–31.

Gratton, L., Hope Hailey, V.H., Stiles, P. and Truss, C. (1999). *Strategic Human Resource Management: Corporate Rhetoric and Human Reality*. Oxford University Press.

Hamel, G. and Prahalad, C.K. (1994). *Competing for the Future*. Harvard Business School Press.

Hayashi, A. M. (2001). 'When to trust your gut', *Harvard Business Review*. February, 5–11.

Huselid, M.A., Becker, B.E. and Beatty, R.W. (2005). *The Workforce Scorecard*. Harvard Business School Press.

Jacobs, R.W. (1997). *Real-Time Strategic Change*. Berrett-Koehler Publishers.

Kaplan, R.S. and Norton, D.P. (1996). *The Balanced Scorecard*. Harvard Business School Press.

Kent, S. (2003). 'Inside the best place to work in Britain', *Personnel Today*, 8 July, 18–20.

Mind Gym. (2005). *The Mind Gym: Wake Your Mind Up*. Time Warner Books.

Morgan, G. (1996). *Images of Organization*. Sage Publications.

Morgan, G. (1997). *Imaginization: New Mindsets for Seeing, Organizing and Managing*. Sage Publications.

Owen, H. (1997). *Open Space Technology: A User's Guide*. Berrett-Koehler Publishers.

Porter, M. (1996). 'What is strategy?', *Harvard Business Review*. November–December, 61–78.

Schlender, B. (2004). 'Ballmer unbound: How do you impose order on a giant, runaway Mensa meeting? Just watch Microsoft's CEO', *Fortune*, 26 January, 66–75.

Waters, R. (2003). 'Microsoft reaches middle age: can Steve Ballmer reinvent the company to guarantee its long-term dominance?', *Financial Times*, 28 July.

Weisbord, M.R. and Janoff, S. (2000). *Future Search*. Berrett-Koehler Publishers.

8

HCM Measurement

Introduction

Reader: *'I'm almost surprised that you've set aside a whole chapter for measurement given what you've said before.'*

Author: 'I certainly argue that creating value in HCM is more important than measuring the value that is created. However, this doesn't mean that measurement is unimportant. Measurement needs to be part of any effective approach to management. But, I propose an approach to measurement that's very different from most of what is written elsewhere. A lot of what I read seems to suggest that people and people management should be measured almost for the sake of measuring them.

For example, the CFO Research (2003) report that I referred to in Chapter 6 asks, 'what is your return on aggregate investments in human capital?' I hope I have already shown that this isn't a terribly sensible thing to expect people or organizations to know. I'm certainly not against a broad understanding of return, but I don't believe that distilling this down to a single metric helps. What does help is using an appropriate measurement framework that enables a conversation to be had about aggregate investments, the sorts of outputs that have been achieved, and the financial return that may possibly be linked to this.

Similarly, the CIPD comment that in a 2004 survey only 10 per cent of companies could put a financial cost on their level of labour turnover (Brown, 2005). So what? Knowing the financial cost of turnover may help some HR teams convince their Boards to invest in their people. But this is hardly the central issue in HCM.'

Reader: *'Just how different is the approach you describe from what most organizations do in HCM?'*

Author: 'That obviously depends on the organization, but for most, it's a lot different. This is the reason why I've already spent so much time describing the HR scorecard, talentship and so on and why I describe Kirkpatrick's model in this chapter too. I hope that comparing and contrasting these models will really drive home why the HCM value matrix is such a good tool to use. Very few organizations are using it or anything similar to it and I truly believe they would gain a lot of benefit if they did ...'

The Importance of Measurement

The importance of measurement is also supported by research. For example, surveys conducted by consultancy William Schiemann & Associates have shown that what they called 'measurement-managed' companies outperformed other organizations. In measurement-managed companies, senior managers use agreed criteria to measure how successfully their business strategies are being implemented. In addition, managers review performance data in at least three of six categories of measurement at least twice per year. Comparing measurement-managed companies to other businesses, Lingle and Schiemann (1996) found that:

- Seventy-four per cent of measurement-managed companies versus 44 per cent of the other companies had been identified as an industry leader over the previous three years.
- Eighty-three per cent of measurement-managed companies versus 52 per cent of the others had financial performance in the top third of their industry.

■ Ninety-seven per cent of measurement-managed companies versus 55 per cent of the others self-reported success at major cultural or operating change.

Schiemann also found that a focus on employee measurement was the single biggest single factor differentiating successful firms from less successful ones.

Sixty-seven per cent of the responding executives said that they valued employee performance data but only 16 per cent said they would bet their jobs on its quality. This might suggest that the value of employee measurement comes from its use in learning, where data acts as a guide, rather than in control, which requires data of a high quality.

This conclusion is also supported by another piece of research. In a study of 157 companies, Ittner and Larcker (2003) at Wharton found that only 23 per cent of firms had developed causal models linking non-financial drivers to financial performance. However, these companies had nearly a 3 per cent higher return on assets and more than a 5 per cent higher return on equity to companies that had not developed these models.

The researchers conclude that it is not just measuring which is important, but measuring the important factors in the value chain. They explain that more successful companies link measures to:

> Causal models, also called value driver maps, which lay out plausible cause-and-effect relationships that may exist between the chosen drivers of strategic success and outcomes.

A linked finding was that measuring intangibles helps improve a company's approach to measurement but only if the company has selected the right intangibles. The researchers found that many companies had adopted 'boilerplate versions' of scorecards without really trying to understand the intangible factors that influence their particular businesses.

As well as measuring intangibles that are causally linked to business performance, the researchers found it was important to validate these links. They gave an example of a company that set a target of 100 per cent satisfaction for each of its customers:

> However, the company never attempted to discover whether a correlation actually existed between a customer's level of satisfaction and the

revenues and profits that customer generated. We discovered, in fact, that the expected relationship did appear – but only up to a point. Customers who were 100% satisfied spent no more money than those who were only 80% satisfied. In short, getting to 100% required considerable investment, with little or no payback.

I also talked to Steve Langhorn, Change Director for Whitbread, about the need to identify and validate measures for a particular business. Talking about one of Gallup's Q12 questions which has been shown to correlate with high performance in most organizations, Langhorn commented:

> It's important that organizations understand and create evidence on this for themselves. For example, one of the questions is 'do you have a best friend at work?' In parts of our outlet workforce, which is often young, and transient, our findings suggest that too high a score on this question can have a negative impact on financial performance. This kind of statistical relationships are often difficult to explain, and are usually indicators of some other factors present in the business. In this case, for example, it could be a poor mix of age profile within the workforce, with a large group of young people, possibly all good mates together, but not necessarily the most productive team overall!

Another interesting finding is included in the CIPD's report on *Evaluating Human Capital*. Scarborough and Elias (2002) find that the activity of measuring is even more important than choosing the right measures if this results in enhanced understanding about the role of human capital. Kaplan and Norton (2004) also point out that:

> Even if the measures are imprecise, the simple act of attempting to gauge the capabilities of employees, information systems, and organizational capital communicates the importance of these drivers for value creation.

However, organizations should not get too carried away with measurement. I talked to Ben Bengougam, the new HR Director at DSG International, the specialist retailer of consumer electronics with brands including Currys and PC World, who explained that, even in a sector so focused on metrics as retail, measurement has very much a supporting role:

> In Retail we measure everything that helps describe performance, the culture is very focused on KPIs. So we measure and report on a lot of

HR activities and outputs: our spend on training, turnover, retention, absenteeism and so on. We try to improve on these metrics. In some areas we try to measure intangibles as well, so for example, the climate and engagement in the business. It's very high on the agenda for our leadership, from the Board to a local level. We look at correlations in engagement and customer satisfaction and can demonstrate that there is almost a 100 per cent correlation. It means we don't have to prove the need for HR, the business understands that effective management of people delivers results. But I think there can be an unhealthy, obsessive focus on measuring the value of HR – on navel gazing and introspection. In general, HR puts too much time and resource into measuring its value. It would be better to spend the same time and resource on doing HR and doing it well, not measuring it. Measurement is only worth doing if it results in action and in positive business results.

Measurement in the HCM Value Matrix

Just as Kaplan and Norton's strategy map developed from their balanced scorecard, so the HCM value matrix grew out of a framework initially designed for measurement. It was only when I started using the value matrix to help clients develop HCM measures that I realized most companies needed to structure their people strategies using the matrix before we focused on developing measures for their strategies. The result of this realization is the broader use of the value matrix that is the basis for Part 2 of this book.

However, this chapter will focus on the matrix's original use as a measurement tool and I first want to describe the way that I developed it, working with a group that included Richard Finn and Geoff Pye from Penna; David Weiss from consultancy Knightsbridge GSW in Canada; and Nick Starritt, formerly at BP. Our objective was to extend Penna's existing approach to HCM (Finn, 2002) to respond to the increasing interest in measurement generated by the Accounting for People report.

Looking for inspiration, we reviewed existing thinking and experience and focused on training and recruitment, as it tends to be easier to separate measures of these processes from all the other things going on in an organization. One of the approaches we reviewed was the evaluation model developed by Donald Kirkpatrick in 1958. Although the validity of this model has been criticized by some researchers, the technique's longevity indicates its face validity and robustness.

Kirkpatrick's Levels of Evaluation

Kirkpatrick identified four levels of evaluation, which are:

- *Level 1 – Reaction.* This type of evaluation measures how participants respond to a training programme in terms of their immediate reaction to the course itself, to materials and to any communications concerning the programme. The evaluation takes place immediately after the programme, usually by 'happy sheets'. Kirkpatrick (1998) explains that: 'Evaluating reaction is the same thing as measuring customer satisfaction. If training is going to be effective, it is important that students react favorably to it.'

- *Level 2 –Learning.* This level evaluates what participants know and remember as a result of a programme. It involves testing participants' knowledge and attitudes before and after the training. Where possible, a control group is used to provide additional data for comparison. Kirkpatrick explains the significance of this level: 'It is important to measure learning because no change in behavior can be expected, unless one of more of these learning objectives have been accomplished.'

- *Level 3 – Behaviour.* Level 3 measures whether participants are applying new skills and demonstrating new behaviours. It involves surveying or interviewing participants and others who have observed their behaviour. This type of evaluation needs to take place long enough after the training for changes to have taken place.

- *Level 4 – Results.* The results level reviews whether the programme has delivered the planned business impacts. It is measured at organizational level. Kirkpatrick thought that this was the most important but also the most difficult level of evaluation. In my view, the difficulty of level 4 evaluation depends on the way it is done. If an organization designs a course with no particular business need in mind then of course it will be difficult to identify the business impact. If the course has been identified through a process like the strategic HCM planning cycle, then the intended business consequences will be fairly clear and it should be a much easier job to evaluate whether they have been achieved.

- *ROI.* More recently, Jack Phillips (1997) has added a fifth level to Kirkpatrick's levels of evaluation. This extra level converts Kirkpatrick's level 4 business impact measures into monetary values enabling them to be compared against the cost of the programme leading to the calculation of a financial ROI.

Developing the HCM Value Chain

Kirkpatrick's model seemed a lot simpler than most approaches to HCM measurement (a good thing!) and could easily be extended from training to other areas of people management. Doing this, the Penna group developed the value chain that was described in Chapter 6:

- Input was added as an initial step in the value chain because we felt that it would be important to measure financial investment, time spent and HR function effectiveness (note also Lev's comments about the need to report on investments that were quoted in Chapter 6). The main units of measurement used in the input step are money, time and capability.
- Activity includes Kirkpatrick's reaction and learning levels, as these refer to the effect, rather than the output, of activities. The main units for activity are quantity, quality, time and user satisfaction.
- Output includes Kirkpatrick's behaviour level, which refers to changes in what people do and is an output of the activities. An output can be a tangible or intangible resource, or an intangible capability if it is something that investors would pay for. The main units are numbers of people or days, capability and engagement.
- Impact includes Kirkpatrick's results level because this refers to changes in the business that are caused by changes in people's performance. The main units are quantity, quality, customer satisfaction and money.

The two main differences between Kirkpatrick's model and the HCM value chain relate to the scope of the models and whether they are built up or down. Kirkpatrick focuses on a training and development event and looks further down the value chain for an impact on business result. The HCM value chain covers the full spectrum of HCM activity. It looks at human capital and the business impact of this capital, and then the activities which are needed further up the value chain. As Lauri Bassi at HCM firm, McBassi & Company explained to me, this provides a more strategic approach:

> Kirkpatrick's levels haven't gotten us what we need to know. Rather than asking: 'is this a good course', we need to operate at a different level, to use a different evaluation structure. We should be asking: 'how is our learning strategy supporting our business goals and how

might we demonstrate that?' We need to ask bigger questions that are more strategic.

Kirkpatrick notes that his higher levels of evaluation require extra data collection and significant investments of time and effort so should only be conducted for programmes that are strategic, expensive, long standing and involve a large number of people. These are all typical attributes for an HCM programme which suggests that, where there are appropriate measures for an HCM programme, it is worth conducting evaluation at each level in the HCM value chain.

ROI is slightly different however. Calculating ROI can cost as much as 10 per cent of a training project and up to 5 per cent of a total human resources budget. Given my concerns about ROI expressed in Chapter 6, I would suggest that in most cases ROI is simply not worth calculating. The case study of measuring an HCM (leadership development) programme at the BBC provides a good illustration of when calculating ROI may and may not be appropriate. Under Greg Dyke's leadership, ROI was not seen as relevant. With the BBC's renewed focus on accountability, it is now being seen as a much more pertinent approach. But I would still question whether, once the BBC has calculated their ROI, they will actually be able to do anything differently as a result.

However, where appropriate, ROI and other ratios (calculated by comparing two metrics, generally in different columns of the value chain, to each other) can be included in the column furthest down the value chain. So ROI, which is calculated as return (impact) minus investment divided by investment (input), can be included in the impact column of the value chain. As another example, cost of recruitment per new joiner, calculated as cost (input) divided by numbers of new joiners (output), can be included in the output column.

One reason why the HCM working group thought the value chain worked well was that we had wanted to simplify what seemed to be unnecessarily complicated and confused. For example, a 2002 survey by *Personnel Today* and Deloitte, which was repeated in 2004, identified five main 'methodologies' for measuring HCM (Berry, 2004):

- HR benchmarking and HR metrics was the most popular approach with 47% of organizations using it. These approaches are defined as looking at the substance of policies and practices together with indicators and measures which are compared across organizations.

- Balanced scorecard methodologies were used by 29% of organizations. These were defined as a suite of people-based key performance indicators that supports the organization in achieving its corporate objectives.
- HR practice effectiveness models involve the assessment of the contribution of the HR function and HR practices on business performance.
- Accountancy-based evaluation creates a numerical value for human capital using accountancy terms.
- Economic value-added approaches provide a process of measuring overall corporate performance based on the total cost of capital employed in the business (for example ROI methodologies).

Deloitte found that 27 per cent of organizations did not use any measurements of HCM and that, as a contributing factor to this, 32 per cent were not sure about what they should be measuring. However, Deloitte failed to provide the missing clarity by pointing out that their five approaches attempt to measure different things and meet slightly different needs. I realized that the HCM value chain provided one of Deloitte's methodologies (HR practice effectiveness) and could be used to link the other four 'methodologies' together too.

- The HR scorecard (balanced scorecard methodologies) forms part of the input step in the value chain.
- HR benchmarking and metrics fit within the activity step.
- Accountancy-based valuation forms one approach to measuring output (see Chapter 4).
- Economic value-added approaches are an example of measuring business impact.

Developing the HCM Value Triangle and the Value Matrix

As well as the value chain, the HCM working group identified three levels of measurement and evaluation, linked to the value triangle, that we called competitive differentiators, added value measures and efficiency metrics (Finn and Ingham, 2004):

Competitive Differentiators are measures of strategic programmes and initiatives which the organization believes will provide it with competitive advantage. These differentiators often focus on specific talent or leadership groups, or long-term cultural change, that define the future and would be hard to imitate by others.

241

> Added Value measures focus on HCM activities required to meet the objectives in the business plan. These are often key HR processes and outcomes related to people capability, motivation and engagement.
>
> Efficiency measures relate to those hygiene activities which need to be performed effectively and efficiently but which offer little competitive advantage.

These levels relate to the three levels of information identified in Chapter 1, but here they describe different types of information rather than different levels of understanding contained within the information. The relationships between the two types of levels mean that whereas efficiency metrics like headcount and absence should be measured and reported using quantitative data, strategic differentiators like leadership capability need discursive and meaningful reporting.

Combining the three levels of measurement and evaluation with the four steps in the value chain gave us a measurement-focused version of the HCM value matrix. We then proceeded to validate this model through a survey of 202 UK-based chief executives and HR directors and 44 Canada-based HR professionals (Weiss and Finn, 2005). We were pleased to find that 82 per cent of UK respondents agreed that HCM is critical to the fundamental success of a business. Reflecting the increasing focus on measurement, 80 per cent of respondents also agreed that measurement is key to the delivery of HCM. Suggesting two measurements for each box in the value matrix (Figure 7.1), we asked participants to indicate which of these 24 measurements they reported on in 2003 and which they wanted to report on in the future. We found that there was a strong desire to increase the amount of reporting and that the only boxes in which respondents expected to reduce reporting were efficiency – activity (box 2) and efficiency – output (box 3).

Reviewing the overall expected increases in reporting at each of the three levels of measurement and evaluation, we found that:

- Fifty-four per cent of the overall expected increases in measurement were for competitive differentiators;
- thirty-eight per cent of increases were for added value measures;
- only 8 per cent of increases were for efficiency measures.

Conducting the same analysis for the four steps in the value chain, we found:

- Twenty-three per cent of the overall expected increases were for input measures;
- only 4 per cent were for activity measures;
- thirty per cent were for output measures;
- forty-two per cent were for impact measures.

These findings implied that CEOs and HR directors knew that they would need to make a substantial shift from measuring activities to measuring impacts and higher value outputs. Our respondents also expected to increase their reporting on input step measurements, underlining the importance of measuring financial investments, management time and HR function effectiveness.

The survey also validated our belief that the HCM value matrix provides an intuitive and useful framework for measuring HCM; that it can help organizations clarify what they are measuring and why; and that it helps ensure organizations focus on high value, strategic differentiators; not the efficiency metrics that are normally the most easily available.

The matrix also shows that measurements need to use the units that are appropriate for the sort of things they are trying to measure. So people can be measured, but not usually in financial terms (there are some exceptions, for example absence costs). People management as an activity can also be measured, but generally in terms of quality, time and user satisfaction, not in monetary terms. It is the impact of people and people management that can be understood in financial terms.

Table 8.1 provides some example of measures within each box of the value matrix.

Developing Creative Leadership at the BBC

The BBC's 20 000 employees and 7500 contract and freelance staff produce TV, radio, web and other services that are used by around 90 per cent of the UK's population each week. These services cost £3.5 billion per year and are funded largely by the licence fee. The BBC's Director-General, Mark Thompson, is focused on increasing accountability and

Table 8.1: Examples of measures in the HCM value matrix

Box 9:	Box 10:	Box 11:	Box 12:
■ Mindsets of leadership team ■ Quality of decision-making ■ Effectiveness of strategic alliances	■ Senior level succession strategy ■ Clarity of organizational communication ■ Use of new people, technologies, e.g. Appreciative Inquiry, Neuro Linguistic Programming	■ Degree of organizational learning ■ Composition, background and diversity of the Board and executive team ■ Strength of leadership pipeline	■ Success in creating change ■ Innovation ■ Customer advocacy
Box 5:	**Box 6:**	**Box 7:**	**Box 8:**
■ Capabilities of HR business partners ■ Management and leadership development budget ■ Management time	■ Senior and line manager satisfaction with people management processes ■ Executive coaching ■ Use of variable pay at senior level	■ Employee diversity ■ Percentage of shares held by employees ■ Turnover in senior management levels	■ Success in managing change ■ Customer satisfaction ■ Economic value added
Box 1:	**Box 2 (e.g. for recruitment):**	**Box 3:**	**Box 4:**
■ HR costs/total costs ■ Degree of standardization in HR processes across the organization ■ Contact centre abandonment rates	■ Average number of vacancies ■ Ratio of direct to indirect recruitment ■ Performance of new hires versus targets	■ Involuntary termination rate ■ Lost time occurrences ■ Percentage of workforce in Union	■ Employee productivity ■ Market share ■ Profit per employee

responsiveness to licence-fee payers and the BBC's recent Charter Review has emphasized the importance of public value. Therefore, the BBC has a clear obligation to secure best value for money in all aspects of its day-to-day activities, including its investment in training and development.

I talked with Nigel Paine, Head of People Development, Ian Hayward, Head of Leadership Development and Josie Barton, Evaluation Consultant about the BBC's leadership development programme. Launched in September 2003, this programme would cost a total of £35 million over five years and would need to have a major impact on the BBC's culture and the quality of its productions.

The Business Imperative

In 2002, the BBC's former Director-General, Greg Dyke, launched 'Making It Happen', an initiative that supported his vision of 'One BBC', an organization that would be 'the most creative in the world'. The challenge was about getting the whole organization to be more innovative, audience-focused and comfortable with uncertainty. This meant creating an environment where power and knowledge were shared more equally, where people would not feel inhibited from being creative and in which ideas would be dealt with according to their merit rather than the seniority of the person proposing them.

Dyke felt that the BBC had become 'over-managed and under-led'. Hayward explained:

> Two things struck him – firstly that there was a huge amount of bureaucracy and secondly that there was a lack of managers who saw themselves as leaders. He wanted people to work collaboratively and was shocked at the amount of competition for air time and resources. He was very apolitical himself and was frustrated that people at a senior level acted in that way.

A survey showed that the Corporation's employees shared Dyke's perspective, feeling that there was too little collaboration and too much bureaucracy, silo thinking and internal competition. Only 28 per cent of employees believed the Corporation was exploiting their full potential and talented new recruits were frustrated with how long it could take to rise through the ranks. Hayward summarized this situation saying, 'Overall, the existing strategy seemed to be about recruiting people with a spark and then draining this creative energy out of them.'

As a result of these requirements, it was clear that the BBC would need to change more rapidly over the next few years than ever before. To help articulate and gain commitment to the change, the BBC ran a series of Appreciative Inquiry sessions named 'Just Imagine'. These sessions asked staff about what they had experienced at the BBC when it was at its best. The key themes from these experiences informed the leadership capabilities that would underpin the new leadership development programme.

Programme Outline

The programme is a compulsory requirement for 7000 BBC managers with more than three direct reports. Every month for a period of five years, 120 managers will begin the six-month, £5000-a-head programme. The BBC's executive committee has sponsored the creation and development of the programme and its delivery is led by a steering group of line managers and executives. Hayward believes that this group's work has been crucial in helping to achieve buy-in from the diverse parts of the organization and to avoid the programme being seen as an HR initiative. The programme has been supported by staff from Ashridge Business School but has been delivered mainly by in-house staff, including people seconded to the programme for six months to work as tutors.

The programme has been run during an interesting time in the BBC's history. Key events have included Lord Hutton's criticism of the BBC's news reporting process followed by the resignation of Dyke, who had been the programme's prime sponsor. More recently, the BBC have announced 4000 redundancies and outsourcing of some non-core services including certain activities within People Development. These events have clearly impacted on the leadership programme.

The programme was designed to support the broader transformation by changing managers' own behaviours, and through the management of their teams, the experience and behaviours of all the BBC's people. Hayward explained the programme's key role saying that, 'Greg wanted to unleash people's creativity. This was about creative leadership and leading creativity.'

Paine commented:

> We needed to create a sense of leadership that all managers needed to exhibit. Leadership was previously an alien concept apart from just one leader. We needed to raise the flag, to raise the profile of leadership.

Programme Design

The programme blends a rich mix of development opportunities and real-life assignments, responding to people's different learning styles. The philosophy of the programme is that people learn best when they are doing, reflecting on their experience, sharing with each other, and working with the everyday challenges they face, as opposed to sitting in a classroom being taught. First of all, participants complete a 360-degree appraisal and receive feedback from a professional psychologist. This feedback is then used to identify individual development needs that are subsequently addressed in a variety of ways during the programme.

All participants then attend a two-day large group session to learn about what it means to be a leader at the BBC. This workshop brings managers together from different parts and levels of the Corporation and participants are often unaware who are the most senior people in the group. Hayward explained that: 'Their name badges show their names and that's it – there are no job titles. In conversations during the two days, a sense of seniority will only slowly be revealed.'

Three weeks later, participants return for a shorter session providing a more in-depth review of their personal styles of leadership. This is followed by:

- a series of two- and three-day workshops including role-plays using actors to explain how to handle difficult situations;
- a divisional day where managers can assess what they are learning in the context of the area they are working in;
- individual face-to-face coaching sessions looking at various elements of the managers' jobs;
- action learning, in which participants meet to share and solve the day-to-day problems they face as leaders;
- e-learning using Ashridge's virtual learning resource centre and an online leadership 'wiki', set up by the BBC and to which over 6000 people have contributed stories and articles.

The programme concludes with a final two-day group event where managers assess what they have learnt and how they are going to implement this.

Individual Measurement and Evaluation

The programme focuses on helping individuals to change their own behaviour so the BBC has tried to stimulate managers to evaluate their own experience on the programme. Feedback from participants includes the following comments about individual performance improvements:

- 'Sickness levels have decreased as I am now more assertive in addressing this issue. The department is performing well due to staff morale being high.'
- 'I am able to get more out of the team by way of performance in dealing with them in different ways. This is to the benefit of all parties.'
- 'Direct feedback to presentation team has made a marked improvement on the show I am responsible for.'

Hayward explained the process and rationale for collecting this information:

> We encourage managers to focus on a personal challenge, particularly on the back of the 360-degree feedback. We get them to ask themselves: "What are the priorities I should be addressing as I progress through the programme?" We suggest that they track their own learning, recording improvements in their knowledge and self-awareness, changes to their behaviour and the resulting influence this has on their performance. Across the organization, we try to track some of this qualitatively, through stories. In the final, large group event we ask managers to discuss with their colleagues two or three stories representing a success, a brave attempt or a failure to address their leadership challenge. We've struggled with this so far but we're trying again as the organization has changed. It was rather counter-cultural but now there's more focus on accountability and value so managers understand what we're trying to do.

Organizational Measurement and Evaluation
Approach to Organizational Evaluation

In tandem with the programme, the BBC developed a comprehensive evaluation framework for all formal development activities. The framework is based on three of Kirkpatrick's four levels to provide the trunk of an evaluation hierarchy. The BBC decided not use Kirkpatrick's

'Learning' level as they wanted to focus on behaviours and performance. However, they did add two other levels: a pre-evaluation level
called 'Inputs' and, at the top of the tree, 'Return on Investment'. A level
called 'Process' (measures like actuals against forecast, financial
performance, utilization rates and cancellation rates) was also added as
a means of measuring how the BBC's Training and Development
department was performing as a function and to inform future planning
decisions.

In summary, the BBC's framework consisted of the six levels shown
in Table 8.2 that can be seen to have a direct relationship to the HCM
value chain:

Only 'strategic' development activities with the greatest potential
impact on the organization's performance will be evaluated at all levels.
The BBC training evaluation policy explains how they distinguish
between 'strategic' and 'maintenance' activity:

> Strategic development is activity aimed at building key corporate
> capability. This includes activities that would impact the way the
> organization works, either through altering the behaviour of a large group
> of people in a way that fundamentally affected the culture or through
> changing the way the organization used technology/processes in a way
> that affected their core product: making TV and radio programmes.
>
> Maintenance: these were defined as activities aimed at maintaining
> current performance. They included compliance activities such as health
> and safety and legal training as well as core skills such as the use of
> existing editing and craft equipment.

There is a direct read across from these levels to creating/adding
value and value for money in the HCM value triangle.

The BBC has planned to track a range of KPIs to support the evaluation framework. At process level these would include measures like
appraisal penetration, personal development planning and instances of
the capability procedure and at output level things like hire failure rate,
loss of key talent and level of intermittent absence. Unfortunately,
measurement systems for most of these indicators have not yet been set
up. Barton explained:

> The evaluation framework is deliberately aspirational – it needs systems
> and processes to be set up in the business that don't necessarily exist as
> yet. This is partly about assembling pressure on the business. We would
> evaluate even more robustly if we had the data.

Table 8.2: BBC evaluation framework

BBC evaluation framework level	Description	Equivalent level in Kirkpatrick model	Equivalent step in HCM value chain
Inputs	What are we delivering? When are we delivering it? Who are we delivering it to? How much is it costing?		Input
Process	What is progress against forecast? Key performance indicators		Process
Reaction	What is the reaction to what we are doing? Is it relevant to people's roles? Can they use it in their jobs?	Reaction	
		Learning	
Transfer	Have skills and knowledge improved? Has there been observable behaviour change/ performance improvement? What is the business climate for supporting transfer?	Behaviour	Output
Business impact	What is the change to business performance? What is the change to organization culture?	Results	Impact
ROI	What is the quantifiable return on the investment? What is the benefit to cost ratio?		

Measurement systems for KPIs that have been set up, like retention, have been heavily influenced by changes in the organization and the BBC has not been able to draw any conclusions from this data.

Results of Organizational Evaluation

Input. Inputs to the programme have been monitored and reported in monthly briefings to the programme's steering group, the BBC's Leadership Board. Hayward explained:

> The Leadership Board is populated by senior executives from different areas of the business. They hold us to account and ensure that what we do aligns with other areas of the BBC's leadership strategy. They champion and argue the case for the programme, in their divisions and elsewhere. They hear very quickly if one programme doesn't go well and will tell me about it.

However, this degree of governance has presented challenges:

> It forces you to be more reactive than you might want to be. They'll ask what are you doing about it when there might not be a real problem at all. There might just be one isolated, although influential, voice. We could have been more sanguine about some things raised at this level – the programme has developed people's self-awareness and sometimes this puts them in an uncomfortable position. Some of the issues that have been raised have simply related to the discomfort some people need to go though during the programme.'

Process. Reaction data was obtained for each of the main development events. This feedback has generally been very positive, although some employees have been sceptical about the benefits, which is understandable given the compulsory and far-reaching nature of the programme. However, the BBC has struggled to make reaction data meaningful as feedback tends to follow the mood in the organization at least as much as it does the absolute quality of the programme. Hayward explained:

> The overall reaction score was very high during the conflict over Hutton – staff were just very happy to have the opportunity to be together to discuss it. It was much lower when Greg left and continued low in the interregnum between director-generals. It got higher when Mark was appointed, higher again upon his arrival and then sank again when people realized how much things would have to change. The data's useful, but it does need to be interpreted.'

Of more use has been tracking engagement in the programme and this has remained consistently high. Of the optional components of the programme offered to delegates:

- Seventy per cent of eligible delegates have taken up coaching;
- ninety per cent have taken up action learning;
- twenty-two per cent have taken up mentoring.

Output. Output measures monitor progress in developing creative and collaborative leadership and an inclusive, unbureaucratic culture:

360 Data on Behavioural Change. The BBC has data on 360-degree feedback taken before and after the programme. The data is broadly indicative of changes in the performance of managers as a result of the programme. Across the leadership competencies, between 74 and 86 per cent of staff considered that their manager had improved by at least some extent.

However, the Corporation is aware that these results need to be reviewed with care. The initial 360 was ipsative, focusing on the individual's three priority development areas to inform the rest of the leadership programme and beyond. The latter data was obtained, three months after the end of the programme through an optional online process in which respondents were chosen by their managers. This process used normative scoring of behavioural statements that related to the leadership competencies but cannot be matched directly to the earlier ipsative 360 data.

The BBC's management and the Training and Development team had felt there were strong cultural reasons for not using the same 360 system pre and post the programme even though they had understood that not doing this would limit the opportunity for evaluation. The Corporation did not want their desire for evaluation to interfere with the developmental objective of the programme. People were quite nervous of assessment and the ipsative review was seen as a more appropriate way to start it off.

This is a common issue experienced by organizations in their evaluation of people management and development activities. The evaluation of results is always a secondary concern to the achievement of the results, which often limits the ability to evaluate in a way organizations would do in an ideal world.

Controlled Evaluation Study. The BBC also tried to evaluate the programme more formally. To isolate the impact of the development, distinguishing between the benefits gained on the programme and from elsewhere, including the leadership experience itself, the BBC ran a controlled study using a more formal evaluation procedure comparing the leadership skills of a hundred participants on the programme to a control group of another hundred managers not on the course.

Self-perceptions of managers and feedback from a total of 600 direct reports were collected before and after the programme to investigate whether individual managers' leadership competencies and behaviours had improved as a result of the programme. The BBC used SSPS analysis software to review the data but the results were unfortunately inconclusive. Barton explained that:

> The principles were sound but between the two rounds of feedback we announced there would be 4000 redundancies. This was bound to have an impact, for example people were obviously nervous when they were asked to assess their managers. We think it resulted in a self-selecting and untypical set of managers who were confident enough to participate.

Again, the BBC's experience is not unusual. Formal evaluation is often impractical given the frequency and scale of change in organizations. Other changes impact on individual HCM programmes and the objectives of programmes often change significantly well before the target date on which the objectives were planned to be achieved.

Transfer of Learning Survey. The BBC wanted to understand how the organization was using and supporting learning during the development processes. Using a set of qualitative data collected from focus groups with development programme delegates, the BBC developed a set of 60 survey questions centred on the key influences on transfer of learning in the business. The survey was sent to the first 650 people who had completed the programme of which 250 were received back giving 95 per cent confidence that this was sufficiently representative. The results showed that, for example:

- Eighty per cent of managers considered that the programme had raised their awareness of their leadership style;
- sixty-one per cent considered that their performance as a leader had improved;
- seventy-three per cent had implemented changes in the workplace that led to improvements in their or their team's performance.

Barton commented:

> It's self-completed but it tells a good story. In several competency areas people say they have changed their behaviour and improved their performance. We have tracked the areas where there has been least change and fed those back into the programme design.

In terms of how the organizational climate and other barriers in the business have hindered the transfer of learning to enable changes in performance, the survey demonstrated that feedback from a participant's managers as they return from the events is the most important factor. However, the survey showed that this happens in only 50 per cent of cases. Barton explained:

> It's not enough for the programme to deliver change – there needs to be fundamental change within the business as well. People say that they come off the programme and think they can do anything. But it's not going to happen if they have a conversation with their boss about how they can change things and their boss doesn't understand what they've just been through. We tried to deal with this by skewing early attendance on the programme towards more senior managers and, in fact, nearly all senior managers have attended in the first two years. It was the best we could do – we couldn't have used a cascade process as the mix of levels was a critical part of the notion of shared experience and people attending the programme definitely approved of this.

Staff Surveys. In addition, as the focus of the programme is to deliver a step change in the BBC culture and leader effectiveness, perceptions about specific organizational capabilities such as communication, creativity and leadership are tracked in monthly climate surveys and through 24 questions relating to leadership or management in the annual staff survey. The results of the first annual survey run in January 2004 indicated that manager behaviours (for example, providing feedback, creating an environment in which staff can be creative, etc.) and the outputs of good management (for example, whether staff feel positive about their job) had improved. Forty-two per cent of staff responded to the survey, which Barton explained is much lower than the BBC would like but quite positive given the difficult period they were going through at the time.

Hayward commented on the survey results:

'We have to use the data quite conservatively, but it certainly gives a sense of whether people as a group think their management are improving. We can see they think we are OK at creativity and developing people but rubbish at performance management. And there has been improvement – 75 per cent of people say there has been at least some improvement in the Managing People Performance competency. The results have been fed back into the programme. The survey showed we are not using external thinking, there are not many people forging into external organizations. So we've introduced examples of people contacting other organizations into the programme and this has created more interest in creating joint alliances. Proving a direct causal link would be impossible but there has definitely been some improvement.'

Summary of Evaluations on Programme Outputs. Hayward explained how the different evaluation activities have given the BBC confidence that the programme is meeting their needs:

We look at how we have met our business challenges – mostly in a narrative and qualitative sense. This fits the BBC's culture. We are programme makers and storytellers – this is our core business. Whether it's news stories, drama, whatever, the business responds well to stories and not that well to figures. But we also look at where we can measure changes in leadership behaviour and its impact in a quantitative sense, for example, through the staff survey, the proportion of people who agree that their manager cares about their development.

Further benefits that were not linked to the programme's original objectives have also been identified. Hayward lists these as:

A vastly improved coaching capability, the ability of action learning facilitators to support teams in problem-solving and networking. We've also developed a very powerful sense of a community of leaders. It came out again and again – it's not 'them and us' – it's 'we', and I'm not alone.

Paine supported this perspective:

Leadership is part of the ether now – we breathe it. People talk about it, they ask each other, is this your profile? Previously, getting them to think about leadership was mostly like pulling teeth.

Business Impact. The final impact of the programme will be to improve TV/radio programme quality and audience satisfaction. The BBC has identified a small number of business indicators that should be most clearly impacted by the leadership programme, for example, the amount of TV/radio programme output that is generated from collaborations and partnerships. However, the BBC understands that many other factors are involved in arriving at these impacts and in any case the development programme was not intended to deliver overnight results and will require time to bed in for change to take effect. Paine noted:

The evaluation has given us an appreciation of the impact but it would be disingenuous to try and make a direct causal link between the culture change programme and any particular business indicators. Evaluation is such an impure science. The BBC is an open system so variables cannot be controlled in the way we would have liked.

Despite these problems, the BBC's evaluation has enabled the Training and Development team to update the programme, keeping it aligned with changing needs. Paine explained:

'It is formative, and significant modifications to the programme have occurred as a direct result of the evaluation data that have been generated. The programme has moulded and changed over the last seven or eight months in response to evaluation and the need to flex in content as the BBC itself continues to change. It's a very different programme now.

Key changes to the structure of the programme have included:

- a change in the balance between large group events and smaller group workshops;
- increased coaching and facilitated action learning;
- alumni events have been introduced for past participants, including master classes and networking opportunities with other organizations.

Changing Requirements and the New Focus on ROI

The BBC's experience also demonstrates the need to measure and report in a way that fits the business. Hayward described how the company's focus has changed since Dyke's resignation:

> Greg had almost blind faith in the programme. It was almost build it and they will come. Evaluation was still important and ROI would have been interesting but Greg wasn't that sort of a person. It wasn't that he wasn't interested. He was very interested in how much it was costing us. But he just knew that this had to be the thing to do. He would ask, 'Can anybody think of a good reason why not to do it?' He would say he could walk round the BBC and talk to a few people and that would tell him better than any evaluation whether the programme was working or not.

However, Hayward explained that the BBC's perspective on ROI has changed since Dyke's resignation:

> Since Mark Thomson has been here the business environment has changed. We're much more aware of our public focus and need for transparency. It's not the same environment that existed two years ago.

Given this new focus, the BBC has renewed efforts to calculate a return on investment for the programme. They have asked Jack Phillips's ROI Institute to work with them and believe Phillips's robust methodology will help them evaluate further cultural change. Hayward commented:

> They have a very clinical and conservative approach that will be hugely constructive for us. Our evaluation strategy really came after the start of the programme and ROI Institute's methodology says that if those indicators were not in place then they can't evaluate it, they can't tell you whether there has been an ROI or a business impact. The idea is that we'll track at least one business area and get the participants from that area to estimate the business value of them applying their learning – whether this is reduced operating cost or increased audiences etc. We'll ask each individual to look at the chain of impact and say as a result of the programme: 'I did this which resulted in this impact and this is the pound figure I put on it'. Some things should be fairly easy and others not – a lot of what we do is so intangible. And it's going to be a big leap culturally – the capability and willingness of the managers to spend time on it will be the biggest hurdle.

Why is the BBC's Experience an Example of HCM?

The BBC's programme displays many of the elements that appear to be common in HCM programmes:

- Being triggered by a business imperative to change the culture.
- Being visibly sponsored from the top with extensive involvement from the business through the Leadership Board and seconded staff.
- Requiring a significant investment in time, resources and money.
- Involving a combination of development interventions.
- Being executed well and evaluated appropriately.
- Producing 'creative leadership' as an intangible capability.
- Resulting in significant shifts in behaviour and performance at organizational, team and individual levels.
- Resulting in further learning and improvements in the organization's approaches to leadership development and to measurement and evaluation.

The BBC's attempts at evaluation have demonstrated a lot of the common issues that surround this field. In many ways, the evaluation does look quite amateurish compared to the sophistication of measurement at RBS and elsewhere. However, I think this is more about the extent of change the organization has had to contend with than anything else. Most importantly, the BBC's evaluation has succeeded in maintaining business sponsorship during a very testing time and changes in business sponsor. It has also enabled them to fine-tune the programme to keep aligned with changing business needs.

Would better evaluation actually have enabled the BBC to do anything differently? Given the BBC's renewed focus on public value, it is understandable that they want to demonstrate a positive ROI. But again, once they have this number, what will it change? Can ROI really be any more powerful than comments like this?

> In the six months since I have done this programme I have involved my team more, we have been more creative, and all their ideas have really started to play into the programmes we make. I don't think it is a coincidence that my viewing figures have increased dramatically during this time. It isn't magic – it is that we are making better TV programmes as a result of working differently. That is what this is all about.'

However, the leadership programme has also been robustly criticized by Paul Kearns, whose focus on putting a financial value on intangibles and investing purely on the basis of ROI has been referred to earlier on. Kearns has accused the BBC's leadership programme of being a 'fiasco', 'cobbled together', a 'misuse of the licence fee', 'badly designed' and has also recommended rather publicly that it should be scrapped. His main issue with the programme appears to be that it had no link to any clear performance objectives:

'In terms of whether they were going to be more creative, more efficient or make better programmes, it was all very vague. Nobody had pinned it down. It was just this woolly thinking about "shifting the culture" at the BBC, he said adding that "the programme was based too much on the views of junior staff as to how their bosses should behave'. (Leonard, 2004).

To me, this inclusive approach played a large part in making the programme a success. Hayward also commented:

The principle behind the programme was about developing distributed leadership as opposed to the previous over-control. Greg wanted everybody and anybody to see themselves as a leader, to see themselves as part of a community. The Just Imagine process was central to giving all BBC managers and staff a voice in this.

How can two HCM consultants judge the effectiveness of the same programme so differently? Kearns clearly has a very different perspective on HCM to me:

'Although this course is about values, creativity and innovation – considered intangibles – at the end of the day, the BBC's bottom line is about viewing figures, and I don't see how these are linked,' said Kearns. (*People Management*, 14 October 2004)

I take a diametrically opposed view to the importance of intangibles. To me, HCM is largely about the development of these very things. It is this intangible value – in this case, creative leadership – that will enable an organization to succeed. It has clearly been a key enabler to success at the BBC.

Ashridge Research on ROI

As well as supporting the BBC's leadership programme, Ashridge Business School has conducted interesting research into evaluation of executive education (Charlton, 2005). This research found that, nearly

50 years after Kirkpatrick published his model of evaluation, only a small minority of organizations regularly evaluate anything other than at the level of individual participant reaction. Only 11 per cent of Ashridge's 270 respondents evaluate the impact at the organizational level and only 3 per cent regularly assess the financial ROI of their programmes. Despite these findings, over half of Ashridge's respondents stated that they were happy with their current approach to evaluation.

Reflecting the increasing interest in HCM measurement, Ashridge found a growing expectation that the value of development activities needs to be demonstrated. Eighty-five per cent of HR respondents agreed with the statement that 'HR professionals will have to get better at proving the worth of executive education in the future'. But given the low proportion of organizations conducting higher-level evaluation and respondents' satisfaction with their current, lower-level approaches, is there a real need to prove the value of development activities? Or is this just a reflection of a mindset that has been developing in the HR community that is out of alignment with actual business needs?

Ashridge's view (in Charlton, 2005) is that it is almost impossible to quantify ROI around management development as there are so many variables involved. Their research found that more sponsors of executive education (44 per cent) than HR professionals (32 per cent) agreed with the statement that 'If there is clear evidence that individuals have benefited from a programme, that is enough to prove a positive return on investment'. These sponsors seemed much more interested in what they should be doing to help people apply their learning than evaluating it. Ashridge's report summarizes this debate stating:

> There would appear to be a 'ROI hard core' who see the pursuit of what has been described as 'the Holy Grail' as worthwhile and necessary, and who in some cases are putting in effort to try and achieve their goal. However, there is also a significant section of organizations where there is a rather pragmatic approach and a more rounded view of what outcomes are needed from evaluation. For this group, 'pure' ROI is less interesting than developing a better understanding of how individuals have benefited from a programme and how they have been able or unable to apply learning at work.

Ashridge's conclusions from the research are that trainers need to be less 'hung up' about ROI and to focus on whether people are taking their learning back into the workplace and applying it properly.

This emphasizes the need to review the 'learning transfer climate' within the organization to understand why some people are putting training into practice better than others. Over 90 per cent of survey respondents agreed that 'Evaluation needs to look at the organization's climate for learning transfer, as well as the programme itself.

The research implies a move from measuring the return on investment to maximizing that return.

Adding Measures to the HCM Value Matrix

As part of the strategic HCM planning cycle, the value matrix should be used to examine whether a small number of measures can be identified for each of the HCM objectives (developed in the HCM strategy development process described in Chapter 7) and these measures included in the matrix. It is important to keep the number of measures down as low as possible as too many measures create noise in the system and can make it difficult to see real performance issues. So sometimes this may mean that it is not appropriate to identify any measures for an objective. Most often it will mean identifying just one measure per objective. However, it may also sometimes be useful to identify a number of measures, using different methods and data sources, to support an objective. Just as we use a variety of assessment approaches in an assessment centre, doing this will increase the overall reliability and validity of the results. This is in direct contrast to some advice that measurement systems should only use measures that are exclusive, 'eliminating redundant measures from the list' (Coffey, 2005a).

Peter Howes, Chairman of benchmarking consultancy InfoHRM (see Chapter 12), supports the need for this sort of triangulation, explaining to me that:

> You shouldn't design interventions just around the quantitative data. It provides the first broad test but then you want to look for qualitative confirmation – from interviews, focus groups, employee opinion surveys and so on as well. For example, you might look at labour turnover, see that you've got a problem at around three to five years tenure, and draw a hypothesis about lack of career opportunities. You would need to look at post-exit surveys to find out why people had left – did they leave because of career opportunities? You might run some focus groups to

find out what people think about the company. This would validate whether you have planned the right intervention or not.

I also advise against the use of indexes combining measures to reduce the total number of metrics that need to be managed (Coffey, 2005b). This advice also applies to the use of ratings like the VB-HR rating, developed by Nicholas Higgins at Valuentis, and the Newbury Index Rating (NIR), developed by Paul Kearns. These ratings attempt to apply the methods used by credit-rating firms like Standard & Poor's to HCM. This might possibly be useful for external reporting if confidentiality is an issue because meaning is hidden deep within the metric. But disguising this information also means that these indexes and ratings are not suitable for internal reporting purposes.

Once the measures have been defined, the next step is to make sure that they can actually be measured. There is nothing worse than planning to measure something and finding out at the end of the year that the measurement system does not provide the information in the way that it is needed. This still happens a lot more often than we would want. The measurement system may also enable benchmarking and this is dealt with in Chapter 9.

Once this measurement system has been set up, measures can be measured and used to monitor progress against the measures and objectives in the value matrix. Correlations between measurements can be used to link measures together in a dynamic simulation of HCM and business performance. The measurements can also be used to validate the expected correlations between measures at each step in the value chain.

Summary

Reader: 'I was expecting you to provide a bit more about the statistical analysis that can be used to validate correlations between measures.'

Author: 'Sorry, that's not really my thing. In any case, I think anything on this would drop down into adding value very quickly. To me, validating correlations is part of a measurement approach to HRM, it's not part of creating value HCM. And to tell you the truth, another reason for not including more on this is that I'm not terribly sure I believe that strongly in the benefit of doing it.

Do you remember that in Chapter 4, I mentioned that Sears had replaced its measures of personal growth and development and empowered teams by responses to its employee attitude survey. Well, if you also remember Charles Handy's McNamara Fallacy that was discussed in Chapter 1, this was a potentially dangerous action for Sears to have taken. Measuring attitudes was likely to mean that Sears would start managing attitudes rather than the personal growth and empowered teams they had envisaged were important. As Rucci states (Rucci *et al.*, 1998), Sears still believes that personal growth and empowered teams are important, so why not measure them? Just because Sears's 'statisticians could find no direct causal pathway' to their two original measures doesn't mean that these measures aren't important. In a complex environment, just because measures don't result in visible correlations it doesn't mean that, acting indirectly, they're not driving performance.

More importantly, whatever statistical analysis you do, this mustn't be allowed to detract from the quality of dialogue and conversation using the value matrix; from your judgement about the way people are driving performance in your organization.'

References

Berry, M. (2004). 'Business must use delay to make sure people count', *Personnel Today*, 2 November, 8.

Brown, D. (2005). 'Get in position to bring accountants to account', *Personnel Today*, 22 February, 17.

Charlton, K. (2005). *Executive Education: Evaluating the Return on Investment – Bringing the Client Voice into the Debate*. Ashridge Business School.

CFO Research (2003). *Human Capital Management – The CFO's Perspective*. CFO Research.

Coffey, J. (2005a). 'Three steps to successful measures', *Balanced Scorecard Report*, May–June.

Coffey, J. (2005b). 'Using indexes as measures', *Balanced Scorecard Report*. July–August.

Finn, R. (2002). *Unleashing the Chain Reaction: Using Human Capital Management to Tap the Power in Your People*. Penna Consulting.

Finn, R. and Ingham, J. (2004). *Taking Measures: Harnessing People Measures to Drive Business Performance*. Penna Board Partnership.

Ittner, C.D. and Larcker, D.F. (2003). 'Coming up short on nonfinancial performance measurement', *Harvard Business Review*, November, 88–95.

Kaplan, R.S. and Norton, D.P. (2004). 'Measuring the strategic readiness of intangible assets', *Harvard Business Review*, February, 52–63.

Kirkpatrick, D.L. (1998). *Evaluating Training Programmes: The Four Levels*. Berrett-Kohler Publishers.

Leonard, T. (2004). BBC's 35m training course is a fiasco, says expert. *The Daily Telegraph*, 2 October.

Lingle, J.H. and Schiemann, W. (1996). 'From balanced scorecard to strategic gauges: Is measurement worth It?', *Management Review*. **85**(3), 56–610.

Phillips, J. (1997). *Return on Investment in Training and Performance Improvement Programmes*. Butterworth-Heinemann.

Rucci, A.J., Kirn, S.P. and Quinn, R.T. (1998). The Employee-Customer-Profit chain at Sears. *Harvard Business Review*, January–February, 83–97.

Scarborough, H. and Elias, J. (2002). *Evaluating Human Capital*. Chartered Institute of Personnel and Development.

Weiss, D.S. and Finn, R. (2005). 'HR metrics that count: aligning human capital management to business results', *Human Resource Planning*, April, 33–8.

9

HCM Benchmarking

Introduction

Reader: *'Can benchmarking really be used as part of a strategic approach to HCM? I've always thought that benchmarking is about weaker companies understanding and catching up with their stronger competitors. It's difficult to see how benchmarking would provide a company with competitive advantage as by the time the company has adapted and applied its learning, its competitors will have already moved on to something else.'*

Author: 'Doing this might not provide competitive advantage but it can still be an appropriate strategy for these weaker competitors. The problem comes when this slightly haphazard approach to benchmarking is used by the stronger competitors as well. Gary Hamel (2000) did an interesting study on this. He asked 500 CEOs whether they believed the strategies of their major competitors had been getting more alike or more dissimilar. Most responded that strategies within their sector were converging. Excessive benchmarking is an obvious reason for this. This isn't good news because it cuts down on choice and results in lower margins across the board.

But no organization can possibly lead innovation in all areas of business, or even all areas of HCM, so benchmarking can also be a useful activity for stronger players as well.

The difference is that a higher performing organization needs to be smarter in its use of benchmarking. It needs to be clear about what it would like to obtain from a benchmarking study and how this information will support decision-making. And its aim should not be simply to copy best practice, but to stimulate thinking about new possibilities that fit its own particular requirements. This means that benchmarking needs to be part of a strategic measurement process like the one I've been describing in the last two chapters.'

Reader: '*How do you see benchmarking being used within this strategic process?'*

Author: 'An organization's HCM strategy should be based upon its long-term business strategy, the potential capability of its people and the requirements of the external customer, investor and talent marketplaces. However, comparing the organization's HCM measures against benchmarks provides a further source of potential insight. It helps understand how good an organization's performance measurements really are in comparison to other organizations.

But benchmarking doesn't have to be about comparing one organization with another. It can just mean internal benchmarking which involves comparing different parts of an organization with each other. And it can also mean longitudinal benchmarking, which is about comparing the same part of the organization at different points in time. So measurements can be taken at the same time every year, or before and after a change, or on an ongoing basis through some form of pulse survey.

So just about every measure can be a benchmark, and benchmarking as it's addressed in this chapter is really about taking the measurements of the measures that have been identified in the HCM value matrix. Some of these measures might be able to be compared externally, some just internally and others just longitudinally. Others might be capable of being measured only once, for example where a 'yes, it's happened or no it hasn't' type of measurement is required ...'

Three Levels of Benchmarking

From this point on, I will refer to the organization wanting to benchmark its own measures as the 'benchmarker'. The measures it wants to compare are the 'benchmarks'. These can be benchmarked against one or more organizations that I will call the 'benchmark organization(s)'. Benchmarks can also be contained in a benchmark database, using data that has been obtained previously from a number of organizations. Additionally, benchmarks can refer to information obtained from other sources. For example, the benchmarker might want to compare its employee profile against local labour statistics.

The benchmarking literature refers to two approaches to benchmarking which focus on 'what' other companies have achieved, and 'how' they have achieved this. Focusing on the 'what' can help raise aspirations about what might be possible and provides objective data that can be useful in convincing sceptics of the need to change. A good example is provided by Michael Hammer (1990) who discusses Ford's accounts payable department. This group of over 500 people had planned to reduce headcount by 20 per cent until they looked at Mazda's department of just five people.

Learning about 'how' leading organizations achieved what they have provides more qualitative information that may be more helpful for action planning. At its most practical, the approach can involve benchmarking a process with the same process, and in benchmark organizations within the same sector. More risk but potentially greater benefits are involved in benchmarking against the same process in a different sector, or against a different process. For example, Toyota's learning about the ability of US supermarkets to replace stock quickly provided the inspiration for its *kanban* or just-in-time manufacturing system. Examples within people management include the application of techniques from supply chain management to resourcing, and external customer services to HR administration processes.

Becker *et al.* (2001) express their preference for benchmarking processes and practices (how) rather than levels and metrics (what):

> Benchmarking studies can be grouped into those that focus on specific
> *levels* of a particular variable or attribute (e.g., What is our cost per hire

relative to other firms in our industry?) and those that focus on specific *processes* … Our experience has been that studies that benchmark *processes* can provide a rich source of information, understanding, and often inspiration. While some have ridiculed such studies as 'industrial tourism,' we believe that observing exemplary processes *in situ* can be a very important learning experience for teams that have the responsibility for designing and implementing new processes within their organizations. In contrast, we are less enthusiastic about studies that benchmark *levels* of a particular variable.

The Confederation of British Industry (CBI) extends this analysis from 'what' and 'how' by identifying three broad levels of benchmarking which depend upon the size of the benchmark sample and the amount of process detail included within the benchmark, as shown in Figure 9.1:

- The bottom level is based on surveys and comparisons against key performance indicators (KPIs). This level of benchmarking enables benchmarkers to compare themselves to objective and quantifiable benchmarks based upon large data samples but which often include quite low levels of meaning and value.
- The next level is best practice benchmarking. Compared to a survey, this form of benchmarking adds value by working at a deeper level of process detail and narrative description. However, doing this generally reduces the number of organizations that can be included in the benchmark sample.

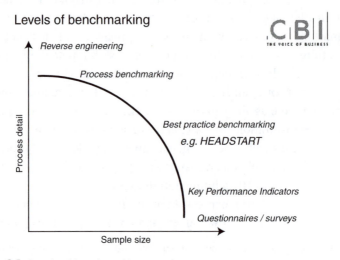

Figure 9.1 Levels of benchmarking

■ The CBI's highest level consists of process benchmarking and reverse engineering. These approaches focus on studying particular aspects of a small number of other organizations. Doing this helps a benchmarker really understand how the benchmark organizations gain the benefits they do and gives the benchmarker the knowledge they need to gain the same level of benefits themselves.

Types of Benchmarking

The three different levels of benchmarking relate closely to the HCM value triangle. Figure 9.2 shows how different types of benchmarking may be relevant to different levels of value/benchmarking, and also to different steps in the HCM value chain. This suggests that no form of benchmarking is better than another but will have more or less relevance depending on the 'box' in the value matrix that is being considered.

Because HCM benchmarking spans inputs and outputs as well as process/activities, I have also updated the names given to the levels by the CBI to survey benchmarking (value for money), diagnostic benchmarking (adding value) and strategic benchmarking (creating value).

This chapter will review each of the different types of benchmarking shown in Figure 9.2.

HCM benchmarking

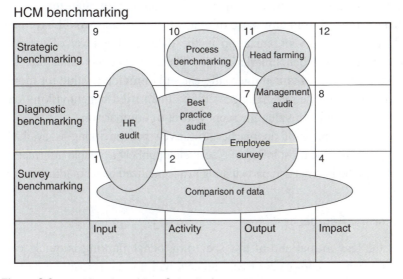

Figure 9.2 HCM benchmarking. © Jon Ingham 2006

Comparison of Data (Mainly Box 2, Also Boxes 1, 3 and 4)

This type of value for money, survey benchmarking focuses on collecting and comparing data and metrics, obtained from the company's management information system. The benchmarker's own data can mostly be obtained from the company's Management Information System (MIS). Benchmark data is obtained from datasets that have been put together from surveys of other organizations' data. These datasets typically contain data for several hundred other organizations and can often be narrowed down to provide a more relevant comparison, for example with organizations from the same sector, country or size of organization. Some benchmark datasets are very focused on one particular people management process. Salary surveys fit this description and are probably the most popular form of people management benchmarking (and are also generally most useful when they are sector specific). Other datasets cover the full range of people management processes and activities.

Data benchmarking is usually quick and simple to carry out. As long as the data has been defined and measured consistently, its reliability and the validity of the comparison is high. The fact that the data is numerical also helps its face validity – senior managers typically feel able to place confidence on the data and take decisions based upon it. However, because this data is generic, by definition it cannot provide much insight into how well a company is executing its strategy or differentiating itself from its competitors. In addition, because the data has been removed from any sense of context (the context would have been different in every organization in the dataset), the level of meaning included in the benchmarks is low. Therefore, in the same way that quantified data obtained internally can only provide a value for money perspective on people management, so quantified benchmarking data can only provide a value for money level of comparison.

A broad range of approaches to survey benchmarking is available, ranging from the most informal – accessing publicly available information, often on the internet – to participating in a formalized benchmarking survey.

Informal Approaches

At the less formal end of this spectrum, benchmarking is quick, easy and cheap, or completely free. The data will not necessarily be particularly accurate, as there is often little control over how metrics are defined, or how data is collected and reported, but it is generally good enough to provide ball-park comparison. Greater accuracy can also be obtained by comparing benchmarks from several different sources.

A lot of useful data exists in the public domain and can be found in books and articles, is discussed at conferences, and can be taken straight off the internet using a search engine or an HR website. More benchmark data is also available for purchase at a small charge and is often free for participants who have contributed data. Within the UK, good sources of data include the CBI Annual Absence and Labour Turnover and Employment Trends survey reports; the CIPD Labour Market Outlook; IRS Employment Review reports on labour turnover and the HR function; Incomes Data Services (IDS) reports; Cranfield's Recruitment Confidence Index and the DTI's labour market statistics. More interpretative reports are available from the Institute of Employment Studies; the Work Foundation; Corporate Executive Board; Corporate Research Forum; Human Capital Institute; HR Planning Society; Business Intelligence; Best Practice Club; Best Practices LLC and the American Productivity and Quality Centre (AQPC). Useful websites include HR.com and Xperthr.com. Deeper information is also available within most sectors. For example, in local government, there is the IPF HR Benchmarking Club and various benchmarks are available via the Public Sector People Managers' Association (PPMA) previously known as the Society of Chief Personnel Officers (SOCPO). In financial services, a lot of information is available via Complinet.

One very useful source of data is HR Benchmarker, which features in *Personnel Today*. This is a benchmarking service operated by the employment law consulting team of DLA Piper Rudnick Gray Cary. People metrics are collected from organizations across both the public and private sectors and the analysis of the data is published in two reports each year. The HR Performance Indicators survey covers an extensive range of metrics about the HR function including HR head-count ratios and costs; key HR initiatives; perceived effectiveness; level of HR outsourcing; and recruitment and training costs (boxes 1 and 2). The Workforce Performance Indicators survey covers a wide range of measures focusing on the engagement of the workforce and also the way in which this is managed, including equality and diversity; employee consultation and involvement; stress and occupational health; perform-ance management; and discipline and grievance cases (mainly box 3).

Slightly more formal benchmarking is available through a number of HR and more general benchmarking clubs that enable their members to interact with each other and access benchmarking data that is important for them. Benchmarking clubs are run by various consultancies; Corporate Executive Board/Corporate Leadership Council; European HR Forum; HR Benchmarking Association and Best Practices Institute. The clubs often provide a broad range of services and increasingly offer higher levels of benchmarking support. One example is FiSSInG, a sister network of the HR Society, that lays on meetings, networking, case studies, research and papers that review subjects of interest to its members. The group's HR Benchmarking Club provides a scorecard for each member enabling them to assess key aspects of organizational and HR performance. The group's chair, Chris Nutt, explains:

> We started up using the UK offshoot of the Saratoga Institute to provide the benchmarking metrics. Later, members wanted a more flexible approach and more discussion, so members developed additional, bespoke measures and dropped others. Sometimes it is just too difficult, costly or time-consuming for members to get the data, so we would drop this measure. For example, the cost of training sounds simple for formal, off-site courses but to include workplace coaching is very challenging to quantify with confidence. Having started with 12 KPIs, we've now got a suite of 49 KPIs (a mixture of lead and lag indicators covering both operational performance and future-oriented human capital measures). There are actually 149 separate measures in all from which we have chosen the 49. This ensures that members have a good choice of KPIs that are most appropriate to their own businesses. Furthermore, the KPIs change over time. For example, to measure gender diversity we started 10 years ago with the proportion of all managers who are female. When this equated to the same proportion as the females in the workforce as a whole, members became more interested in the proportion of women in senior management positions. We therefore started to measure the percentage of the top 10, 20 and 30 per cent of jobs (by salary) that are occupied by women. We chose 30 per cent as a KPI, and then moved to 10 per cent as the world changed.
>
> But that's only part of the story. People want to check out each other's developments, organizational successes, capabilities and policies. They quite often have ad-hoc queries and we go round and share each other's inputs on this. Since members are active benchmarking partners who get to know each other personally and organizationally – not just data providers – there are opportunities to network and provide more in-depth

reviews of developments and initiatives in each member company. For example, a meeting was held recently in Edinburgh, hosted by Standard Life, to share experiences of HR service centres, the practical issues, costs and benefits and so on. It's what I call casual benchmarking – Standard Life talked about their experience and then everybody had an opportunity to talk about what they had been doing as well.'

Formal Data Surveys

More formal approaches to survey benchmarking rely on using proprietary tools and databases. The greatest advantage of these approaches is that the benchmarking firms provide common taxonomies and greater control over the quality of data entered into the database to help ensure that exactly the same type of data is being compared (an apples to apples comparison).

The best-known proprietary service is provided by PwC Saratoga which was formed by Jac Fitz-Enz who started producing human capital metrics reports in 1985. Saratoga has a dataset of about 150 metrics, although the firm has always emphasized the need for organizations to select a smaller number of metrics that inform their individual strategy. Saratoga (2006) also suggests that there are 12 generic metrics that most companies can use. One of these metrics is the Human Capital ROI that was referred to in Chapter 6 and is also referenced in the case study on BT in Chapter 10.

Fitz-Enz's new vehicle is called Human Capital Source. This benchmarking firm provides a Workforce Intelligence analytic process that uses about 15 people measures and a similar number of business measures to enable benchmarking across the organizations in the dataset and also with lists of best companies to work for. The difference here is that as well as benchmarkers seeing how they compare with other companies in each metric, they will also be able to review their performance in the metrics that show the greatest correlation to business results.

Other benchmarking companies include InfoHRM (see Chapter 12) and the Hackett Group.

The Hackett Group. Another tool is provided by the Hackett Group, a benchmarking company that covers Finance, IT, Procurement and other functional areas as well as HR. Over 3000 organizations have used

Hackett's benchmarking services within at least one of these areas and there is currently data from about 200 clients in its HR process database.

Data is self-reported by the client although clients can ask Hackett staff if they need help in understanding and responding to requests for particular types of information and this assists in maintaining the comparability of the information in the dataset. Stephen Joyce, Managing Director of Hackett's HR practice, explains that in addition to this:

> We also hold about half a dozen interviews with executives in and outside of HR. This provides another voice in the process. It doesn't end up in the metrics, these depend purely on the benchmarking tool. But it validates the survey responses.

Hackett's HR benchmark covers four process groups: transactional data, employee life-cycle data, planning and strategy, and management and administration of the HR function. Hackett also benchmarks Payroll as a specific process at a greater level of detail, but other than this the firm believes their general HR benchmarking provides sufficient depth of information. Joyce comments that:

> We seek to provide insights based on data rather than just provide data so we've kept things to a fairly high level. It's enough to provide a baseline of information that can point an organization in a direction to look further into things themselves. Organizations don't want or need additional information to tell them what they already know. Too much data will just result in analysis paralysis.

Hackett benchmarks organizations against a relative standard of performance they call 'world-class' and a peer group of companies experiencing similar complexity and rate of change, or volatility in the business, to provide a meaningful and relevant comparison. 'World-class' is defined as the level of performance exhibited by companies that rank in the top quartile in both 'efficiency' (cost and productivity) and 'effectiveness' (quality and value) metrics.

Hackett also reviews a range of other factors including processes, technology, organization, strategic alignment and readiness to partner with customers and suppliers. By correlating take-up of these factors with the performance metrics of world-class organizations, Hackett has identified and 'certified' a range of best practices. When Hackett presents the results of its benchmarking reviews, the recommendations often relate to implementing specific certified practices that will impact on a range of processes. Joyce explains:

> It's not just about improving processes. We'll look holistically at these other dimensions and investigate the things clients can do to improve their performance. We'll look at something like self-service that's important to a number of process groups and we'll isolate the correlation between higher levels of self-service use and lower cost of service delivery. Or can they leverage technology better while they're redesigning processes? Or do they have the right skill sets in the people working on the processes?

But this review of potential best practices needs to be balanced by what is right for the particular client and their own business context. Joyce comments:

> We do worry that some companies take a case study and just apply it without enough thinking and the issue may not actually be a problem for them. We ask, 'Why do you want to do that, have you done an analysis?' They need to establish the right practices rather than all possible ones. These are the practices where there are definite correlations to world-class performance. But it's equally important to assess in an organization what sort of impact implementing a best practice will have and how achievable is it. It's all well and fine to tell an organization to put in automated workflow technology but if they don't have a technology backbone in place it's not very achievable. Organizations need to assess the best practices and develop a picture of high impact and high achievability. And then decide which of the practices they will implement.

Hackett publishes summaries of the benchmark data and its broad conclusions in a cross-functional *Book of Numbers* and separate books that take a deeper look at each functional area. As an example of Hackett's findings, the firm indicates that overall HR cost per employee is 25 per cent less for world-class companies than for their more typical peers. Of particular relevance to the subject of this book, Hackett (2004) has also found that:

- world-class companies are 159 per cent more likely than typical companies to have mature balanced scorecards in place;
- the full benefits of effective scorecards are not being realized for more than 80 per cent of typical companies;
- companies report an average of 132 metrics to senior management each month (83 financial and 49 operational metrics) – this is nearly nine times the number of measures suggested as being appropriate;

- half the metrics companies rely on are driven by internal financial data which places too much weight on historical performance.

Joyce commented:

We've not done any specific analysis on the use of HCM measurement but we do tend to see that world-class companies put in place effective measurement systems for key change processes and use more measurement tools.

We finished the conversation with Joyce adding:

There's one more thing that's worth mentioning. Most of our clients are after a simple answer to a complex problem. We provide a great benchmarking tool but it's not the holy grail. Benchmarking provides the information clients need to figure out what they need to do. It's not an end in itself.

Employee Satisfaction and Engagement Surveys (Boxes 2, 3, 6 and 7)

Surveys of this type are based on the perceptions of employees. Whether these surveys can be used to measure activities (boxes 2 and 6) or outputs (boxes 3 and 7) depends on whether they focus on satisfaction or engagement.

Satisfaction surveys look at how much people like things in the organization. Although the data is obtained from employees, the focus of the questions is the processes and practices within the organization which are then judged by employee satisfaction with them. For example, a survey might ask, 'have you had a performance review', 'did your manager explain your performance rating?' and 'did you agree a development plan?' Responses to these questions say very little of value about the people completing the survey but can be useful in improving the performance management process. A particular form of employee satisfaction survey focuses on specific groups experiencing particular stages in the employee life cycle, particularly joiners and leavers. Joiner surveys provide very specific information about recruitment processes and employer branding. Leaver surveys provide more general data on the employee experience from a particular perspective, in which the organization's offer has no longer met the employee's requirements.

Engagement looks at how much people want to exert extra effort and will engage in the discretionary behaviours that contribute to business success. Although data is still gathered on processes and practices, the focus is on the difference these practices make to employees.

Both sets of survey can be valuable but engagement surveys generally provide a lot more usable information to inform change. Because the surveys help identify the practices that drive engagement, they help link activities and output (boxes 2 and 6 with boxes 3 and 7) and form an important component of a causal model, as demonstrated by RBS, Standard Chartered, Microsoft and other organizations.

Whether surveys provide value for money data (boxes 2 and 3) or more valuable information (boxes 6 and 7) depends on how they are constructed. Surveys add value by focusing on an organization's own drivers of performance.

This is the approach that Penna has taken to employee engagement surveys. Penna has forgone the benefits of having a large dataset of benchmarks and, instead of this, focuses on an individual organization's needs. The survey process consists of two stages. The first and qualitative stage is where broad insights about the organizational environment are gained. This will typically consist of interviews with senior managers to help define the priorities and context of the benchmarking exercise. Focus groups are also held with a cross slice of key people. These are run loosely and often use pictures rather than descriptions of issues to stimulate creativity and engagement with the survey process. E-focus groups are also used when the organization wants a lot of staff to participate or where the qualitative stage needs to be completed quickly. This activity also allows the survey to be tailored to the particular issues of the organization and to be written in an organization's own language.

The second, quantitative stage adds detail to this output through use of a survey. The surveys all use the same set of outcome questions focusing on satisfaction ('I am satisfied with my current job'); advocacy ('I would recommend working at this organization to my friends') and intention to stay ('I intend to be working here in two years time') and these are benchmarked. Other questions are determined based upon the issues raised in the qualitative work. Instead of asking people about what is important to them (as they tend to say that everything is important), this approach uses advanced statistical techniques to derive importance by identifying which items correlate with the outcome questions. This allows organizations to focus on the actions that will have the most direct impact on engagement rather than on areas where there is the lowest satisfaction. Low satisfaction in particular questions is not an issue if these questions are not correlated with engagement outcomes.

Increasingly, surveys are being run on a more regular basis. For example, an organization can survey one-twelfth of its workforce every month or run a short, regular survey in addition to an annual questionnaire. This 'pulsing' approach provides the same level of reliability and the same level of involvement but also provides some information on trends. It is an ideal approach for organizations going through change. Some tools also allow real-time measurement of engagement to enable individuals, teams and organizations to implement immediate improvements. Margaret Savage, previously HR Strategy Director at BT, told me about BT's use of a tool called eepulse, developed by Theresa Welbourne at Michigan, which asks team members to rate the extent to which they feel energized by their work:

> In my top team (and in other areas across BT) we have been using eepulse to provide an instant weekly touch point on energy levels in the team. The team defines what they interpret energy levels as – so it means what they want it to mean. We can see if the team is at peak performance or low performance. Everyone can see their own profile and this is aggregated to a team profile. Every week team members say how the team is operating. What were the high points this week and what pissed us off. And we have a look at whether we are below or above the zone. We look at the verbatim responses that are presented back and we have a weekly call when I ask whether I can do anything to shift things. We want to be working at optimum peak performance levels but you have to start with the Herzberg stuff. People don't trust you until you get through this. They don't believe you just because you can show them the policy; they want to see the evidence. The tool allows you to take action as their boss; it helps in 'connecting to the edge'. The team can interact with you. You can't get round the world to see them all but this helps you put your finger on what's happening.

The approach focuses less on data and more on meaning, moving towards the top of the diagnostic benchmarking level. In actual fact, as pointed out in Chapters 1 and 2, organizations probably do not need as much data and information as they think. For example, Ulrich and

Smallwood (2003) describe how engagement surveys only formalize information that is often already quite well understood:

> Useful as studies are, they're often unnecessary. You can find out much about commitment by simply observing it. When we teach classes on employer commitment, the participating executives often seek precise, rigorous, and trackable measures that they can use for management action. Then we ask those who visit multiple sites how long it takes them to discern the employee commitment level of a unit they are visiting. Without exception, they reply in terms of hours rather than days and they refer to dialogues, not data.

Popular examples of surveys include the *Sunday Times* Best 100 Companies to Work For Survey run by Best Companies Ltd and sponsored by the DTI, and the FT Best Workplaces Survey which is also run in about 30 other countries. Other well-known survey providers include research companies like Gallup, Gfk NOP, ISR, MORI, ORC and consultancies including Hay, Hewitt, Mercer, and Towers Perrin.

HR Audits (Boxes 1, 5 and 9)

Some people, for example Kearns (2004), believe that HCM should not be concerned with measuring the HR function. I think this is almost as big a mistake as only evaluating the HR function. The HR function plays a vital role in managing people for human capital. Measuring the effectiveness and even the efficiency of HR in performing this role needs to form part of a strategic approach to HCM measurement.

In an *HR Magazine* article, Becker and Huselid challenge the HR function to focus on their performance relative to their business strategy (box 5) rather than efficiency metrics and survey benchmarks (box 1):

> HR professionals have routinely relied on benchmarked comparisons of cost and other efficiency-based performance outcomes associated with activities of the HR *function*. But reliance on these types of benchmarking measures not only fails to measure HR's important contributions to firm success, it can also encourage an approach to human capital management that is counter-productive.
>
> Instead, HR professionals should judge their performance relative to their firm's own *strategy* rather than the HR efficiency of other organizations.

Defending the use of HR efficiency metrics and benchmarking, my response to the article was also published in *HR Magazine* (Finn and Ingham, 2004):

> Just because HR efficiency measures do not measure impact on business performance does not make them worthless. Benchmarking and efficiency metrics provide powerful supporting arguments for strategic decisions. If HR is inefficient it will be unable, or certainly less able, to make a strategic impact.

A range of tools that resemble or form part of the approaches to data surveys (box 2), best practice diagnostics (box 6) or process benchmarking (box 10) can be used to assess individual as well as functional HR capability (boxes 1, 5 and 9).

An example of box 1 is the assessment of HR professionals against the competencies developed in the University of Michigan's 2002 competency study. This assessment can be conducted online at SHRM.org. An example of box 5, also using the Michigan competencies is RBL Group's HR 360 competency survey. In this survey, 360-degree feedback is obtained on an organization's HR function and its HR professionals and contextualized feedback is provided via a workshop and follow-up coaching.

Best Practice Audits (Mainly Box 6, Also Boxes 5 and 7)

Best practice benchmarking is based on the use of facilitated interventions and diagnostic assessment tools. Value is added to the benchmark information by framing it as a set of best practices. In this way, a benchmarker is able to compare itself with an articulated description of best practice (that can also be described as a 'standard') as well as with the other organizations in the database. Value is added to the benchmarking exercise by contextualizing it in terms of the benchmarker's own situation and business/HCM strategies. And value is added to the process through the facilitation of powerful conversations to extract insight and meaning from the benchmarks.

The output of the benchmarking is information an organization can use to do something about the issues that have been raised and facilitation is often extended to the development of action plans linked to deeper implementation of some of the best practices. However, the process of taking part in best practice benchmarking is often as useful as the actual results detailed in the final report.

Best practice benchmarking focuses on activities but some tools, for example the European Foundation for Quality Management (EFQM) Excellence Model, also address the outputs of the activities. The Excellence Model is a non-prescriptive self-assessment developed as a framework for assessing applications for the European Quality Award. The framework uses nine criteria covering five enablers including leadership and people, and four results areas including people results and key performance results.

More specifically within people management, Investors in People (IIP) is a best practice standard that describes the role of managers in leading, managing and developing their people. The standard now covers 40 per cent of the UK workforce and organizations in other countries such as France, Denmark, Austria and South Africa are also adopting it. The standard was first launched in 1990 and has been regularly reviewed since then. I helped facilitate the latest review that was completed in November 2004. The updated standard focuses on the whole employee life cycle rather than just performance management and development. It mirrors the business planning cycle (plan, do, review), enabling organizations to fit use of the standard to their own planning cycle. There is also more emphasis on continuous improvement, encouraging organizations to review and improve their people development plans.

The standard consists of ten indicators which must all be met but can be achieved in different ways. Achievement of the standard involves a rigorous assessment process which for a 1000 person organization involves about 5–10 per cent of the workforce. This rigour provides a high level of reliability but it means that the assessment takes quite a long time and is relatively expensive to complete.

The standard is supported by three modules covering leadership and management, recruitment and selection, and work–life balance. In addition, as well as using the standard and modules, organizations can benchmark themselves against the performance of other organizations in each of the indicators using the Investors in People Profile tool. Profile provides four levels of achievement within each indicator, ranging from Level 1 which refers to performance that meets the requirements of the standard, through to Level 4 which represents excellence. It is not expected that many organizations would ever reach level 4 in all areas and doing so would probably mean that they had not focused enough on aligning people management behind a differentiated HCM strategy (including making trade-offs).

CBI Headstart

Another example of a best practice people management standard is Headstart, one of the CBI's benchmarking tools which are collectively called PROBE (standing for Promoting Business Excellence). These tools date back to 1992 when Phil Hanson, IBM's practice leader for industrial consultancy, and Chris Voss, Professor of Total Quality Management at London Business School, developed a framework to measure a company's maturity on a journey towards a vision of world-class manufacturing performance. This framework later became Manufacturing PROBE. Developing a related tool, Service PROBE, Voss *et al.* (1997) found that companies which performed less well in benchmarking tended to be the most complacent, believing their competitiveness was better that it actually was. Benchmarking helps to remove this complacency, which tends to hold a company back, by pointing out the gap between the benchmarker's and benchmark organizations' performance.

Headstart was developed by the CBI, using the same framework as the Manufacturing and Service PROBEs, and by looking at academic research and best practice in CBI members. Like these other tools, Headstart focuses on two areas of activity: practices and performance. Practices refer to the established processes which an organization has put in place to deliver business results. Performance refers to the measurable results of these processes.

The benchmark tool is based upon a self-assessment questionnaire containing 73 questions focused on practice and performance in four critical areas of people management: leadership and culture, employee development, employee involvement and work organization. The questionnaire is completed individually by people who have been selected to provide a representative, cross-functional, multi-level team from the organization. This team then meets together with an independent CBI facilitator who helps the team come to a consensus score for each question and will then produce a comprehensive diagnostic report. Value is added to the diagnosis through the conversation of the team, aided, supported and validated by the facilitator.

For each of the four elements, feedback is provided against both practice and performance comparing the benchmarker against a standard of world-class performance (defined as scores of 80 per cent or more on both practice and performance) and other organizations in the database that have been selected for comparison based upon having a similar industrial classification.

I talked to Phil Hanson about the development of the Probe tools:

> We believed that surveys provided a rather shallow level of questioning and that our approach would provide much better quality. Having the right group of people in the room and a facilitator to manage the process ensures more integrity in a company's responses to a set of questions. And it's a self-assessment, not an audit. Who owns the integrity of an audit? It's the auditor. For a self-assessment, it's the participant. Occasionally a facilitator says he or she is not happy with an organization's answer – they're kidding themselves about something – so we don't put the data in the database.

Headstart provides an effective and efficient means of generating employee feedback which lends itself to short reviews before and after change and to comparing the effectiveness of people management across different parts of an organization.

CBI Headstart at Firstplus. Firstplus Financial Group plc was set up in 1997 and has been an operationally independent business within Barclays since 2000. The company currently employs 300 people and is still growing.

Firstplus started using the EFQM Excellence Model from day one and has found using its self-assessment process very useful. In 1999 the company decided to drill down further into the people aspect of the model. Claire Hurley, who was the company's Head of Business Excellence, chose Headstart to help it do this.

The results of the company's first Headstart review indicated that Firstplus was a 'contender' (defined as scores of 60 per cent or more on both practice and performance). Hurley explained to me that these scores were not as high as she had hoped, but she was pleased that they were balanced, that is practice and performance were about equally as well developed, meaning that practices were sound and were starting to play dividends. Hurley was also pleased that some of the strengths highlighted in the assessment reflected what the company was trying to achieve (for example Firstplus scored highly in 'creating a performance culture' that supported its focus on 'high performance, high reward').

The benchmarking review also identified a number of areas for improvement. For example, the CBI facilitator noted that the company had a fairly inflexible policy on working hours and that growth targets were potentially incompatible with existing recruitment goals. However, the facilitator also noted that the areas where Firstplus had the potential to make the greatest gains were, to a large extent, already being addressed. These outputs were reviewed alongside the company's staff satisfaction survey, employee focus groups, an EFQM internal benchmarking exercise and feedback from an IIP assessment. All these different types of information were combined to develop an action plan and also informed the development of the following year's people management strategy.

Firstplus repeated the benchmarking in 2001 (using a facilitator), and in both 2002 and 2003 (through a self-assessment against the world-class standard but without access to an updated benchmarking dataset). In all three years, Firstplus was firmly in the world-class category and in 2003 its scores were 92 per cent in both practice and performance. The team conducting the self-assessment was still able to identify some areas for improvement. For example, although recruitment practices had improved substantially, their performance was still seen to be 'mildly unattractive' as the company occasionally found it difficult to fill positions. The team also noted that the company's greatest challenge for the future would be avoiding complacency and slipping backwards.

The following year Firstplus went through extensive change which involved further integration into Barclays, the departure of several members of the previous top team and a new CEO. Hurley explained that she had thought about not using Headstart again that year as she knew things would have deteriorated, but she wanted to understand the extent of this. In fact the 2004 review still indicated world-class performance with 82 per cent in practice and 80 per cent in performance.

The CBI facilitator who had been brought back in for this fifth Headstart review commented that:

> Practice is marginally ahead of performance. This would imply that Firstplus Financial Group plc have a wide range of policies and procedures in place and that in part, due to the changes in senior management and the period of transition for all employees, performance may have been affected during this period.

Figure 9.3. provides a graph from the Headstart feedback report. It shows the practice (pr) and performance (pf) scores for the two areas within employee development: recruitment and selection, and the training and development cycle. Within both these areas, practice is ahead of performance and all four scores are still in the top quartile of companies in the overall dataset sample.

The assessment report commented:

'Recruitment and Induction – Here Firstplus Financial plc sees practice ahead of performance (96/90). In place are robust recruitment polices and procedures to take the business forward. There has been a high level of recruitment activity in the last year which has resulted in a key number of senior appointments and the CEO is committed to ensuring that in terms of talent management they attract high calibre people into the organization. This may involve some delay in filling key positions such as the HR Director and IT Director role. The recruitment strategy needs to not only include a clear succession planning remit but also look at how specialist positions, e.g. IT/telecoms etc., can be filled so that the time lag is not detrimental to the business.

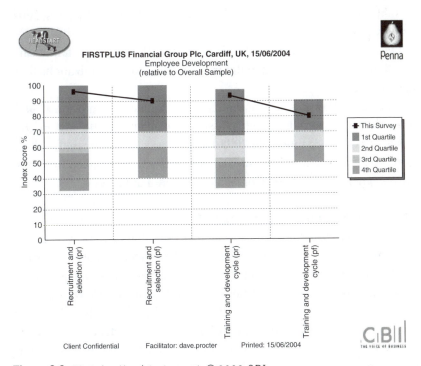

Figure 9.3 Firstplus Headstart report. © 2003 CBI.

As indicated above, the review highlighted that a number of challenges which had been identified in earlier reviews still remained present, or had resurfaced during the transition period. In particular, the company was still facing difficulties in responding effectively to their continuing fast growth. Karen Martin, HR Director, explained that this situation was being made even more challenging because neither she nor the Chief Executive were prepared to compromise on quality or recruit someone unless they were sure they had found the right person. Because of this approach, which meant that Firstplus was not always able to find talent, the company had a small number of long-term vacancies on the executive team. To resolve this situation the company is now seeking to reinforce its branding as an employer of choice.

As well as using Headstart, Firstplus has tracked its performance in people management against a range of benchmark metrics. Sickness absence has consistently stayed below 2 per cent (compared with the national sector average of 3.5 per cent) and with the exception of the hiatus in 2004 turnover has been kept well below the industry benchmark.

Table 9.1 provides some of the results from the company's 2004 employee survey.

Over the last few years, 100 per cent of staff have consistently said that they are more satisfied with Firstplus than other organizations they have worked for.

Since 2004 Firstplus has concentrated on continuous improvement and, most recently, has graduated up to assessment against the broader EFQM business excellence model. In 2005 Firstplus was an award winner of the European Quality Award and in 2006 the company was ranked twelfth in the *Sunday Times* Best 100 Companies to Work For survey.

Management Audits (Boxes 7 and 11)
The executive search firms, a few other consultancies, private equity firms and investment banks have developed a variety of tools to measure and benchmark executive talent. These tools vary in focus from a psychological assessment using psychometrics and an interview with a chartered occupational psychologist (for example YSC's benchmarking and management audit) to a business audit based on competency-based interviews (rather than psychometrics) using the search firm's regular recruitment consultants (for example Egon Zehnder's management appraisal).

Table 9.1: Firstplus employee satisfaction survey results

Employee satisfaction with	Percentage satisfied
■ Their job, company and the product	97
■ Communication	93
■ Training and development	92
■ The performance management system	86
■ Reward and recognition	83
■ Management style	92
■ Processes	87
■ The working environment	91

Other tools include Heidrick & Struggles' strategic leadership review, Korn/Ferry's strategic management assessment, Mercer Delta's leadership audit, Russell Reynolds's executive assessment, Spencer Stuart's human capital assessment, Whitehead Mann's management assessment valuation and Hay's talent audit.

These various audits allow executives to be assessed against a best practice standard, other executives within the organization and executives in other organizations, usually within the same industry. The assessments can also be consolidated to provide an overview of the management group as a whole. Although the datasets of best practices are the focus of the assessment, it is the judgements of the experienced psychologists and executive search consultants that makes this form of assessment added value (box 7). To be created value (box 11), management audits need to be tailored to the benchmarker's own competencies and involve a comparison of other organizations against these competencies.

Process Benchmarking (Box 10)

Process benchmarking is concerned with gaining insight and in-depth understanding about how a particular process in one or more benchmark organizations could be adapted to fit and create value within the benchmarker's own organization. The effectiveness of processes often relies on nuances and systemic issues that can only be detected by

287

examining them via detailed observation and analysis. For example, Ulrich (1997) describes his experience at GE:

> When working with General Electric, I witnessed the pilgrimage to GE by a number of companies seeking to learn more about GE's practices in succession planning, culture change, development, and employee involvement. Many of these visitors, enamored of the GE programs, returned home only to find that they were impossible to implement in their given work settings.

Tools like McKinsey's 7S or Hammer's Change Diamond (Hammer and Champy, 2001) can be useful to ensure all the appropriate elements of an organization's approach have been considered.

Like Headstart, process benchmarking has its roots in manufacturing but this time, experience goes back at least as far as 1979 when Robert Camp at Xerox initiated a process called competitive benchmarking. Xerox had suffered a huge deterioration in market share and profitability with the loss of its reprographic technology patent. Benchmarking was the beginning of the company's fight back. Xerox sent a team of staff to visit some of its Japanese competitors and examine its competitors' processes and technology. Xerox also compared a number of its products with competitors' models that had similar features and capabilities. These products were broken down and each component reviewed against Xerox's product.

The following year Xerox broadened its benchmarking activities to study organizations outside the reprographic industry. For example, the company studied American Express's billings and collections process and LL Bean's warehousing operations. Camp (1989) explained why Xerox focused on process rather than survey benchmarking:

> First, benchmarking can be divided into two parts, practices and metrics. Practices are defined as the methods that are used; metrics are the quantified effect of installing the practices. Benchmarking should be approached on the basis of investigating industry practices first. The metrics that quantify the effect of the practices can be obtained or synthesized later. One cannot determine why the gap exists from the metrics alone. Only the practices on which the metrics is based will reveal why. The reverse is not always possible, and it could mislead or defeat the purpose of benchmarking.

Process benchmarking usually involves only one or two benchmark organizations and is often done on a reciprocal basis. Choosing to benchmark competitors can provide the most directly useful information but this may need to be done covertly (perhaps more of a case of industrial espionage than industrial tourism). Choosing another organization within the same industry makes it easy to share issues and concerns. However, the most innovative ideas and therefore the greatest benefits are likely to come from choosing an organization outside the sector.

Phil Hanson described to me some of his observations and experiences in process benchmarking:

> It's basically about taking one process and unpicking it, then comparing this in detail against another organization. Suppose you want to study a particular manufacturing or an administration process – responding to queries or something. The first thing you need to do is to draw the process flow and improve what actually goes on compared to what should. Secondly, you can remove large amounts of nonsense by seeing the process flow drawn out and by mapping the value stream. Most waste reduction can be done without reference to other companies. Thirdly, it may then make sense to go and interface with other people who use the same process. For example, at IBM we looked at taking waste out of our logistics processes and compared them to other electronics companies. Then someone said we should compare our processes against food companies downstream of Tesco and Sainsbury's. They're in a very savage situation where they're delivering perishable products to very difficult and demanding customers with huge purchasing power. So if something arrives a minute late it's sent away and if the shelves are empty you get fined for the time they're not stocked. We looked at these companies' processes and realized we weren't quite so good after all.'

In an HCM context, you could use process benchmarking to study value creating people management processes. For example, if your organization focuses on creating innovation through teamwork you might want to go to Skandia to study how their values support success in innovation. Or if you focus on developing individual potential you could study the way that Microsoft develops people's strengths.

At one client I was involved in, the client wanted to study the recruitment processes of five other leading companies it had already identified. The client wanted to do this covertly (none of these five organizations were or had ever been our clients). We identified people we knew who had previously worked in one of these organizations or had otherwise been touched by their recruitment processes, for example having unsuccessfully applied to the organization. We were able to uncover a lot of information about the five companies' processes.

This type of benchmarking is not always appropriate. To be carried out effectively, strategic benchmarking requires considerable amounts of time and trust in the other parties to divulge all relevant information. It also requires a willingness to learn. In the CIPD's book on benchmarking people management, John Bramham (1997) has suggested that:

> Perhaps the main reason for failure is the rejection of ideas for change coming from outside the organization – 'not invented here'. Benchmarking depends on a willingness to look at other organizations intelligently, and to learn from them ... If your organization is obsessed with 'territory' and 'turf wars', if there is an obsession with pride as to what has been done in the past, you will not be able to make use of benchmarking.

Head Farming (Box 11)

As its name suggests, process benchmarking focuses on processes (box 10), not the outputs of these processes (box 11), on HCM rather than human capital. However, it is also possible to use a process benchmarking approach to benchmark a competitor's human capital. In the same way that process benchmarking focuses on key processes, this approach typically focuses on comparing key individuals, probably those in the leadership team or core talent group, with other similar people not currently working in the benchmarker. However, process benchmarking goes beyond comparing processes to other companies to include bringing aspects of these processes back into the benchmarker. Similarly, companies that make the effort of comparing their internal core group against external talent are generally going to want to take the opportunity to try to recruit some of these people into their organizations. Therefore this approach to benchmarking becomes the basis for the type of proactive recruitment described as head farming in Ernst & Young's case study in Chapter 5.

Summary

Reader: *'Interesting, I hadn't thought of IIP and Saratoga as providing different forms of the same thing.'*

Author: 'No, I don't think many people do. And I think this is why many organizations struggle to gain value from either of them. Neither of these tools should be implemented as a separate activity. The driver should be the HCM strategy, the measures in the strategy, and what these measures mean in terms of what needs to be compared externally. Some of the time, an organization may not need a benchmark, some of the time they may be best using Saratoga. At other times it may be IIP. And I think probably much more of the time than is currently the case, strategic benchmarking will provide the organization with the level of knowledge and value that it seeks.'

Reader: *'And how would an organization know where it should focus?'*

Author: 'I think there are two main issues here. The first is about using benchmarking to support the measures in the value matrix. Once an organization has developed its measures, it can review these and think about how confident it feels about them. If it's not sure about whether the targets it has selected are appropriate, then benchmarking might be useful.

The second issue is about using benchmarking to support creativity. And here, you don't know what insight benchmarking is going to give you until you've benchmarked. I think the key here is to benchmark measures for objectives within the primary areas of focus. So if you're considering value for money, benchmark the activity (box 2) by using survey benchmarking, for example Hackett or Saratoga. If you're looking at adding value, use a best practice audit (box 6) like IIP, but focus this on the needs within the business plan. For example, if the business strategy is about reacting to market opportunities more quickly, you might want to get an IIP Profile assessment done, but focus on indicator 7: 'People are encouraged to take ownership and responsibility by being involved in decision-making'. If it's created value you want, use a management audit or a head farming approach to improve your knowledge about the capability you've got.'

References

Becker, B. and Huselid, M. (2003). 'Measuring HR? Benchmarking is NOT the answer!' *HR Magazine,* December, 57–61.

Becker, B., Huselid, M. and Ulrich, D. (2001). *The HR Scorecard*. Harvard Business School Press.

Bramham, J. (1997). *Benchmarking for People Managers: A Competency Approach*. Chartered Institute of Personnel and Development.

Camp, R.C. (1989). *Benchmarking: The Search for Industry Best Practices that Lead to Superior Performance*. ASQC Press.

Finn, R. and Ingham, J. (2004). 'United Kingdom mulls HR metrics', *HR Magazine*, April, 27.

Hackett Group (2004). *Balanced Scorecards: Are their 15 minutes of fame over?* The Hackett Group.

Hamel, G. (2000). *Leading the Revolution*. Harvard Business School Press.

Hammer, M. (1990). 'Reengineering work: Don't automate, obliterate', *Harvard Business Review*. July–August, 104–112.

Hammer, M. and Champy, J. (2001). *Reengineering the Corporation: A Manifesto for Business Revolution*. Harper Business.

Kearns, P. (2004). *One Stop Guide: Human Capital Management*. Personnel Today Management Resources.

Saratoga (2006). *Key Trends in Human Capital: A global perspective – 2006*. PricewaterhouseCoopers.

Ulrich, D. (1997). *Human Resource Champions*. Harvard Business School Press.

Ulrich, D. and Smallwood, N. (2003). *Why the Bottom Line ISN'T!* John Wiley & Sons.

Voss, C., Chase, R. and Roth, A. (1997). *International Service Study*. London Business School.

10

HCM Implementation

Introduction

Reader: *'We've looked at developing HCM strategy, developing measures to support this strategy and using benchmarks to validate and inform these measures. So now this chapter must be about taking action to implement the strategy and achieve the targets set in the measures and benchmarks?'*

Author: 'Yes, that's largely correct. But because organizations need to take the same types of actions to implement HCM strategies and business strategies, this chapter is really more about managing through people rather than managing the implementation of a people management strategy. The key thing we will consider in this chapter is that organizations need to consider the time horizons that they should be acting in. Some implementation issues can be dealt with in the short term and some take much longer.

However, there is a complication in this. Implementation requires contradictory actions to be taken at the same time. In other areas of the strategic HCM planning cycle this isn't such a problem. You can conduct survey benchmarking and process benchmarking together and the fact that they're focused on different levels of value doesn't matter too much. The actions don't interfere with each other. Implementation actions do interfere. For example, in the short term, measures can be used to control what people do. Longer term, they can be used to support learning about HCM strategy and how people management drives business performance. But, of course, you actually need to use the same set of measures for these two different and potentially conflicting purposes.

You need to find a way around this contradiction. There's often no perfect solution to how you do this. And the best solution is about what's right for a particular organization at a particular point in time. What's best fit for them. It's about balancing the pros and cons between different options. And this often requires replacing actions, for example moving from centralization to decentralization and back again. It means I can't say this is the right way to implement your HCM or business strategy, for example how you should link measures to reward. It all depends…'

Time Horizons for HCM

To implement their HCM strategies, organizations need to think about the actions they are taking within three different time horizons: current state, short term and long term.

Current State

Managing in the current state is about managing basic standards of performance. Think about the way that performance in the high jump has increased over time. Figure 10.1 provides a deeper analysis of the graph we looked at in Chapter 7 (Figure 7.3), It shows that at any point in time, there are three levels at which personal, team or organizational objectives can be set. One level of objectives, 'stretch goals', aims towards the next sigmoid curve. The next level, 'SMART objectives', continues the current sigmoid curve. I will explain both of these types of objectives later on. At this point, we just want to look at the lowest level of objectives, which are actually not objectives at all but standards. Standards represent the basic levels of performance that are required within a particular field or function.

The dotted line in Figure 10.1 indicates how standards change over time, being increased fairly infrequently and often only when mental

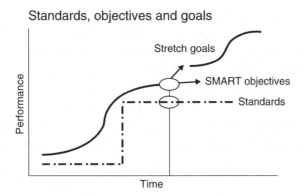

Figure 10.1 Standards, objectives and goals. © Jon Ingham 2006

models about what is possible have changed. This usually relates to periods when standards are increasing rapidly within a new sigmoid curve or in response to another exceptional event, for example, the Olympic Games every four years. So before Fosbury came along, high jumpers were doing well if they reached about 2.25m. During the decade after Fosbury, a new standard was introduced. Any jumper who was serious about their sport needed to be using the 'flop' and be jumping at about 2.35m just to stay in the game. So whereas SMART objectives and stretch goals tend to relate to roles and individuals, standards can exist right across organizations, sectors, countries or the world.

In terms of people management, standards describe activities (box 2 in Figure 7.1) that are required aspects of people's roles and are often explicitly included within their role descriptions. Standards describe base expectations and people are rewarded for performing to standards by a base salary. Standards should only have to be included in someone's performance management objectives when the standard has changed, just to highlight the change, but only then for one or a maximum of two years. When I moved into one business unit as an HR Director, the organization had a bonus objective of not being more than a month late in completing performance reviews. It was crazy – they had been rewarding people for performing at a lower level than the standard they had set (completion to time) and this sent a very strong message about the low importance of people in this business.

Standards are usually only updated in response to a new strategy or restructuring. They are not linked to particular business objectives that change over time, so they relate to value for money activities (there are exceptions where an organization's standards are so far ahead of the competition that this does create the basis for differentiation and creating value). Standards should be managed through behavioural control. Organizations need to communicate their expectations and take corrective actions if these expectations are not being met.

The management charter in the BT case study provides a set of standards for managing performance. The charter ensures that managers know what the organization expects them to do. It is also supported by a range of monitoring tools which make it very visible when a manager is not meeting the standards. This will affect their reward and increasingly their future in the organization.

Short Term

Gratton (2000) suggests that there are 'five possible process levers that can be realigned quickly to meet subtle, annual adjustments in the business goals'. These are: recruitment and selection, performance objectives, performance metrics, reward and recognition, and short-term training.

The performance objectives Gratton is referring to here are the ones I have identified as SMART (specific, measurable, achievable, realistic and timebound) objectives. These objectives continue along the current sigmoid curve, extrapolating current rates of improvement in performance. They also need to be aligned to objectives in the business plan (box 8). SMART objectives tend to be relatively similar for all people within a role, which enables their performance to be compared. In the high jump, an example of a SMART objectives would be a target for members of the British high jump team to each improve their performance, measured as the height they are jumping, by 5 per cent at the next Olympic Games.

Short-term performance is managed by ensuring that people understand what they need to do and motivating them to do it. Linking SMART objectives to variable reward can help meet both of these cognitive and humanistic requirements. For example, Kaplan and Norton (2001) state that:

> Employees should feel that when the organization has been successful, they share in the rewards; conversely, when the organization has been unsuccessful, they should feel some of the pain. Incentive and reward

systems provide the linkage between organizational performance and individual rewards.

We know that reward can influence what people do. For example, a recent report by the Conference Board (Gates, 2003) found that while only 39 per cent of companies reward managers against human capital measures in their bonus plans, 48 per cent believe managers will decide differently about people investments when people metrics are included. However, alongside many other commentators, Purcell believes this approach can be overplayed. Referring to Kaplan and Norton's position, Boxall and Purcell (2003) state:

> They tend to place too much faith in incentive remuneration (the 'balanced paycheque') ... The principle of aligning employer and employee interests is, of course, absolutely fundamental but this doesn't mean that bonus systems are always desirable ... There are many situations in which the better focus a scorecard can bring will work well alongside high wage levels but without mechanistic bonuses.

In fact, Kaplan and Norton (1996) do understand that a link is not always appropriate. Explaining that some companies have linked scorecard measures to compensation systems, they acknowledge that the reverse is also true:

> Some organizations, however, have reduced their emphasis on short-term, formula-based incentive systems as a result of introducing the balanced scorecard. They have discovered that dialogue among executives and managers about the scorecard – both the formulation of the measures and objectives and the explanation of actual versus targeted results – provides a better opportunity to observe managers' performance and abilities. Increased knowledge of their managers' abilities makes it easier for executives to see incentive rewards subjectively and to defend those subjective evaluations – a process that is less susceptible to the game playing and distortions associated with explicit, formula-based rules.

In general terms, rewards succeed at ensuring temporary compliance but they do less well in creating lasting change in thinking, attitudes and commitment. Some research has even shown that people who expect to receive a reward do not perform as well as if they do not expect to receive a reward.

In addition, tying rewards to objectives will open up any cracks there might have been in the performance management system. If measures do not capture all of the key requirements of the organization effectively, and other aspects of performance management such as the use of competencies do not support the white space between the objectives, then this increased focus can result in dysfunctional and unaligned behaviour and may result in unintended consequences as people play the system. We should not criticize them for this. All this means is that people have changed their behaviour in line with what we have been paying them to do. This is exactly what we wanted to happen, just not in the way that it has played through.

An example of this problem is provided by Shell's experience in setting targets for replenishing oil and gas reserves. In the late 1990s, Shell made this a formal performance target and rewarded managers if they achieved it. The company's oil reserves showed a healthy increase until end of 2003. Then in January 2004, the company confessed that it had overstated the reserves by 23 per cent. A contributing factor to this seemed to be that the reserve replacement measure had triggered some reward for managers in two of the previous five years. Reporting on an interview with Shell's President, John Hofmeister, Lester (2004) comments that:

> There was suspicion that the inclusion of reserves on the scorecard was partly to blame. Reserves are, after all, the future of Shell's business, and intangible in the sense that they are managers' estimates. The snag was that they were linked to individual reward structures … the reward system has now been changed to put more emphasis on the group and less on the individual.

If this type of overstatement can be made about physical resources, the same type of problem can certainly occur with intangible resources and capabilities. This means that in most situations, the introduction of incentives should be delayed until the system is already working well or at least until the strategy is clear and measures have been validated, checked and piloted to ensure as much as feasibly possible that the system cannot be manipulated.

However, Norton's Balanced Scorecard Collaborative inadvertently point out a further problem in linking performance objectives to reward:

> Of course, you should avoid changing targets during the year. Otherwise, employees may conclude you're 'gaming' the system – and lose all motivation to perform. (Frangos and Johnson, 2005)

But of course, given the complexity in environment, few organizations would want to be tied to objectives they cannot change. This limited flexibility is probably the most significant challenge to be overcome in tying SMART objectives to reward.

Long Term

The first requirement to manage the long-term horizon is a long-term vision or strategic intent. Gratton (in Gratton *et al.*, 1999) notes that:

> A long-term vision is a particularly crucial aspect of people strategies because the time cycles for people resources are considerably longer that those for financial or technological resources.

Developing a long-term vision is not easy in a complex environment, but paradoxically it is probably even more important. People need a picture of the future state to help give them meaning and to reduce ambiguity that can interfere in their performance. Stiles (in Gratton *et al.*, 1999) explains:

> Though the cause of failure of organizational change programmes is often laid at the door of poor implementation processes, we have seen in our research that a major factor in aligning employee behaviour to the new value and image of the organization concerns the way the organization manages the sense making activity of employees. Changing the mindset of employees is a difficult and often lengthy process.

Complexity also means that organizations need to make ongoing, rapid fundamental changes in their businesses and organizations to keep up with, and pull ahead of, environmental change. Fundamental change is more likely to be produced when planning backwards from the future state than planning forward from the current state. Planning backwards enables people to think more laterally, opening up people's mindsets to new possibilities, potentially resulting in breakthrough changes in performance.

Pfeffer notes that the need to think long term about people is the main reason why organizations, while talking about putting people first, often fail to translate this mantra into an operational reality. The easy problems are seen as quick wins and given time and attention. The harder problems require organizations to have the courage of their convictions, even if this means breaking with tradition and doing something their competitors are not doing. Because of this, these areas are avoided even though they will provide greater leverage once they are addressed:

> The point is, it takes a certain willingness to violate what everybody else is doing, and beyond that it requires tremendous courage to put people first. It takes tremendous courage to be who you say you are, and it takes tremendous courage to live your mission statement. (Pfeffer, 1998)

A long-term vision is supported by stretch goals. These point towards the next sigmoid curve. They are not SMART, as it is impossible to know the extent of the breakthrough that might be achieved, but they can be directional (for example, 'improve' or 'maximize'), or set within a broad range. Alternatively they can be qualitative and deliberately ambiguous. What is most important is that these goals are focused on capability (box 11) and expressed in sensory terms. This means that people are clear about what someone will see, hear and feel when they have achieved what they want. One of the benefits of having objectives is that this creates a psychological priming effect in which what someone thinks about influences what they get. This effect is magnified when objectives provide a sensory understanding rather than just a logical appreciation of the desired outcome. An example goal for the high jump would be something like: 'What would it be like if you could jump centimetres past the current world record? Can you imagine what you would hear, see and feel? Now, let's find a way to make it happen.'

Performance in this environment is managed through conversation, helping people construct new mental models and make sense of their organizations, its environment and strategy. This is one reason why managing long-term implementation processes is more difficult than those operating in the shorter term. Gratton (in Gratton *et al.*, 1999) notes:

> Those elements which link to the longer term are rather more opaque, more complex, and made up of clusters of processes.

In this environment, reward and even more importantly, recognition, need to be tied to stretch goals very loosely, if at all. Gratton (2000) describes three key people processes which support the delivery of a longer-term vision:

- The capability to transform the leadership cadre of the organization.
- The capability to transform the skills and behaviours of the workforce.

- The capability to create organizational structures, roles and responsibilities aligned to the longer term goals.

I think the most important of these are the organization's management and leadership skills. Increasing complexity, the need for transformational change and the need to personalize employment relationships all add to the challenge of leadership and line management. Line management also provides a key point of leverage within the system, the centre of the CIPD's black box model, where interventions have multiple benefits in improving the line manager's capability and, through them, the capability of all their people. In addition, most line managers' capability, or at least their motivation, to manage people is not that high so there is plenty of opportunity to make a difference.

Ghoshal and Bartlett (1998) believe a 'simple yet profound change' is required in organizations:

> That management is, above all else, about achieving results through people. Not that there is no value to crunching numbers, analysing trends, or restructuring activities. But these traditional responsibilities have, for too long, distracted managers from their most basic and most valuable role – being able to attract, motivate, develop, and retain individuals with scarce and valuable knowledge and skills. It is a role that is, at the same time, both enormously simple and incredibly difficult.'

The mindset change that is still required in many line managers in many organizations is that managers need to manage people first and then fit in the other things they need to do around this, rather than the other way around.

The other key requirement for me is learning, and this is where use of the measurements that are being collected comes in. In a complex environment, using measurement for control is likely to be ineffective. The resulting search for data can also be seen as overly intrusive and controlling by employees. Organizations that say they trust their staff but monitor all their work are unlikely to be seen as authentic. Employees who know they are being monitored in this way are less likely to experiment and so this will reduce creativity and innovation. It will also reduce the organization's ability to learn and improve its strategy.

Instead, as much as possible, measures should be developed by the teams and individuals which will be performing the work – not be handed down to them by top management. The measures should be used not for control but to help the individuals and teams achieve their objectives. Senior management need to be involved to support, not to find fault. If a team falls behind target, it might be due to poor performance, but it may be down to a whole range of other factors as well. Judgement is needed in making sense of these outputs and what corrective actions may be required. And it needs to be OK to say that you do not know. Sveiby (2004) develops on the point:

> When is a system control and when is it learning? When does learning become control? Admittedly, this is not easy, but here are a few pointers. First, the process of developing the metrics is different. The metrics are produced bottom-up, with heavy involvement from all relevant groups. No trumpets from the accountants' ivory tower! Secondly, the indicators are used by the same people who produce them and they use them to improve their own processes, not somebody else's. Third, the indicators are reported openly to everyone. Fourth, when the indicators suggest a difference between say, a high-performing and a low-performing unit, the units in question are required to meet and the difference becomes the starting point of a dialogue to discover hidden value; are we measuring the same thing? What is it that we can do better? Fifth, the indicators are never the basis of a reward system. If rewards are to be distributed at all they should be group-based and allocated to those who make the highest value improvement, i.e. possibly the previous low-performing unit!'

Maximizing Performance at BT Global Services

BT Global Services (BT GS) is BT's global communications and technology business. It operates worldwide, with more than a third of its 30 000 people working outside of the UK. In 2003, the company had just been through a period of downsizing, restructuring and uncertainty, including the possibility of initial public offering hanging overhead. Today, the BT GS business is recognized internally as BT's growth engine and externally as a major player in the business services and solutions space. Behind these dramatic changes were a small number of programmes or campaigns driving a standard operating environment across businesses and countries, maximizing the contribution of all BT's people and changing people's behaviours to support its new brand values and GS's new strategy.

Figure 10.2 shows how BT matched their updated external brand vision, promise and values with a set of internal people values.

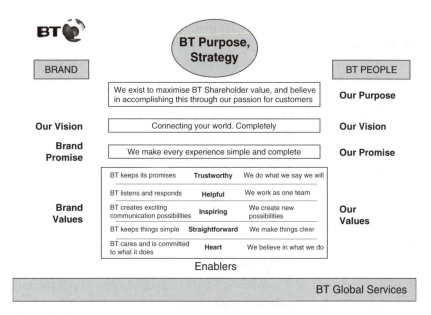

Figure 10.2 BT brand values and people values

Starting from the bottom and working up, the enablers are the things that support people and reinforce the values day to day – including performance management. On the left hand side are the brand values and on the right the people values: they are a mirror image of one another – how people act on the right drives how the company is seen on the left. The titles for both sets of values spell out 'THIS Heart' as an easy to remember summary. A set of leadership capabilities has also been developed that cascades from the people values. When people live the values, the brand and people values are truly aligned and BT delivers on its promise to the customer of a simple and complete experience. By succeeding in delivering the brand promise for all its customers, BT realizes the vision and delivers on the strategy of the business.

The Maximizing Performance programme was central to creating this transformation. Working with two of Penna's Directors, Robin Davies and Richard Finn, I was Penna's programme manager for this work, and also facilitated a number of the 170 workshops that we ran.

Programme Objectives

The first requirement was to remove the fragmented ways of managing, developing and reviewing employee performance and behaviour which had emerged from a legacy of partially owned joint ventures. Eleven different performance management approaches needed to be refined to one single system. In addition, employee engagement survey results showed that although employees believed they understood the business strategy, they often felt that this was not clearly reflected in their individual objectives. And because of the strong focus on the bottom line, managers were sometimes not fully engaged in managing the performance of their teams through effective appraisals and feedback. Changing this would require a broad-brush improvement in the quantity and quality of line manager engagement with their teams.

Addressing these issues, the key objectives for the programme were:

- for everyone to have SMART objectives, aligned with the business strategy and with their peers;
- to develop a single way of reviewing the performance of people and a single approach to differentiating performance;
- to share the same language regarding what makes an outstanding, good, or poor performer and to support them appropriately.

The expected outcomes were that duplication of effort and time wasted would be reduced by at least 5 per cent, hence contribution per full-time equivalent (FTE) would be increased, also by at least 5 per cent.

Programme Approach

One critical success factor was reducing the number of key HR programmes to four, of which this was one, and ensuring each programme was effectively led, managed and resourced. The programme team took a holistic approach by ensuring there were tight links through to other programmes, particularly to reward and recognition. We were also proactive in the use of communication, developing and issuing a series of briefings and updates including new web pages, a brochure, posters and postcards that were sent individually to every employee.

Tina Beeden is an HR Director who had responsibility for leading the programme. She explained that:

> We treated it as a change programme, putting a lot of work into stakeholder analysis and planning how to deal with blockers and resisters. We did a lot of planning up front so that we could hit the ground running

and not just end up reacting to problems as they presented themselves. The branding element has also been very important.'

Business Ownership

The programme was launched in April 2003 when Penna and BT GS's HR team co-facilitated an event with the GS Executive. Maximizing Performance was a major change project and we all knew it would require the engagement of senior managers in order to succeed. It took several meetings to get the level of sponsorship we required but it was worth the investment of time, creating energy for the programme that remains to this day.

I talked about how this sponsorship had helped us with Frances Allcock, BT GS's Vice-President of Organization Capability. Allcock thought the programme's joint humanistic and commercial focus contributed to its success, and linked this to HR's need to balance its strategic partner and employee champion roles:

> Right from the early stages, the leadership were clear that there was a commercial imperative to maximize performance, but they also felt very strongly that, considering the contribution people were already making, 'our people deserve to be managed better'. They wanted managers to increase their contribution without working any harder and to manage our people asset in the business as any other asset, but not in a cold way – but because they deserve it. There was a lot of integrity in this and it helped us enormously.

The Workshops

To build upon the executive's enthusiasm for the programme, the programme team designed, facilitated and co-ordinated the delivery of 170 two-day workshops for BT GS's top 2000 managers worldwide. The programme was organized in a cascade with each manager attending a workshop led by their own manager before leading the workshop for their own team, supported by an HR practitioner and Penna consultant. The workshops were run as business meetings in intact teams and focused on helping managers to see people performance management as an opportunity to improve business performance rather than an administrative chore. One session focused on ensuring that personal objectives reflected opportunities for stretch in individual roles and within the business as a whole, and that these were aligned between team members. So managers were asked to share their objectives with

305

their peers, challenge each other's objectives and develop an understanding of where there were gaps and duplications between each other's and with the team's overall objectives. The intent here was to close the loop between business performance management and people performance management, ensuring that stretch in people's individual objectives would deliver the required business results.

The performance management system had been designed to be simple, clear and easy to understand because it was going to be used across 26 countries and 13 different languages. Supporting this, we wanted to show that managing people better did not require any new or sophisticated approaches, just doing very simple things consistently well. So the workshops were built on solid, commonly understood performance management principles. A highlight of the workshop was an exercise using Herzberg's theory on motivators and satisfiers (dating back to 1959!) that helped the line managers internalize the benefits of managing performance based upon their own experiences of being managed.

As well as defining 'what' people needed to do, Maximizing Performance was developed to focus on 'how' people needed to operate during this period of change. This was achieved by using BT's new leadership capabilities which were aligned with the business strategy and the group's values. To help managers experience living the values and to develop skills in giving feedback and coaching for performance, the workshops also incorporated role plays (using actors to ensure that scenarios were realistic) providing participants with accurate and valid suggestions for improving their performance in managing their people.

Management Charter

To help make performance management 'simple and complete', BT GS introduced a Management Charter outlining nine critical commitments they wanted line managers to make to drive the Maximizing Performance programme forward:

- All their people to have agreed roles and responsibilities.
- Ensure their people have 'SMART' objectives in place and that these are regularly reviewed (quarterly at a minimum).
- Proactively ensure that 1:1s do actually take place.
- Ensure that honest feedback is given and development needs are discussed.

- Ensure that their team's Development and Performance Reviews (DPRs) are completed on time and that 'levelling' takes place.
- Have regular people agenda items at their team meetings.
- Actively manage poor performers and poor attendance cases.
- Ensure that their own objectives are aligned and their behaviours are consistent with the BT internal brand values.
- Be open to the diverse nature of the organization.

Beeden commented:

> The Charter helped ensure managers knew exactly what they were being expected to do to make the programme a success. It also acted as a bill of rights helping everyone understand what they could expect from their managers. It's influenced what people are prepared to accept. If their managers are not displaying the right behaviours people are able to and do challenge.

Auditing Adherence to the Process

There has also been an extensive audit process. Every spring and autumn a high proportion of objectives are audited for SMARTness (actually only the Specific, Measurable and Timeliness aspects of the objectives are reviewed – the Achievable and Realistic elements not being easily audited).

The audit process has helped BT GS take action in areas where Maximizing Performance was not being applied effectively. It is, however, an after the event review, and GS have now also introduced an IT management system that audits and intervenes in the completion of quarterly reviews on a real-time basis. Beeden explained:

> We've introduced a tool across Customer Services which represents about a third of the GS organization, that drives the review process by flagging the need to do a review to managers. So when it's the end of quarter one and you need a review, you both get an email. Then if the review is overdue the system prompts you again. If it's still overdue the system reminds you again, and reminds your boss. When the manager puts the rating in the system you get an email telling you this and asking you to confirm the rating. If you get a Needs Improvement the system doesn't allow you to go forward until you've done a formal improvement plan. The system also asks, by the way, how was it for you? Was it good, very good, or outstanding? If it was poor or very poor you need to add a reason to explain. We get reports on this and can instantly see whether

managers are behaving in a way we would expect. Managers who have more than eight people can request reports on feedback within their team as well.

Measuring, and Performance Managing, Adherence

To ensure managers remained committed to the programme, all managers were given bonus-related objectives around Maximizing Performance. In addition, a Performance Metrics Dashboard (PMD) was developed for the senior managers and those managers who manage a significantly sized team, that is they had 70 or more total reports. This showed how managers had performed using one overall rating developed from four different areas of people management:

- experience: a clear sense of direction;
- capabilities: performance reviews and talent management;
- culture: completion of SMART objectives, DPR ratings and performance improvement plans;
- image: living the values.

Allcock explained:

> The power of the PMD is in its simplicity. It has a huge amount of face validity. The Charter says what people should have and the PMD measures the things in the Charter. There's a clear line of sight between what's important, what managers are measured on and what they need to do differently. They're all things that are actionable as well. If the PMD says that people don't think their people get one to ones, the manager has only got two issues: either their people do get one to ones and there's something wrong in the way they're doing it, or if not then their people need to have them! A lot of HR metrics are too complicated – managers don't know what they need to do.

The PDM is not hardwired to reward but does form part of a manager's annual performance rating and pay could be directly affected as a result. Oleh Godun is an HCM Manager who had previously worked in EP First (now part of PwC Saratoga) and has been working on measurements within BT Group and GS. He built on Allcock's comments on the PMD:

> It's a very powerful tool. Critically, it's got the strong backing of the Chief Executive – it gives him a top level view of all his managers.

We have lots of metrics about the business and each team but this one gives him an unbiased appreciation of how well each manager is managing people performance in their area. Although it is not hardwired to reward managers do pay attention to it, querying their scores and scrutinizing the variables contributing to the overall rating. PMD has a very clear formula behind it and every component is in the managers' control to influence.

Measurement and Reporting

Working with Godun and the programme team at BT, and in tandem with other work at Penna, we developed a reporting system, tracking progress at the four levels in the HCM value chain. Figure 10.3 illustrates the sorts of outputs and business impacts that were identified and measured to support each of BT GS's four key HR programmes. Godun explained:

It's really a summarized view of the HR strategy. But presented like this, it's provided us with a really good way of managing and monitoring our campaigns. We look at whether the milestones and deliverables are achieved in the context of the desired outputs and bottom line

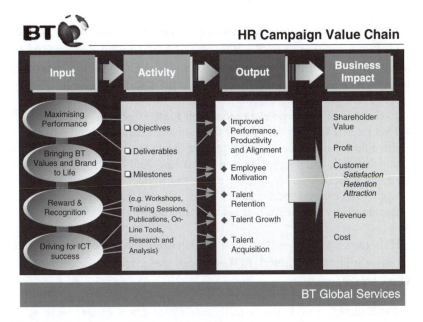

Figure 10.3 BT Global Services HCM value chain

business impact. When these improve that gives us confidence that the campaign has worked as expected. It's difficult to pin down that one thing has caused another, but if the output measures are deteriorating that gives that extra stimulus to review the effectiveness of the campaign and, if required, introduce remedial action quicker.

BT was clear that few of their Business Impact or Output measures (for example, overall employee engagement, attendance-related pay, absence rate, and cost and resignation rate) could be directly linked to just one campaign. Instead, many are likely to be impacted by and should be shared across all four programmes. Godun commented:

> You can measures inputs, activities and outputs for each campaign. But it's extremely difficult to attribute any particular impact measure to any campaign. The closer to the bottom line the vaguer the link because there are so many contributing factors.

Beeden also commented on the difficulty in measuring the more intangible aspects of the programme:

> Measurement is a blunt instrument. It's fine on the 'what' but you can't have the same level of measurements for the 'how'. This is personal and subjective, there's not always a right or wrong.

Each of the measures was associated with a mechanism to provide the information. For example, BT's people engagement survey (CARE) provided an overall view of engagement. Margaret Savage, who was previously acting as chief HR officer for BT GS, commented:

> Every team of more than eight people gets CARE feedback in team form. I get the HR functions as head of the function. I can delve into some of the differences between areas in terms of team behaviour, participation and feedback, and then get into action planning. And I get my own team's results as well. I can see whether we are managing change well as a top team. I can ask what particular results are, check what is happening, and use the survey meaningfully to set goals to improve.

BT's measurement system also demonstrated how benchmarks like Saratoga's Human Capital ROI support the internal measurements. Allcock explained:

> The Human Capital ROI ratio really shows people how we are managing people compared to other leading organizations in the sector, and how

much return we are getting for our investment. It really captured people's interest.

However, as Godun explained, benchmarks were only included where these were seen to make sense within the value chain, not just because the benchmarks were available. He pointed out that:

> Saratoga provides us with a very useful top-level reference which is the starting point for the investigation. But it is the understanding of the underlying mechanisms that adds real value. The data we're interrogating using our recently implemented data warehouse enables us to undertake this sort of complex analysis.

The Results

Effective design, facilitation and programme management ensured a real change in line managers' behaviour and a corresponding impact on business results. BT GS's Executive links these results directly to the outputs from the Maximizing Performance programme.

Input

At the input level, we managed to keep levels of sponsorship and engagement high, and ensured budget spend was producing value for money. The first year required the greatest, pump-priming expenditure of over £1million and in this year, GS's Chief Executive, Andy Green commented that:

> If I had any spare budget I would only consider giving it to the HR team during 2003/04 as they have demonstrated such an efficient use of budget to date and have such a clear strategic requirement.

I am sure most readers will agree this is not the sort of remark that Chief Executives usually make about HR expenditure!

Activity

At the activity level, the Maximizing Performance programme was implemented successfully all over the world within the agreed timescale. Business teams commented positively on the excellent support they received from the programme team in raising their performance.

Verbatim comments were consistent and include comments from line managers such as:

- 'Excellent, well worth the investment of my time.'
- 'Very thought-provoking.'
- 'This highlights opportunities for everyone and I look forward to taking my team through the process.'

Green summarized the feedback, saying:

We've had excellent feedback. People are saying that this focus on our people and enabling them to work better, has come at the right time. The content of the workshops is right and if anything people want to spend longer on it!'

The quality of SMART objectives has been audited for each of the last three years and average scores have improved from 0.87 to 2.05 out of 3. The distribution of performance ratings has also improved dramatically (see Figure 10.4). Allcock thought that this was one of the most significant results of the programme:

We tend to forget the enormity of the change – I don't know of any other organizations where we've seen this scale of change.

Increased Performance Deifferentiation

Penna

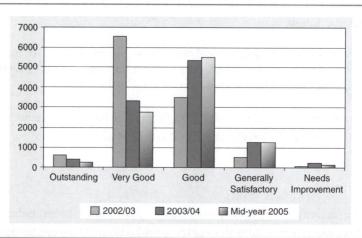

Figure 10.4 BT Global Services distribution of performance ratings

Note that BT have not enforced a normal distribution curve. The graph is a distribution of ratings that has moved towards a normal distribution through effective management of performance. Allcock explained:

We don't have a forced distribution. Yes, managers are targeted on getting something close to this, but we give them a generous, slightly skewed distribution to aim at, and although this is a factor in their PMD, only 8 per cent of the PMD score is based on the distribution and they can still get 'best in class' in their PMD and score zero in this particular piece.

Changes in the distribution of annual ratings mean that BT is able to deal with lower performers and generally raise the bar on performance. The company can identify the 20 per cent of people who receive a rating below 'good' and have targeted business leaders on managing up 90 per cent of these and managing out the other 10 per cent, which is 2 per cent of their total employee population. From a base of practically no one, the numbers of people being managed out has increased to several hundred per year as a result of the programme. Beeden commented:

We've got a benchmark of this for other high performing businesses of between 4 and 5 per cent. But we think that 2 per cent is an appropriately challenging target for a more paternalistic business like BT. And our real focus is managing up the other 90 per cent in an environment where everybody's contribution is increasing.

Allcock added that:

Active management of poor performance is a fairness thing too. Our people deserve not to have to carry other people because their managers aren't doing what they should. Our engagement survey shows that managers agree that poor performance is being tackled.

Output

In terms of output, BT GS know that as a result of the programme, their people are more aligned with and more engaged in the business. Measures for the individual senior managers have indicated very positive changes in behaviour. BT's annual CARE survey has demonstrated continuing improvements over the period of the project, for example, those responding positively to the item 'I clearly know how my work contributes to the success of the company' increased from 84 to 91 per cent from 2002/03 to 2003/04.

Savage commented on this:

> The survey has given us plenty of evidence that the 'how' is changing. The way that managers are talking to people is showing more focus on the 'how' as well as the 'what'. People are saying they have more awareness of the corporate strategy, of business performance in the context of the strategy, they have more belief that senior managers know what they are doing and that they are managing change. They have better relationships with their line manager, they feel they understand their job and have the capability to do it.

The programme has also helped to extend HR's credibility in the business. For example, the BT GS Executive recognized the success of the Maximizing Performance programme by awarding the HR team the prestigious 'Excellence' award on the basis of the implementation and outcomes of the programme (the first time HR had ever won it). Andy Green, BT GS's Chief Executive commented:

> The Maximizing Performance campaign along with the other HR strategy interventions are the best HR programmes I have seen in the past decade.

Impact

Best of all, measures for business impact show clear and significant improvements in business performance. Between 2002/03 and 2003/04:

- BT's benchmark for HR effectiveness, the Human Capital Return on Investment increased by 92 per cent;
- revenue/employee increased by 17 per cent and earnings before interest, taxes, depreciation and amortization/employee by 45 per cent.

At the outset when the first workshop was run in April 2003, the BT GS Executive commented that they would know if this was a successful project if, unlike other performance management programmes before it, it was still thriving one year on. Three years later, BT GS is still progressing on Maximizing Performance, which also points to the successful development of engagement and sponsorship for the programme within and throughout the whole organization. Allcock explained:

> It's an essential piece of our current transformation. The senior managers have said, 'Let's not reinvent the wheel – we'll use Maximizing Performance'. Three years later, they still see the programme as an enabler. A lot of organizations still need to understand that deep change takes this long. They think that one year they can do this and the next year reward or whatever it might be. Well yes they can as long as they keep their existing programmes moving forward too.

The company has seen other, unexpected benefits of the programme with their recent phase of acquisitions and the new Connected World strategy that requires teams to work together much more than in the past. Beeden explained:

> Maximizing Performance has now been extended to all of our acquisitions and joint ventures. It's become an integral part of the employee proposition, helping to create allegiance and driving the behaviours we want, ensuring we can form teams for all areas of the business. People still talk about it, I still get emails saying 'when we did Max Performance you mentioned ...' The fact that people are still talking about it shows that it's in the lifeblood of the organization. And this wouldn't be the case if it hadn't had the impact that it has.

Why This is HCM

BT is well down the road to HCM. They already have several years' experience of collecting, analysing and using measures for people management. As an example, they have identified that average employee absence is about 13 days per year (which in 2002 was costing them £89 million per year). However, employees working part-time or at home took just three days' sick per annum. This has provided powerful evidence to support the extension of their work–life balance programmes. Most recently, the company has been building a data warehouse linked to a new PeopleSoft 8 HR system and topped with self-service reporting tools. It means that BT can now manage all their people data internally and can organize the data from the PeopleSoft system and other databases for effective reporting and interrogation. BT believes that the analysis from this data will help them identify new opportunities for making improvements in people management. The company has also incorporated people data in external reporting and, in 2005, won PwC's annual Building Public Trust Award for people reporting practices.

Most importantly to me, BT has demonstrated the ability to be highly innovative in their people management thinking and tight in its execution. I was particularly impressed by the way the HR team focused on the needs of their customers to develop a set of people values that aligned with the company's brand values in order to align their people activities with customer needs. BT also uses measurement intelligently as a means to support their innovative approaches.

I could not say that I knew Maximizing Performance would be an example of HCM at the start of the programme, but looking back, it is clear that this was not a normal HR project with a typical set of HR achievements. I think the most important aspects of the programme that make it stand out as an example of HCM are that:

- there was a clear business imperative (of improving contribution per FTE by at least 5 per cent);
- there was extensive commitment from senior leaders and participation from across the business (through a small number of champions involved in delivering the workshops, and from managers spending time in attending their manager's workshop and then in leading a workshop for their own team);
- the programme involved a broad range of people management activities (for example, reward and communication as well as the development workshops) and was executed well;
- the HCM value matrix was used to measure and improve its execution;
- the programme focused on producing intangible value, in this case, performance management capability;
- there were tangible and very impressive business results;
- there has been learning, and improvements have been made over time.

Allcock commented on her learning over the last few years:

> We underestimated the amount of re-education that would need to be provided. People lose sight of why we're doing something. If I ask them to explain what Maximizing Performance is here to drive forward they'll sometimes say it's about a fixed distribution – no, that's not the answer! And when this happens they focus on the actions rather than the spirit of the original intent. Every year we need to invest as much time if not

more than we did at the beginning, or the programme starts to become mechanistic and we lose its spirit. There are still things we can do better. For example, we've got a lot of leakage. We really need a first-time manager programme to be provided on promotion, and induction of new managers. We have put all of our acquisitions through Maximizing Performance but not our new recruits!

I especially like the use of performance management to illustrate HCM because this, probably more than any other HR process, tends to be seen as an administrative chore, an HR bolt-on that is part of the bureaucracy that has little to do with how managers run the business. In fact, performance management is absolutely critical to HCM. It is the key process that translates strategy into actions and is, or should be, one of the top two or three business priorities for any line manager. BT's experience has proved the impact that performance management can have on business success.

The project was also a good example of best fit. Everything revolved around the alignment of objectives within BT's project structure and increasingly complicated matrix and the need to drive out inefficiency.

I have put the case study in Chapter 10 because I think that the implementation of the HCM programme is, above all, where BT GS have excelled. They have used measurement not just for reporting but to influence and drive changes in behaviour in line with the programme's objectives. This includes their use of the People Metrics Dashboard, quarterly review monitoring system and eepulse (mentioned previously in Chapter 9).

Summary

Reader: *'I think that's a great case study, and clearly demonstrates some impressive results. If there was one thing that helped BT achieve these results, what would that be?'*

Author: 'I think more than anything, it was their desire and effort to make a difference; to transform the business; to find the new sigmoid curve. I think this is shown in the resources they devoted to this programme, the fact that the programme is still in place several years later on, their emphasis on both SMART and stretch objectives, and so on. Of course, given where BT was at the time I got involved, the company didn't really have any choice but to transform. That's why I list one of the attributes of an HCM programme as dealing with something that's mission critical – something that keeps the CEO and the company's investors awake at night. The real key, remembering Handy's advice in Chapter 2, is to create your own sense of urgency to transform your business before you get this far.'

References

Boxall, P. and Purcell, J. (2003). *Strategy and Human Resource Management*. Palgrave Macmillan.

Frangos, C.A. and Johnson, L.K. (2005). 'Creating a strategy-focused workforce by aligning key HR processes', *Balanced Scorecard Report*, September–October, 10–11.

Gates, S. (2003). *Linking People Measures to Strategy*. The Conference Board. Report Number: R-1342-03-RR. December.

Ghoshal, S. and Bartlett, C.A. (1998). *The Individualized Corporation: A Fundamentally New Approach to Management*. Heinemann.

Gratton, L. (2000). *Living strategy: putting people at the heart of corporate purpose*. Pearson Education.

Gratton, L. (1999). People Process as a Source of Competitive Advantage. In *Strategic Human Resource Management: Corporate Rhetoric and Human Reality*. (L. Gratton, V. Hope Hailey, P. Stiles and C. Truss, eds) Oxford University Press, pp. 170–198.

Kaplan, R.S. and Norton, D.P. (1996). 'Using the balanced scorecard as a strategic management system', *Harvard Business Review*, January–February, 75–85.

Kaplan, R.S. and Norton, D.P. (2001). *The Strategy-Focused Organization: How Balanced Scorecard Companies Thrive in the New Business Environment*. Harvard Business School Press.

Lester, T. (2004). 'Measure for measure', *Financial Times*, 5 October.

Pfeffer, J. (1998). *The Human Equation: Building Profits by Putting People First*. Harvard Business School Press.

Stiles, P. (1999). Transformation at the Leading Edge. In: *Strategic Human Resource Management: Corporate Rhetoric and Human Reality*. (L. Gratton, V. Hope Hailey, P. Stiles and C. Truss, eds). Oxford University Press

Sveiby, K.E. (2004). 'When measuring fails – try learning!' *Journal of Learning and Intellectual Capital*, 1(3).

11

HCM Reporting

Introduction

Reader: *'I take it that reporting is the last stage in the strategic HCM planning cycle?'*

Author: 'Yes, although it's not the end of a chain but a link to the next cycle of strategy development, providing the information that all those concerned with an organization's HCM activities need to make appropriate decisions. Also, of course, in reality, the processes are likely to take place in a rather more integrated fashion than is suggested by this rather sequential process. But I do think that getting as close as possible to this sequential cycle makes sense. Doing this ensures that organizations are reporting on the right information to the right people. It also helps organizations move away from the far too common situation in which they use their data warehousing and reporting capabilities to provide data to people, vaguely hoping that someone will find it useful.'

Levels of Reporting

This chapter will look at three different levels of reporting ranked in terms of the value they provide. The lowest level refers to compliance reporting to regulators and focuses on data, basic practices and value for money. The next level is reporting to investors on how people management adds value to the business plan. The highest level of value in reporting is obtained by internal reporting on value creation to employees, managers and the Board.

Putting the audiences for reporting in this order may surprise some readers. The fact that HCM focuses partly on the needs of investors can be taken to mean that they are also the most important stakeholders. For example, Kearns (2004) states that whereas HRM is focused on managers and employees: 'The most important stakeholders in HCM are external – the City, government, shareholders.' If this is true, then investors should also be the prime focus for creating value from reporting.

However, I do not agree that investors are the most important stakeholders in HCM. It is true that creating value HCM is about developing people and organizational capability to delight investors, as well as other stakeholders. But the most important stakeholders in creating this value are the people in an organization. And investors are only ever going to be delighted by transformational results, not wonderful reporting. This suggests that the concerns I expressed in the Preface and Chapter 1 about the accidental linking of reporting and the term 'HCM' were well founded. Investors want information about how people are being managed to deliver objectives in the business plan. They do not expect organizations to report on how they are creating value through their people. External reporting to investors is about HRM not the creating value level of HCM.

Compliance Reporting

There is an ongoing need to report to government and regulators using efficiency metrics and standards. These bodies are not generally interested in strategic information but need to ensure that basic minimum levels of performance have been met and that they are made aware of other key issues affecting the business. Examples include notification of redundancies to the DTI, production of a remuneration report by listed companies (including salaries, fees, bonuses, expenses, compensation for loss of office and other benefits paid to Directors) and reporting of injuries, diseases and dangerous occurrences (RIDDOR) to the Health and Safety Executive. Other requirements exist within particular sectors. For example in financial services, this level of reporting relates to the tick box approach to compliance against training and competence standards required by the Financial Services Authority (FSA).

Reporting to Investors and Stakeholders

This level of reporting relies on information about adding value activities and added value resources and capabilities, aligned with the business plan. Investors are not particularly looking for, and companies are unlikely to report on, the more transformational actions they are taking to create value through their people. Some companies even think that reporting adding value information will result in releasing too much sensitive internal information. In fact this is unlikely to be the case. As covered earlier, knowing what one company is doing and trying to replicate it are two different things. Referring to 'There's more to cooking than reading the recipe' (a paper by Autier and Durand, professors at E.M. Lyon, and Gates from the Conference Board), Hayashi (2003) reports that because human capital is embedded in complex social systems:

> When it comes to human resources, competitors may know the ingredients and recipe, but that doesn't mean they'll automatically be able to prepare the same dish.

This is why companies feel able to volunteer themselves as case studies and talk about their experience at conferences. The potential for raising their reputation easily outweighs concerns about losing competitive advantage. In any case, companies already report a range of non-financial information. For example, oil companies report on their proven oil reserves and pharmaceutical firms report on their 'pipelines' of new drugs and the remaining life of patents.

However, only a small amount of information on people management currently gets reported to investors. In Penna's research that was reported in Chapter 8 (Finn and Ingham, 2004), only 29 per cent of respondents stated that they reported on HCM measures externally. A recent report by Dave Ulrich's RBL Group and Creelman Research found a similar lack of reporting within Fortune 50 firms:

> Only 10% of Fortune 50 firms reported employee satisfaction/engagement metrics in their Annual Reports or Corporate Social Responsibility Reports. 74% of Fortune 50 firms did not even mention employee satisfaction/engagement results (qualitative or quantitative results) in these communications with investors. (Ulrich et al., 2006)

Companies will not have to report a great deal and nothing above the value for money level to meet the requirements of the new Business Review which has replaced the OFR. However, there is still demand for non-regulated best practice reporting. This demand was demonstrated by the consistently negative reaction from a wide range of investors and business bodies to the withdrawal of the updated OFR requirements. For example, the FT's Accountancy column noted that:

> Not all shareholders have called for mandatory OFRs to be reinstated but they do all agree there is a desperate need for better narrative reporting. (Jopson, 2006)

This indicates that pressure for more meaningful reporting on non-financial issues is only going to increase. In many ways, nothing substantial has actually changed. Standardized or mandatory reporting was only ever going to apply at the value for money level. No form of legislation is going to change how companies report at the adding value level. Organizations will only report on how their HR processes meet the needs of their business strategies if their investors and other stakeholders demand this information.

However, many signs suggest that investors are still not terribly interested in people management information. HSBC organized a conference call as part of the Accounting for People consultation but got only seven Corporate Social Responsibility (CSR) focused fund managers dialling in. Denise Kinsgmill explained:

> Some analysts don't know what we are talking about. We need to educate the investment community on what constitutes the drivers of productivity. Chief executives are a lot further along the road than investors, who are a little old-fashioned. (IRS, 2003)

Grossman (2005) identifies two more factors that explain investors' and analysts' lack of interest: firstly, that they typically have experience in finance and accounting rather than HR; and secondly, that they tend to be untypical of the workforce in many organizations. They typically have very short-term perspectives and find it difficult to understand the value of a lot of people management activities which, as I explained in Chapter 10, is often longer term.

If this is true, then investors' perspectives are going to need to change. Kingsmill referred to a 'spotlight of accountability' falling on investors who, due to the increasing professionalism of the fund management industry, will increasingly be expected to talk about the basis for their recommendations, their own targets and objectives and their remuneration. Investors will also be put under increasing pressure from pension fund trustees prompted by growing shareholder activism, and from chief executives of companies which are reporting effectively on people management and want to gain credit from investors for the information they are providing.

In fact, there are positive signs that investors do already use people management information. One example of this comes from research conducted by Ernst & Young (1997), studying the use of financial and non-financial data in 300 sell-side analyst reports and by 275 buy-side investors. The firm's researchers found that 35 per cent of investment decisions made by buy-side analysts and portfolio managers are determined by non-financial information. The more non-financial measures they used, the more accurate their earnings forecasts proved to be. The ten measures that matter most to sell-side analysts together with the way that these are linked to people management in the HCM value chain are shown below:

- Execution of corporate strategy (this is about managing through people – see Chapter 10).
- Management credibility (refers to the output step in the HCM value chain).
- Quality of strategy (people management adds value to business strategy).
- Ability to innovate (output).
- Ability to attract and retain talented people (activity).
- Market share (impact).
- Management experience (output).
- Alignment of compensation with shareholder interests (activity).
- Research leadership (impact).
- Quality of major processes (output).

The use of non-financial, including people management, information may already be increasing. For example, in 2005, Macquarie, an Australian bank, downgraded the shares of National Australia Bank (owners of Yorkshire and Clydesdale Banks in the UK) from 'buy' to 'hold' after a staff survey which showed very low engagement scores. Another positive sign of this shift was the formation of the Enhanced Analytics Initiative in 2004. This group of institutional investors has agreed to allocate 5 per cent of their broker commissions on the basis of how well brokers integrate analysis of extra-financial issues and intangibles. The group hopes that by doing this it will create an ongoing improvement in the quality and creativity of research and believes that this can reduce risk and may add value too.

The remaining reticence of investors may be down to them not understanding the value of the information that could be provided. It is no wonder they are not interested when they think all they will be getting is bland statements or standard metrics. Once they start to see reports built upon the frameworks provided in this book, I believe they will start to demand similar high value information from all firms.

I talked about investors' perspectives on people management reporting with representatives of two investment firms, Lauri Bassi at McBassi and Rob Lake and Jane Goodland at Henderson.

Perspectives on Reporting at McBassi & Company. I spoke first to Lauri Bassi, previously Vice-President of Research at the American Society of Training and Development (ASTD) and head of the HCM research company, McBassi & Company, and an investment firm, Bassi Investments, that 'invests in firms that invest in their people'.

At ASTD, Bassi used data on thousands of organizations around the world to research the connection between investment in training and organizational performance. In direct contrast to Watson Wyatt's findings (in Chapter 3), investment in employee training turned out to be the single most powerful predictor of stock price increases that Bassi could identify.

Bassi Investments looks to invest in firms that spend at least double the typical 2 per cent of payroll on training and also support their investment effectively through associated HR practices. Data is compiled from multiple sources to support annual direct requests from Bassi Investments to companies' investor relations departments. Bassi's investment company then uses proprietary algorithms to combine per capita training expenditures and a small number of traditional financial measures to develop recommendations about inclusion and weighting in their portfolios.

Using this model, Bassi Investments' overall portfolio of large investing firms has beaten the market by about 33 per cent per annum. However, the invested funds currently consist of just a couple of million dollars. Bassi reports a small but growing trickle of interest.

But major promotions targeted at, firstly, training professionals, and secondly, large union funds, have generated very little in the way of results. This reflects some of the inertia that will need to be shifted if non-financial reporting is going to be effective in changing investor behaviour.

However, the investment arm is primarily there to make a point – that Bassi and her colleagues trust their analysis enough to put their money on it. Bassi explained:

> What it has really shown us is that we should invest in any company that hires us. It shows they're serious about their investment in human capital.

Over the last three years, Bassi's HCM company has extended its analysis from training expenditure to other people management indicators:

> We started out with training because this has budgetary numbers associated with it. The numbers are still not easy to get at, but they do exist. They're the only metrics we currently have that are sufficiently quantifiable to be investor grade. The intention is that, over time, we will develop our broader HCM metrics so that these can also be used as a basis for our investments.

If Bassi's funds can be as successful as they have been based purely on such a blunt measure as training (that could indicate inappropriate investment just as easily as it could a proactive commitment) then they and other investors must surely be able to benefit from the use of a broader set of people management measures and metrics.

Perspectives on Reporting at Henderson. One fund manager that is already active in understanding more about HCM is Henderson Global Investments. I spoke to Jane Goodland, who was a senior analyst in Henderson's Sustainable and Responsible Investment (SRI) team, and Rob Lake, Henderson's Head of Corporate Engagement, who was also on the DTI working group on materiality in the OFR. Lake is working with the firm's conventional financial analysts to understand how a better appreciation of people management can help improve investment decisions, not just in the SRI area but across all of their funds. Lake and Goodland emphasized that the key to gaining investors' interest is providing proof that people management does impact on business performance but that this requires companies to develop a better appreciation of these links first. At the time of writing, Henderson were running an experiment, talking to companies, including their HR directors, and asking about human capital. Lake explained:

> Lack of interest by investors isn't the only issue. Many companies' measurement systems and capabilities are still really shaky. HR has never been accountable the way other parts of the organization have. They've never been asked to provide information on budgets or returns on investment. Even when they do, the starting point is normally about corporate responsibility, it's about showing how nice you are. It's not about how well you're managing this asset. Businesses and HR need to work out what accounts for their success – they need to have a clear position on this if they are going to help investors understand it. Is it health and safety? Is it diversity? What is it and why is this good for their business?
>
> It'll be interesting to see whether understanding these issues adds enough value; whether the time that's spent doing this, rather than doing the things that are usually done, helps us make just as good investment decisions.

Author: 'What sort of information do you think companies need to collect and report to help develop this understanding?'

Goodland: 'You need quantitative data to support analytics and to enable you to compare peers with peers. But you need the qualitative stuff as well. This tends to come out through sitting down with the Chief Executive; it's not the sort of thing that's easy to publish in a report. But then companies will always tell you that they're leading edge and you need the quantitative metrics to challenge this as well. So it's a bit of a chicken and egg thing.

Let's look at engagement as an example. There should be some common, underlying constituents of engagement that are a bit more amenable to reporting. Things like absenteeism; turnover; pay rates compared to benchmark and so on. Of course, these still need to be interpreted. Low turnover isn't always good – down to a threshold it's good and then below this it might be bad. I think you need some sort of sector-based comparison for this.'

Author: 'I was with Bob Stack at Cadbury Schweppes this morning and he was saying, and he is one of the few HR directors that attend meetings with investors, that in his experience investors don't care about anything but outputs. He said that if he could give them a vial of magic liquid that would provide the capability the business needs, then they'd be happy, they'd say take it, get rid of HR. Do you think investors are interested in a range of inputs and activities as well as outputs being reported?

Goodland: 'Ideally I think you would report measures at all those levels. Some investors are interested in all these measures and some aren't. But most are interested in what the companies are doing, how effective their interventions are and what impact these have on business performance. It's important that companies focus reporting on the things that matter most, it's not about providing reams and reams of information. But it's not just about outputs.'

Lake: 'But there's a lot of things investors take no notice of, or just a glimmering interest. To some extent, they do pay most attention to what comes out of the black box, they wait until the earnings drop out at the end, rather than trying to understand what is the company's internal capability to respond to certain things.

It's a huge challenge, not just for human capital. You can take any given issue where it's self-evidently important to do well – it's still not necessarily worth investors trying to understand it. They just don't really have time to get to grips with it. Other things are still as or more important to investors. If Sainsbury's can't get stuff on the shelves this could be about people's capabilities but it could be about computer systems or many other things.

But companies don't like talking about what they are trying to do internally either. It's too easy to run into things that are commercially sensitive or just plain embarrassing. And the relationship between a company and its investors is a very important thing. If they say the

327

wrong thing the investors go back to their desks and sell the shares. Companies manage their relationships with their investors very carefully. It's about communicating good news, or very carefully managed bad news. So the companies keep to the financials as the other stuff gets too difficult.'

Author: 'What about the HCM ratings that are being developed. Do you think these would help investors?'

Goodland: 'Ratings might be useful – it depends on how they are derived. From what I've seen they look very complex. And the same question applies around correlation and causation. Can they demonstrate that a company with an AAA rating is more likely to outperform its competitors? If they could persuade investors that they have a robust and intelligent methodology then they might be onto a winner. If it's just about giving them a tick because they've got a diversity policy in place then great, but actually we can do that ourselves.'

Reporting to Boards, Managers and Employees

This top level of reporting suggests that the main focus of reporting should be internal, not external. Creating value is about developing people and organizational capability to delight investors. Delighting them is about delivering improvements in business results and this can be supported by internal HCM reporting. So this level of reporting is about providing the information that the Board, managers and employees need to be as effective as possible and in particular to help their learning about HCM rather than to support control. Internal reporting should be a learning process and a journey of self-discovery.

Internal reporting focuses on the competitive differentiators that drive the business – these are not measures that will generally be reported externally due to the confidential nature of this information.

Board directors need to understand the changing value of human capital and the actions being taken to increase this value as a key lead indicator of future business success. Line managers need to understand

HCM to support their role in managing people to provide this success. Employees need information on HCM to help understand the return they are getting on their investment of personal human capital, supporting their engagement with the organization and helping them to manage their careers. Davenport (1999) explains:

> Instead of worrying about calculating the worth of human assets, companies should concern themselves with defining what human capital owners get out of their association with a business. In other words, they should focus less on the value of the individual to the organization, and more on the value of the organization to the individual.

Reporting to Internal Stakeholders
The same three levels of reporting are also found internally within large groups. Johnson and Scholes (1984) refer to these levels when they describe three ways a holding company can manage its business units: financial control (value for money), strategic control (adding value) and strategic planning (creating value).

The reporting of government departments to the Cabinet Office provides another example of reporting to internal stakeholders.

Government Department Reporting to the Cabinet Office

Mike Watts is HR Transformation Director at the Cabinet Office. He manages a team of nine people charged with speeding up the pace of change within the HR function and in people management activities across the civil service. I talked to Watts about the capability reviews that the Cabinet Secretary, Gus O'Donnell, had introduced to review the capabilities of all central government departments.

Author: 'How does HCM fit in with the capability reviews?'

Watts: 'The capability review is about whether a department, and more specifically its leadership team, are ready to deliver targets which are important to the elected government, and whether they have the capability to deliver on whatever those targets may be in the future. Can they lead the organization, come up with a decent strategy and deliver that strategy across a value chain that is not just the department

329

creating the policy but includes other people and organizations too? How ready is the organization to drive that agenda? This will give us data individually by department but will also start to show patterns that are emerging across the whole civil service.

I believe HCM is about whether an organization has the people it needs, which, together with the way it organizes those people, helps produce the capability that's required to deliver whatever the organization is there to deliver. This fits in with the capability review because capability is a measure of whether people are ready to deliver effectively. This is largely a measure of HCM. It may not be called that but this is what it is. Especially if we consider HCM to be wider than just skills but also to be about the organization, and therefore about how you bring those skills to bear on a problem.'

Author: 'And what's your view about the role of measurement within HCM?'

Watts: 'Measurement needs to be part of the performance improvement cycle. It needs to be about the things you have to put in place to make something better, not just whether something's better or not. After all, the pig doesn't get any fatter simply because you measure it. You need to measure the things you're giving to the pig like the foodstuffs and its environment. If you measure and quantify the environment in which you've got the pig, and use this to work out what affects the pig, then the pig can get fatter. So, for example, it's not that helpful to measure engagement in isolation without understanding what difference leadership or the performance management process or the way the organization is organized is making to it. The value is in having a discussion about how the patterns of measures are interplaying with each other. This is not always about absolute cause and effect but there will be correlations.

Equally, measures help you get clarity that everyone's actually talking about the same thing rather than having a set of words where everyone's talking about something slightly different. If you have a set of words with a set of measures and a set of targets it becomes very difficult to be talking about things differently. So you need measures because otherwise you're not looking at the same thing necessarily, nor can you necessarily work out the interplay between these things. And doing this is more important than looking at any one measure in isolation.

You can collect data in different ways for different reasons. Absence management is a good example. Some people collect absence data because they want to measure the availability of people. Other people may see it as a measure of productivity or as a measure of line manager capability. So it could be a measure of at least three different things. You need to be clear about why you're measuring it and what else you need to understand for that measure to be useful.

You also need to understand who measurement is for. Accounting for People was aimed at the City and investors. This is a worthwhile and laudable aim because having informed investors is a better place to be. But how can you inform your investors about your measures and the interplay between them unless you have a clear handle on these things for yourself first? You need to make sure you can measure the predictors of success, not measure success itself. That's why I disagree with people who say you can always put a pound sign on human capital. Well eventually, yes. But HCM is about finding more qualitative ways of understanding what you've got, and whether that's likely to turn into a pound sign, as opposed to finding a way of making it equal a pound sign — because that's what's already happened as opposed to what might happen. If you believe that strategy is iterative and emergent you can't spend all your time disconnected from lead measures. Doing so shows limited and deliberate thinking, a belief in absolute cause and effect rather than an interest in correlations that might or might not influence the choices that Boards might make.

Then it's a question of what you can release to your investors to help them make an informed decision. What can you use to prove that the top team are on top of their organization's capability relative to its promises? Just having a set of things being routinely reported without knowing whether the management team are really on top of those things doesn't strike me as something that's going to be very useful. It isn't as if there is absolute comparability between organizations.'

Author: 'Can you explain a little more about your views on the limited and deliberate style of thinking you mentioned?'

Watts: 'There's a school of thought about planning and strategy that sets out an A to B route map. But in practice, while you need this as a start point, a useful metaphor is that once the first shot has been fired it all goes to hell in a handbasket because things change, things happen, things emerge that you didn't foresee. Although, through the planning process rather than the plan, if the planning was very thorough, you will have probably covered lots of possibility. So even if the deliberate plan doesn't necessarily show it, you're more ready for the possibilities. You have to get the right mix between emergent and deliberate planning. And to have a system which allows for emergent issues to be brought into the plan and make the plan live and breathe. It's about getting the right blend between the two things. This is particularly true when it comes to things like HCM. Having a deliberate people strategy is one thing. But what's more important is interpreting and understanding how the factors are interplaying with each other and coming up with some decision that you can test a little bit further down the way to ensure that your hypothesis is working out correctly.

Very little in HCM is hard cause and effect. If you have 50 or 60 of the same retail outlets it's much easier to isolate factors and turn up the dial on a few issues to see what impact something has in branches depending on how well it was done. So a retail network has distinct advantages in terms of more obvious correlation and cause and effect. In less comparable organizations it's a more complex picture than that. You can count the amount of resources that you have available and to a degree that's a level of HCM.

But this doesn't take account of people's skills or motivation, or of the leadership that is going to make sure that people have got the right skills and motivation. Understanding the interplay between measures takes judgement around a whole lot of variables. And the more variables that make up the full picture the harder this is.

These are issues you've got to deal with and this is what makes HCM so fascinating. Perhaps to some people's minds this is not scientific enough. I can understand that if you've got a certain way of thinking about life, then all this feels quite woolly and difficult. And to be honest I don't feel 100 per cent comfortable about it. But I do realize it's something different, something that is quite difficult to explain. But you either have to pretend that it's something that it's not, or live with the fact that it's woolly and ambiguous and try to work out a way of managing it in these terms. There is a new way of thinking, a whole new set of disciplines, that are required for HCM that probably are not prevalent in a lot of top teams. So there's a real issue in getting traction with senior teams. The thing about moving an organization is if you're too much outside the common sense you won't move it forward. So I think you've got to find the language and a way of engaging people who don't necessarily think that way or even want to think that way but who are very powerful nevertheless. If you don't, it's a great idea but it's got no traction.'

Author: 'Other than the capability reviews, what is the Cabinet Office's role in HCM?'

Watts: 'From the centre, I am trying to get agreement that ultimately people and the organization are what turn to results. So while you need to manage current performance, you also need to be putting sufficient time and effort into future desired performance, and building the capability to make that happen. And we need a consistent understanding of HR's role in managing human capital; of HR's role in terms of what a good HR function does in that new space.

333

Understanding whether HR functions are mature enough is one aspect of what we're doing – helping them get better at their role and ensuring they're developing their understanding of HCM, for themselves and with their boards. I believe one of the indicators of whether they're a maturing HR function is that they do have an informed hypothesis about their HCM value chain and that this is regularly discussed at board level. But not just in isolation, it needs to be connected to what's going on in the business. This means that we need to use their set of measures rather than imposing a set. So what you might measure for effective leadership in one department might be quite different to another. It wouldn't make sense to impose a set of measures. Instead of this, we've got a framework we call our 'maturity matrix' to ensure departments have got certain types of measures in place and are working with them in the right way. We're concerned with four levels of measurement: operational effectiveness, making pieces of change happen, aligning the organization in a holistic way with the executive strategy, and informing strategy, which is your 'created value'. This framework provides a much more appropriate set of questions and challenges than 'how are you doing against a measurement 'X' that is set centrally.

The other part of our role is making sure we've got the right HR talent to make HCM a reality. People who can step into the new game and will become leaders of the organization rather than service providers and change supporters. If we've got the right people in HR being led in the right way and dealing with human capital issues in an effective way then we're got a basis for building the capability of the organization. That's why developing the capability of individuals in HR, particularly those individuals who are leaders in HR, does have a lot of leverage on an organization's delivery.

And then we're looking at things like knowledge sharing – being a nodal point for the transfer of learning around these subjects. So that's the type of thing we're doing in the centre to help HCM. Making sure that HR functions have a degree of support to get there, making sure they've got the right people in place, but challenging them as well. That all sounds pretty simple but it's not that simple to make happen. But we're making some progress.'

Author: 'So if all the measures are contextual, are you able to do any benchmarking across departments?'

Watts: 'If you consider operational effectiveness is a precursor to HCM then we do have some common measures. You're very unlikely to be doing a good job at HCM if you're not delivering high quality basic services which are adding value and supporting change in a particular way. So it may make sense to compare things like time to recruit somebody across like-to-like departments, but these aren't really what I call HCM measures.

The Cabinet Office coordinated a process in which more than 20 departments went through a benchmarking review using Saratoga. The data was not assuredly refined but it helped give departments an indication of how they were performing. The purpose was really about galvanizing people to realize that there were such large discrepancies that there was something worth investigating. It meant also that we were able to provide statistics for Gershon's efficiency review.

But you need to be careful about what you measure and what you benchmark. Something like HR to employee headcount is too crude. If you're in the bottom quartile regularly then you need to ask yourself a question. But it might just be part of a deliberate strategy, that you're organizing yourself differently. A measure like this is an indicator of functional performance and it may play out in HCM but I wouldn't just take it on face value – there might be some very good, real reasons that you've decided this is the way it should be.

You also need to be careful comparing yourself to an average – you need to ask yourself: 'what is it about us that makes other organizations' data like ours, what do these

335

organizations look like?' Take absence management again. Just because the national average is 'X', it's suggested that your figure should be 'Y'. But how can we use the same benchmarks for the Prison Service and the Treasury Solicitors? So rather than comparing departments to each other, we need to think about more appropriate comparisons. For example, we could compare the Department for Work and Pensions to a call centre service in a retail bank environment.

The way I try to help people is to say if it's a definite cost, then benchmarking between organizations is really quite important. But if you can separate from the cost the deliberate investment, because it's got a cause and effect correlation with capability in the organization, that's an investment not a cost and benchmarking's not appropriate. So trying to separate the two issues is quite important.'

Author: 'And in terms of creating value/the building capability category of your maturity matrix, what HR programmes in central government are there in this category?'

Watts: 'Like a lot of organizations, we've got lots of really good and intuitively correct initiatives. But are they combining to make sure the organization is ready for its agenda? At this moment in time I couldn't put my hand on my heart and say they are. They're not really that well coordinated and orchestrated yet but they will get better as we get better at HCM. It's almost like the chicken and egg. You can't do nothing until you've cracked HCM because to a degree if you've got nothing going on you can't perfect HCM anyway. So this is about departments improving their understanding of how everything fits together and what's really making things work around here. What do we really believe is going to make the difference going forward? Given that we've only got limited time and resource what are we really going to put all of our effort into?'

Author: 'So do you think that a programme management environment is part of HCM?'

Watts: 'Yes, in one sense it's got to be. The net result is that otherwise you have loads and loads of initiatives where there isn't a clear connection and you're not sure of which ones are working and which ones aren't. Or they might all be working but some of them may be pulling in opposite directions. But until you get into that and look at it as a system rather than a set of initiatives you're not going to understand that.

If you focus on a few good things that you really believe will make the difference you'll be more likely to succeed. So I think it's really important to get a priority list of initiatives. But this should always include skills and organizational initiatives as they are definitely precursors to improving an organization's capability for delivery.'

Learning from Corporate Responsibility Reporting

Although it is still early days for reporting on people management, existing experience in reporting on corporate responsibility may provide some learning that is relevant for HCM. Corporate responsibility has evolved from corporate social responsibility (CSR) which focused on philanthropic or risk-related issues that had little relevance to the management of the business (value for money). In contrast, corporate responsibility is an integral part of the way companies are managed (added or even created value). Similarly reporting on corporate responsibility has become more strategic, relying on conversations on qualitative issues rather than standards and surveys.

Corporate Responsibility Reporting at National Grid

I talked to Ian Gearing, Corporate Responsibility Manager for National Grid, one of the world's largest utilities which currently operates in the UK and USA.

Author: 'Can you describe what you are doing in Corporate Responsibility?'

Gearing: 'We talk about being a responsible business or operating responsibly. We try not to use the term corporate

337

social responsibility. Going back in history, CSR was associated with philanthropic, community investment activities. Some organizations saw it as part of their business but for many it was a bolt-on, something they needed to do as well. Corporate responsibility for us is about everything we do, it's about how we earn our revenue, not just how we distribute some of our profits.

We don't see any contradiction between what we do for our shareholders and our other stakeholders. For example, there is a clear business case for safety. If we break the law we get fined and even more importantly sustain reputational damage. If our employees are injured, they take time off work which means poor productivity and we appear a less attractive employer. There are so many business cases. What's good for our people is good for our investors too.

As another example, some years ago we couldn't recruit enough fork-lift truck drivers so we looked at a pool of labour that was basically untapped. We started a scheme working with Reading Young Offenders Institute, providing offenders with training and a guaranteed job which they start in before leaving the establishment. Plus they have prospects to move forward. There are 11 000 under 21-year-olds in prison and it costs £36 000 each to keep them there. On their release, over 70 per cent of offenders who aren't on the programme reoffend within the next seven days. On our scheme, only 7 per cent reoffend. The programme has now spread to other types of job, for example gas technicians, fitters and engineers; to 14 other young offender establishments and 50 other companies which are using the same approach to meet their own recruitment needs. Including these other companies, over 1500 offenders will have been through the programme by the end of 2006. It's met a clear business need and produced substantial broader benefits to society as well.'

Author: 'And what about reporting in Corporate Responsibility – how do you get this value you are creating across to investors and other stakeholders?'

Gearing: 'We try to have periodic meetings with the investors and analysts from the SRI funds. This works much better than the questionnaire approach they used earlier on. I think they realized they weren't getting very good information from it. I think the recent debate about the OFR regulations is a bit of a red herring as well. We have always tried to comply with the voluntary OFR guidance. Our approach would not have changed substantially if it had been made mandatory. We would still have put fundamentally the same information in the OFR within our annual report.

We've linked our reporting to the GRI standards as well. But the most important thing has been to identify what metrics we need to report on for our business. Investors want to know what are the risks, what are we doing about them and how are we doing in this – not about how we're doing against a set of generic standards. GRI's still important, as we appreciate that some institutional investors find it useful to help compare organizations. But this came last. Only once we'd identified our key performance metrics did we look at how they mapped against GRI's requirements. GRI includes some things we hadn't thought of and we've used them to close the gap down. But there are other things in GRI we don't consider relevant for our business and we haven't put in a process to collect data just to conform to GRI.

We are trying to include more forward-looking information, looking ahead up to five to ten years time. Investors are becoming more interested in what we're going to be doing. You can't report quantitatively on this as such, but you can set targets, and describe qualitatively what you're going to be doing. One thing we find is that institutional as well as retail investors want to know about our people. The feedback we always get is that investors want stories about our people and how they're affected by what we're doing.

A good example is in inclusion and diversity. Something like 20 per cent of our employees are female. And because we're generally in a contracting industry and we don't have huge turnover in employees, these numbers move very slowly.

339

Instead of the numbers we can talk about what we're doing to bring about long-term change. We are starting up women's networks as well as ethnic minority and disabled people's networks so people from across the entire group can talk about the issues and they have started to put actions in place too. We can talk about these actions and provide some case studies about individuals because what we're doing isn't demonstrated immediately by the numbers.

We also plan to produce a separate Employee report this year. Every employee will get a personal copy. It's generally the same information that we send to investors but we'll use a different tone of voice. You can't always celebrate success so easily when you're sharing the same information externally.'

Summary

Reader: 'It's just occurred to me, now that we've reviewed all of these HCM processes – strategy development, measurement, benchmarking, implementation and now, reporting – that these are actually exactly the same management processes as those used within HRM and Personnel, but they're performed in a very different way. Is that right?'

Author: 'Yes, I do think that's right. I think HCM and HRM at least use the same set of management processes, and the same set of 'operational' processes too. What I mean by that is that HCM, just like HRM, uses recruitment, performance management, development and so on. But again, like the management processes, they're delivered differently in HCM. We saw what these differences look like for talent management in Chapter 5. There may also be a different emphasis on these processes in HCM. I think there's probably more focus on things that aren't always seen as part of HR's portfolio. For example, organization design, engagement, risk management, Board development, corporate governance, corporate responsibility, risk management, visioning, organizational values, the work environment and so on.

Another difference between HRM and HCM is that the focus of HCM needs to encompass more people than just those who are an organization's employees. HCM is about attracting the maximum amount of human capital for use by the organization so it needs to extend to the management of contractors, consultants, suppliers, outsourcing providers and other parties and individuals to provide the best possible mix of human capital.'

References

Davenport, T.O. (1999). *Human Capital – What It Is and Why People Invest It*. Jossey-Bass Publishers.

Ernst & Young Centre for Business Innovation. (1997). *Measures that Matter*. Ernst & Young.

Finn, R. and Ingham, J. (2004). *Taking Measures: Harnessing People Measures to Drive Business Performance*. Penna Board Partnership.

Grossman, R.J. (2005). 'Blind Investment', *HR Magazine*, January.

Hayashi, A.M. (2003). 'HR Information disclosure', *MIT Sloan Management Review*, **44**(3), 12.

IRS (2003). 'Measure for measure', *IRS Employment Review*, **783**, 5 September, 18–20.

Johnson, G. and Scholes, K. (1984). *Exploring Corporate Strategy*. Prentice Hall.

Jopson, B. (2006). 'Directors need safe harbour on forward-looking statements', *Financial Times*, 7 February.

Kearns, P. (2004). *One-Stop Guide: Human Capital Management*. Personnel Today Management Resources.

Ulrich, D., Smallwood, N. and Creelman, D. (2006). *Reporting on Human Capital: what the Fortune 50 tells Wall Street about human-capital management*. The RBL Group.

12

HCM Roles and Technology

Introduction

Reader: *'So what roles need to change to support HCM?'*

Author: 'Firstly, there's a big change in the HR role. In some ways, there's nothing that new here. When I first started working on people strategy over ten years ago, I spent a lot of time with HR functions helping them develop their own capability to implement people strategy. But now the bar has been raised, standards have been increased, and there's a much greater imperative to change.

However, HCM is a complex challenge that touches every part of an organization. It cannot be delegated and confined to just one individual or department. So now we need to think about the capability of HR, other functions, line managers and senior leaders who all have an important role to play in an effective approach to HCM. This chapter looks at the how all these roles need to change across the organization in order to deliver HCM ...'

Roles in HCM

HR Roles

HR is going to have an absolutely key role in HCM, at least for those organizations in which the CEO goes around saying, 'our people are our most important asset'. If this is true, it has to have consequences. It means that human capital is not just the most scarce but is also the most important resource. It means that HCM is recognized as the best source of transformation within the organization and that performance management needs to be seen as a key, if not the key, business management process. And it means that HR has a new, strategically important role. This is not just about giving HR equal status to Finance; it potentially creates a role for HR that is second only to the CEO.

Reporting is a good example of life in this new sigmoid curve. An HRM mindset might mean the HR function influencing Finance and the Company Secretary to let HR get involved in people management reporting in the business review. An HCM mindset suggests that HR should play the lead role in non-financial reporting. The need is to focus on intangibles, non-financial measures and future performance. HR understands these issues whereas accountants are generally happier with financial rather than business reporting and are used to focusing on the past rather than the future. HR has a similar view to Finance that spans across the whole business and its additional understanding of people and performance puts it in a position to take prime responsibility for this.

Ed Lawler, founder of the Centre for Effective Organizations at the University of South Carolina, suggests that to take advantage of this opportunity, HR needs to develop into three separate roles (Lawler, 2005):

1. Basic Administration Services and Transactions involved with compensating, hiring, training and staffing. Emphasis on resource efficiency and service quality.
2. Business Partner Services involved with developing effective HR systems and helping implement business plans, talent management. Emphasis on knowing the business and exercising influence – solving problems, designing effective systems to ensure needed competencies.
3. Strategic Partner Role contributing to business strategy based on considerations of human capital, organizational capabilities, readiness, developing HR practices as strategic differentiators. Emphasis on deep and broad knowledge of HR and of the business, competition, market, and business strategies.

Comparing the business partner and strategic partner roles, Lawler (2005) explains that the strategic partner role is key to the development of an integrated people management strategy:

> Although they have some of the same deliverables, the strategic partner role does more. It provides strong input and direction to the formation of business strategy, something that does not happen with the business partner role.

Lawler (2005) also explains that to play this role, HR needs to be represented at executive level in the organization:

> The strategic partner product line is the one that is least well developed in most corporations and the newest. It is also the one that has the potential to add the most value. It is rapidly increasing in importance because of the growing importance of intangibles and human capital. Because business strategy is typically developed at the corporate level in most organizations and the strategy implementation process begins there, this product line needs to be delivered to the senior executives of the corporation.

This role has also been labelled as a business player, which Ulrich and Beatty (2001) distinguish from the role of a business partner, stating:

> To meet these increased expectations, HR professionals must be more than partners; they must be players. Players contribute. They are engaged. They add value. They are in the game, not at the game. They deliver results. They do things that make a difference.

Because the administration services, business partner services and strategic partner roles all involve different focus and activities, Lawler (2005) believes that three separate functional groups are required:

> Research on organization design suggests that to deliver three related, but different, product lines, an organization needs to be structured differently than if it is delivering a single product line. Relatively independent units need to be established to deliver multiple product lines because the skills, competencies, capabilities and relationships that are required to deliver the product lines are different.

Lawler recommends that a new organizational effectiveness unit needs to be created to take responsibility for the strategic player role. This unit provides a multidisciplinary centre of excellence focused on HCM strategy. A similar role is identified by Kaplan and Norton (2004). They believe that the success of strategy maps and balanced scorecards depends on the development of a strategy-focused organization and that this depends on the development of strategic management capability. This is largely about making strategy everyone's responsibility, which I would translate as making sure that everyone is participating effectively in conversations about the future. But the strategy-focused organization can also be supported by a new support function, the Office of Strategic Management. Kaplan and Norton (2004) explain that the functions of this office should include:

- strategy formulation and strategic planning;
- alignment;
- strategic communication;
- balanced scorecard coordination;
- initiative management;
- governance coordination;
- performance review administration;
- change management.

I think that Lawler's organizational effectiveness unit forms a part of Kaplan and Norton's office of strategic management. In fact, as the focus of strategy moves from competitive strategy to resource-based strategy to HCM, and from strategic positioning to internal resources to human capital, these two functions start to look like the same thing, a strategically focused People Management Department. Lawler thinks it is likely that the business partners and administrative services would also report into this department in the way that accounting reports into finance and sales into marketing.

The People Management Director who heads up this department, is part of the business team that shares overall responsibility for people management strategy. The People Management Director will still have a particular role within the top team based upon his or her deep understanding of people's capability and ability to influence people's engagement.

This is the opportunity for the HR function. However, the risk is that HR remains focused on its administrative and operational roles and that another function takes responsibility for HCM. The question for HR professionals and their boardroom colleagues is whether HR can rise to the challenge, or whether they will see HR roles marginalized and outsourced.

To reinforce the point I have already made several times, the key to this new role is not about using financial language and advanced analytics to copy other functions, but for HR to develop a people-centred role of its own. As Ulrich and Brockbank (2005) explain:

> HR professionals need a perspective that is compatible with and distinct from other business perspectives. That is, they must be able to understand and value the finance and sales perspectives, but they must also add their own point of view. Without such a unique and powerful perspective, they are redundant and fail in their aspirations as full business contributors.

This new role focuses on helping to meet the needs of customers and investors by matching these with the capability and potential capability of people in the organization. In this way, the role puts the soft and hard perspectives of HRM back together. HCM needs to be totally aligned with longer-term business needs but it also recognizes that these needs will only be met by creating a context for people to make their investment as effectively as possible, and for the organization to leverage this contribution. This should not be an either/or problem. Employee productivity and satisfaction are not opposites. Yes, sometimes delicate balancing is required, but mostly (with the main exception being ongoing increases in reward) what is good for employees is good for the business too. This means that Ulrich's employee champion or employee advocate role (Ulrich, 1997) is still an essential part of the HR's portfolio. As Ulrich and Brockbank (2005) explain:

> Some in the field argue that HR should move exclusively to business partnering, to help business leaders define and deliver financial and customer goals. We disagree. Employee relations are not just window dressing: employees really are the primary asset of any organization. The treatment employees receive shows in the treatment of customers and, ultimately, of investors. Indirectly, caring for employees builds shareholder value. HR professionals are the natural advocates for employees – and for the very real company interests they embody.

In fact, as Ed Lawler (2003) explains, HCM requires people to be 'cared for' much more proactively than before, to ensure that they are provided with greater return on their investment than that they could receive elsewhere:

> Like financial capital, people need to be treated with care, respect, and commitment if the organization expects them to stay invested. It must also

provide them with the returns they need. Just as in managing financial capital, organizations cannot afford to waste their human capital or risk it going to place where it can get a better return. Like financial capital, human capital needs to be carefully allocated, utilized and managed.

Other Roles

If it is going to avoid the fate of the corporate planning function, the People Management department is going to need to work in partnership with different functions, with each partner bringing different skills and insight. Obviously the most important relationship is with the CEO and the executive team, ensuring HCM is completely aligned with the bigger picture and that the executives understand the potential opportunities that people can provide.

I would suggest that the next most important relationship is with Marketing. Marketing has expertise in eliciting and consolidating insights from customers that can be used to help embed understanding of customers' and investors' needs. Marketing's experience in mass customization of products and services can be reapplied internally to shape attractive, mass personalized propositions for employees. Marketing is also a critical partner for HR in creating an employer brand and projecting this to the talent marketplace.

Another important relationship is with Corporate Communications, using their expertise to help capture the employee's voice and to communicate the objectives, implications and success of HCM programmes.

Another key relationship is with Finance to help monitor costs, build financial evaluation into HCM programmes, and participate in calculations and decisions about ROI where these are seen as relevant. Another key role is to ensure that corporate performance management and people performance management are fully aligned. Finance clearly wants to take on such a role. A survey of 180 senior financial executives by CFO Research Services (2003) found that:

> CFOs themselves tend to think that they should have a greater role in human capital decisions. Our survey found that while 62% of finance executives believe they should play an 'important' or a 'leadership' role in human capital, only 38% have such a role today. Our interviews confirmed that many in finance think they should be more involved.

An ongoing relationship with IT is required to provide a common platform to integrate people management systems and processes and to provide the other technology that supports HCM including intranets, knowledge-sharing solutions and business-to-employee applications.

I think that Facilities Management also has a role to play, in providing practical advice on how to affect the physical aspects of HCM, such as the reorganization of office space to facilitate new working practices.

However, the other key relationship I have not yet discussed is that with line managers. People managers are responsible for attracting, retaining and managing talent and are therefore immediately accountable for HCM. The role of the manager does not look significantly different in HCM but it's based on a different mindset and will feel very different to both the manager and the people they manage. Above all, it requires a personalized relationship based on an authentic desire to help both the individual and the business fulfil their potential.

HCM Technology

HR information systems (HRIS) also play an important role within HCM. Most use of IT in people management has concentrated on improving efficiency rather than effectiveness. For example, the CIPD's 2005 people management and technology survey found that:

> The five most popular reasons for introducing an HRIS are: improving the quality (91 per cent), speed (81 per cent) and flexibility (59 per cent) of information, reducing the administrative burden on the HR department (83 per cent) and improving service to employees (56 per cent).'

While these motives all relate to value for money improvements, they are also worthwhile aims. Whether or not an organization uses an HR module of an enterprise resource planning (ERP) system or another HRIS solution, there is a need to provide a base functionality and a common view of data as efficiently as possible. This is supported by findings from Hackett Group (2005) that world-class HR organizations are 87 per cent more likely than their peers to have deployed a common HR application. This enables these organizations to operate more efficiently, employing 35 per cent fewer HR staff and spending 27 per cent less per employee on HR than their peers.

Typically companies start with their own unique requirements and build, or purchase and then customize an application around their internal requirements. In contrast, Hackett's world-class companies find an application with the closest fit to their requirements and map their business processes to the selected application. The system is only customized if there is a solid business case for doing so. Stephen Joyce from Hackett explained to me:

> To make changes you have to know where you are going, where are the largest opportunities for improvement. World-class organizations never have enough money and resources; they need to make choices, to identify where to make their investment. They're good at standardizing things where they can be standardized.

However, 39 per cent of the CIPD's respondents reported improving productivity (added value) as one of their reasons for introducing an HRIS. The question was not asked but some of the respondents may also have introduced an HRIS to help extend their differentiation and competitive advantage (created value). Moving to these levels of value means going beyond base ERP systems to provide superior functionality in specific areas that support an organization's chosen competitive strategy, strategic intent or intangible capability. Although this need may be met by using modules of existing ERP solutions (and many organizations have bought value added functionality that they do not use), the best functionality is often provided by best of breed systems focused on particular areas of people management.

The opportunity within HCM is for an organization to use best of breed technology to provide best fit with its HCM strategy, and reinforce the intangible capability the organization is trying to create. So within a number of different organizations with the same ERP system, one might use a best-of-breed solution focusing on workforce planning and recruitment, another on performance management and e-learning and another on career development. The need to include flexibility within best fit is increasingly supported in these solutions through the use of software as a service (SaaS). So organizations can easily change their best-of-breed solutions as they create new ways to fit with their environment.

A data warehouse can be used to ensure a single and correct source of data is provided from across the ERP and best-of-breed systems and, where appropriate, combined with data from other systems including finance, sales, marketing and customer service too. Business intelligence or workforce analytics systems can simplify access, monitoring, analysis and reporting on this data and can populate scorecard systems like the HCM value matrix, at least its bottom (value for money/data) row.

Technology can also help with presentation of the data through a portal-based user interface, providing relatively insightful information according to the role and preferences of the user. Information can also be shared through the use of RSS news feeds, wikis and blogs.

The HCM Toolkit at RBS

Supporting the use of RBS's HCM model described in Chapter 2, the Group's client-facing HR professionals have been provided with a comprehensive human capital toolkit that has been designed to help them survey, measure, research, benchmark and report on the management of people. This web-based resource (see Figure 12.1) includes a range of tools, for example on conducting in-house pulse surveys in between the group-wide annual survey. As well as supporting businesses, this has driven greater consistency in questions and saved considerably on costs.

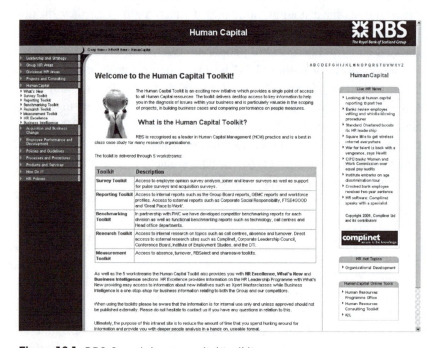

Figure 12.1 RBS Group's human capital toolkit

Greig Aitken, Head of HR Research and Measurement at RBS explained to me:

> We've created a single gateway for over a thousand of our HR staff. Our integrated, consistent human capital toolkit contains resources that allow people to make informed business decisions. It provides diagnostic tools that enable our HR teams to look at a whole range of measures and indicators without the need for complex application skills. So from their desktop they can access key HR data, research reports, project methodologies and diagnostic tools. They can commission research out of Washington, London and Paris to support key projects and two weeks later it arrives at their desk.

Although for the sake of confidentiality most of the toolkit is currently provided only to HR managers, the intention is that in time managers will also be given access to a more concise collection of data to support their direct role in managing people.

HCM Technology from InfoHRM

InfoHRM (previously a joint venture with the Corporate Leadership Council known as CLC Metrics) has combined the use of benchmark metrics with data warehousing and web-enabled reporting technology in order to provide line managers in client organizations with their own human capital dashboards. Managers can use these to track and take action over trends and exceptions in their people management activities.

InfoHRM arranges to extract data on the HR function and HR processes, workforce mobility, profile and productivity from their clients' HR, payroll and other systems, stores this in InfoHRM's own database in Australia and analyses and benchmarks this data. Benchmarking is built around a client's own transactional data (hire date, pay increase date, transfer date, etc.) which means that managers can drill down into the data from an aggregate to a more detailed and more useful level. It also means that benchmarking can be performed based upon a broad range of company characteristics, job characteristics and demographic variables.

The potential benefits of this approach are considerable but Peter Howes, CEO of InfoHRM, believes it is important to create demand for these tools rather than push them out to managers:

> We provide web-based reporting tools but these can be like the web itself. People have to navigate and sift through thousands and thousands of pages. It's a journey of discovery to find out if there are any insights

worth having. But most people don't go in and analyse the information. So it's often better to develop the capability of HR professionals to bring this stuff together and interpret it for managers.

It's a major professional challenge to build the interpretation skills so that someone is able to look at the data and identify what they need to do. People need to understand that if they're looking at labour turnover, they may want to combine this with a career path ratio looking at promotions against transfers. Or the average tenure in position, or the ratio of internal to external recruits by level – are they bringing in too many or too few people at different levels? Doing this will give them more insights about what's behind the turnover rates.

It can take two years to give people confidence in the system, to get it up, make it credible and ensure that people really believe in it. The really advanced stuff can take five years or more.

The HCM Strategy Role at Orange

Orange is a global mobile telecommunications business owned by France Telecom. It employs over 30 000 people and operates in 14 countries throughout Europe and the rest of the world.

I talked to Alison Speak, Head of HR Strategy, Planning and Reporting. Speak has been at Orange for over ten years, joining in the UK and moving through various roles and projects across the global business that have included setting up new businesses in Sweden and Thailand. In her current role, Alison reports to the Executive VP of People and Communications for the group. As well as leading on people strategy and reporting, Alison manages Orange's HR business partner team. She aligns her work to that of the VP for the business strategy area to ensure that HR is fully integrated into business decisions.

Author: 'Can you explain your planning and reporting role in more detail?'

Speak: 'We develop the HR strategy, the strategic themes, the KPIs and the measures against these KPIs that are used to inform the HR Business Partners, to help them work on talent management, on succession planning, alongside the line managers. The measures help ensure that they're going in the right direction. We're only scraping the surface of the real information that they need but at least the numbers are up to date.

Our reports include data aggregated for the group; results presented by group and then by country; an exec summary per area and a scorecard, with all the submitted data; and the results for the group and each of the countries are compared to an appropriate benchmark sample of European telecoms operators. The business-critical KPIs are reported at the monthly executive meeting. This has created a lot of demand – the CEO said, 'Yes, we want more – and make it available to the managers as well.' So we've got a big commitment from the executive team to take this forward.

We're looking at working with CLC Metrics to do this. We think their approach is very sophisticated. We're looking at using them to take, analyse and get our data online. They provide a tool that enables you to use the data you've got and make it available to managers. That's the thing about data – it's not only for us in HR – it's for the line managers to use. And if the data's static, no one will use it. If it's online and you can run reports off it, you as a manager will use it for decision-making, use it for reorganization, for managing your people better. You can cut the data by department, gender, length of tenure and so on. And if you're in Retail or Customer Services then you may want cuts of data that are different to the group – less is more here.'

Author: 'How have you selected the measures that you use?'

Speak: 'It's about picking measures that suit the business, that suit the business size and shape. What will be an indicator of success for one business will not necessarily be an indicator for another. Each business is different so it's not surprising that each business should choose different indicators.

You need to pick the metrics that will give you useful data, that measure the things that give you success. The starting point is our HR strategy. Loads of people miss this step. We've only scraped the surface so far but we've measured what we think are the indicators of success for our strategy. Working with the HRDs from the main countries, we took the HR strategy and the strategic themes and asked ourselves, 'What will success look like, what will indicate it, how can we measure it and what should be our KPIs?' Having all countries use these same measures means that countries can't try to cut the cake in different ways. There's no more scope for arguments about FTEs against permanent employees or numbers with and without contractors.

One of our themes is 'attracting and retaining key talent'. There's loads more competition in the mobile market than there ever was before. There's a lot of change and uncertainty. A lot of the best people are moving into the games industry. So the challenge for us is, how do we keep them? Our measures for this are things like termination rate and involuntary termination. Another theme is 'building leadership capability' and here we look at development training hours per FTE and something we call the executive stability ratio. This is a measure of senior management stability to turnover – calculated as the number of executives with more than three years' service as a proportion of the total number of executives.'

Author: 'And you also mentioned that you've benchmarked your measures against other telecom companies – can you tell me more about this?'

Speak: 'Once we had decided what to measure against the strategy we were able to go out into the market and talk to potential benchmarking providers. We selected to work with EP First [now Saratoga], part of PwC, who have an extensive database from which we were able to select Telco benchmark organizations. This was a useful discipline and we've modified the KPIs to some extent to fit the benchmarks. But there's a trade-off in what's possible if you want to benchmark against Virgin and T-Mobile etc. In the first draft of the KPIs we were quite creative but we realized we couldn't benchmark most of the indicators we'd developed.

We've had some real learning in benchmarking. When we started out on this journey everyone wanted to benchmark ourselves against our competitors to ensure we could have an external perspective as well. It's impressive when you can use external benchmarks to support your arguments in the business, or when making presentations to the Board. To be able to say that Vodafone gets this or that. But it's more important that we see for ourselves what makes a good indicator of success rather than worrying about what they do in BT or Vodafone.

Over a period of three years, what we've learnt is that you don't really need an external benchmark. We have to ask ourselves, do we know the inside of another organization's business well enough to know whether something would be worth benchmarking? Now, we're not so interested in our competitors. We want to use the KPIs that are right for us internally and benchmark within the company and across the group. We can benchmark across 13 or 14 companies within France Telecom, including those previously known as Equant and Wanadoo.

I think you need to be confident that what you're doing is good for your company and then benchmark on this internally, and not get fixated on comparing outside. But it took us two years to get to this point. Perhaps you have to get comfortable by using external benchmarks before you can let go of them and be able and confident to benchmark internally. It's been a key challenge we've made back to the benchmarking firms. The most fundamental thing for me is that I want to measure what my company needs to measure. I don't want to have a whole list of things benchmarked with other companies and which are meaningless to me.

We also do some deeper benchmarking where we select just a couple of organizations outside our sector who are doing something similar to us. And we'll set up a process, not just for HR but other parts of the business, for example Marketing and Customer Service, and we'll look in some detail at the other organizations we've chosen to study. Our UK Business has been especially good at doing this.'

Author: 'How do you use your measures to drive improvements in performance?'

Speak: 'We use the four or five strategic themes from the HR strategy to focus people. Our different country businesses will all have their own HR strategy but these need to be aligned to the Group strategic themes, and to support the direction of the parent company (France Telecom) as well.

We organized a one-day workshop when the benchmarking report came out. We talked about what countries were doing – if they were doing well in a certain KPI and maybe not so well in another. We arranged for the countries to do pair coaching – we'd link up a country that had scored well with one that had not done so well. The pairing worked really well – the HRDs all meet frequently but this got people at a more junior level working together and talking as well.

The weaker country's first reaction tends to be to blame legal constraints. Or they'll say that their culture and employee relations are different. But we can use the country external benchmarks too. If they can see that there is a gap between themselves and the norms in their own country, then we can begin the discussion about what can be done to change for the better.

In any case, when we all have a look at it together, people realize that there are plenty of creative ideas that can be transferred. There's always a way to do it. In a couple of countries we've got them to talk to other companies, in telecoms or general industry. The Corporate Leadership Council arranged some contacts in other organizations that we could go and talk to, which were seen as best practice in a particular area.

The measurement process has given us a vehicle for having these discussions, and for having a better understanding of how we're managing our business. This isn't about top-down control – things don't work that way around here. We encourage two-way, or multi-way, traffic and participative sharing of ideas between countries. We work hard to get buy-in and this takes time. But now when we meet to discuss our plans and measures, everyone's committed to it, and we can spend more of our time reviewing what we're doing.

We've used the process of planning, measurement and reporting through two full cycles now. At the end of the year, we use progress against the KPIs to inform the following year's strategy. The main drivers are still the business strategy of Orange and the parent company as well as external influences such as the labour markets and technology growth in all our countries. But we've used the process to revisit our strategic themes. We've had a better quality discussion, it's been much smoother and easier, and it's raised expectations for next year. So we're going to look to see whether we can do more, and do it more regularly – whether we can review and improve the KPIs more often, rather than just waiting for the annual group strategy once a year.

Also, although we've been able to monitor countries against their KPIs, we've not always had a full picture of all the HR initiatives across the countries. This year, we're asking each country to map their HR initiatives against the strategic themes. We want to see some kind of operational road map. We need to know what they're doing, whether they're moving in the right direction. Is their performance against the themes and measures increasing and creating more success?'

Author: 'And finally, what would you say has been the most important learning on the journey?'

Speak: 'We're not doing anything particularly sophisticated. We tend to beat ourselves up that we should be. We're not as good at it as we want to be. But we are doing a lot more than a lot of people. For example, we know our measures should be linked to our employee engagement measures. They should do but at the moment they don't. They're a bit separated and they need to link. We're a bit further ahead in the UK but not across the group.

And we need to stop saying we're not as good as we could be. We'll never be as good as we could be, we'll never finish the journey. We'll never get to '42' or whatever where everything is perfect. Business is too complicated. There are too many variables. The organization changes, the environment changes. All you can do is to keep on top of it and keep on plugging away. In five years' time it will all look very different to how it looks today. You can't leave it standing still; you need to keep on pushing. Getting people involved and helping them keep engaged.

It is frustrating when there's never an end point but bringing it to an early close by coming down to one ROI metric or rating isn't the right way forward. I can see the attraction of doing this – it talks the language of Finance, or at least the language of Finance people who tend to be those with most clout on the Board. And we do need these hard metrics, but perhaps we also need to educate Board members about the things they would call the soft stuff. We need to show them how we can measure things in different ways that are still valid and can still affect the success of where we're going as a business.

But I wouldn't want people to underestimate how long it takes – to get regular data, to ensure it's sound and validated. Doing all of this and getting it to a stage that we can now start looking at moving it online has taken years. The other thing is that the business is now a lot more stable and mature. We can put more focus on this now. Three years ago, the timing wouldn't have been right. We were going through enormous growth and so much change. It would have been foolish to do this then.

It is amazing how many people I meet at conferences that are also doing this. Their job titles may not make it clear all of the time but if you talk to them, they're doing this type of role. Of course, this is still something that's got to be owned by the HR director but they can't concentrate just on this. They need someone to steer it and dedicate their time to it – although the role may just be a transition one while they get everything set up.

My advice to other people coming into this sort of role would be to keep involving people and ensure that what you're doing is well linked to the business strategy. Previously, our planning group didn't have much dialogue with HR. Now they've become really involved in what we've been doing which helps ensure we're delivering what's needed and that we're aligned with where the business is going.'

Summary

Reader: *'So, we've got to the end. We seem to have come a long way since you covered Penna's Unleashing the Chain Reaction and the UK government's Accounting for People reports in the Preface and Chapter 1. But you still haven't given us a definition of HCM!'*

Author: 'No that's right, and its intentional I'm afraid. I didn't want to provide a definition that would just get shot down. I think Denise Kingsmill was right in her belief that Accounting for People would lead to further evolution in thinking about HCM. I think it has, and this book is evidence of that. I think thinking will continue, and perhaps one day a definition we can all agree with will emerge.

But I don't think that will be easy. Another reason I've not provided a definition is because HCM does look so different in each organization, strategy and context. It is about best fit after all. So I'd struggle to look through all of the case studies and conversations included in this book and say, 'here you are, here's the common thread, this is a definition of HCM'.

What I think I have done though, is illustrate what HCM can look like, and the value this can provide. I hope it's enough to help organizations think through how they can create value themselves; what HCM would look like for them. In addition, within each chapter, we've considered at least one major theme, all connected to other themes, but all slightly different as well. I think that these 12 themes point towards HCM. They don't provide a definition, but I think the more of these attributes that are included in an organization's strategy or programme, the more likely it is that they're doing HCM:

1. Focusing on knowledge and insight rather than metrics and standards.
2. Acknowledging complexity and not trying to understand everything through cause and effect.

3. Using best fit, not just basic or best practices.
4. Focusing on creating value through intangible capability.
5. Integrating people and business strategy, driving and accelerating the business plan.
6. Managing a large proportion of the people management agenda through strategic programmes.
7. Gaining energy from the outside in, matching potential capability with investors' and customers' needs.
8. Measuring strategic differentiators that indicate potential transformation.
9. Using internal, longitudinal and focused, strategic, external benchmarking.
10. Focusing on long-term stretch objectives, and learning from their outcomes.
11. Reporting to employees, managers and the Board.
12. HR acting as a strategic partner (the role that Chief Executives would love to have!).

Table 12.1 provides a more in-depth review of these twelve themes, using the three-level model developed from PwC's corporate transparency triangle that we looked at in Chapter 1, and again as the value triangle from Chapter 6 onwards.'

Reader: *'One final question. Are there any organizations that shouldn't do HCM?'*

Author: 'I don't think there are any particular types of organization that can't do HCM. The only real factor is level of organizational maturity. If an organization is struggling to get core operational and administrative services delivered well then these should probably be the focus rather than HCM. I think in general terms HCM works best where:

■ the organization is a people or people-oriented business;
■ the organization is relatively large;
■ the environment is not simple and stable;
■ the organization has investors or stakeholders who are interested in the medium to longer term (or the management is

Table 12.1: Review of themes within Personnel, HRM and HCM

	Personnel	Human Resource Management = Personnel plus	Human Capital Management = HRM plus
1 Information for reporting	Data, quantitative, objective, 'the number game', metrics and standards, comparability and reliability, basis for analysis	Information, quantitative with narrative, graphs and tables, often industry focused	Knowledge, insight, narrative, qualitative, subjective, stories, fuzzy data, organization specific, validity, basis for synthesis, understanding and judgement
2 Assumptions about business environment, organizations and people management (mental models)	Cause and effect, simple and stable, strategic fit, long-term competitive positioning, people seen as a cost/an expense, behavioural psychology, management by objectives, financial reward	Dynamic systems, negative and positive feedback, circular causality, resource-based strategy and core competencies, long-term strategic intent, people seen as assets/resources, hard and soft HRM, cognitive and humanistic psychology, learning organizations and systems thinking, psychological contract, employment value proposition	Complex processes, 'edge of chaos', emergent strategy, short-term, strategic capability, people seen as investors, social constructionism, participation in conversations, search for meaning

(Continued)

Table 12.1: Review of themes within Personnel, HRM and HCM—cont'd

	Personnel	Human Resource Management = Personnel plus	Human Capital Management = HRM plus
3 Practices (Activity step in HCM value chain)	Basic practice	Best practice, bundling	Best fit, contingent, configurational, agile
4 Intangible value provided by practices (Output step in HCM value chain)	Value for money, tangible outputs, efficiency, compliance with legislation and basic standards, incremental improvements in effectiveness, direct but minor financial impact	Added value, tangible and intangible resources that support the achievement of business objectives, effectiveness, acts in combination with other intangibles and tangible resources, indirect impact on financials (through systems of cause and effect relationships)	Created value, intangible capability, potential for transformation, acts on whole organization, major but unclear financial impact
5 People management strategy development	Separate process, people management largely irrelevant, no connection to business plan, focus on activities, administering	Aligned process, people management has transactional focus, HRM information informs the business plan,	Integrated process, people management has transformational focus, HCM drives and accelerates the business plan, focus on

	HR operations, upholding employment regulations, ensuring efficiency, everyone is talent, people management responsibility of Personnel function	focus on the business plan, and activities and outputs to deliver business plan, creating capability to perform now, focus on talent pools, ensuring effectiveness and alignment, people management a joint responsibility of line managers and HR function	creating capability for the future, focus on core talent, producing truly wonderful solutions, taking advantage of exceptional opportunities, HCM everyone's responsibility
6 People management activities	Focused on service delivery not project management	Numerous, small and tactical projects, projects often annual events within service delivery	Strategic programmes, mission critical, audacious
7 Source of energy	Inside out, improvements to processes, reactive	Business-in, meeting business needs by developing capability and implementing people management activities, annual people management plan, current state looking forward	Outside-in, delighting customers and investors, creating the future and looking backwards, creativity based, people-based strategy
8 Measurement	Efficiency of HR activities, compliance	Effectiveness of HR outputs against business plan	Strategic differentiators, organizational capability, potential for transformation

(Continued)

Table 12.1: Review of themes within Personnel, HRM and HCM—cont'd

	Personnel	Human Resource Management = Personnel plus	Human Capital Management = HRM plus
9 Benchmarking	External surveys, large datasets, little meaning	Best practices standards of performance, facilitated reviews	Internal and longitudinal, focused, external, deep meaning
10 Managing implementation	Current state, standards, controlling behaviour (doing)	Short-term, SMART objectives, managing change, changing attitudes (thinking and feeling)	Long-term, dynamic, stretch, directional, sensory goals, creating change, learning, changing mindsets
11 Reporting	Regulators	Investors and stakeholders	Board, managers and employees
12 'HR' Role	Administrative services, transactional, operational, implementing policies and procedures, service centres, outsourced and offshored	Business partner services, process owner, adviser, change agent, supporting business strategy, developed by senior management, clear differentiation of staff and line functions, HR staff responsive and supportive, line managers responsible for decisions and outcomes	Strategic partner/business player, consultant, project leader, on the Board, leading design and implementation of HCM strategy and programmes, HCM embraces all people-related services, seen as integral to success, line managers assuming HR roles

resilient enough to withstand pressure to sacrifice long-term growth for short-term needs);
- the organization is focused on growth through differentiation rather than cost leadership;
- the organization is managed strategically, with a clear, high-level business strategy, ideally through use of a strategy map and business scorecard, and effective leadership;
- planning is bottom-up as well as top-down;
- the organization acknowledges complexity and is based on networks and relationships rather than structures and hierarchies;
- the personnel and HR levels of the HCM value triangle are working effectively;
- managers take responsibility for people management;
- the culture is relatively sophisticated;
- the organization uses technology effectively.

All apart from the first four of these points are in the organization's control and also within the power of HR to influence. So if the time is not yet right for HCM, these levers can be used to make things more conducive.'

So even if an organization is still currently focusing on value for money, it can still start to influence these factors, to make it easier to move towards HCM later on. And there's no better time to begin than now.

References

CIPD (2005). *People Management and Technology: Progress and Potential*. Chartered Institute of People and Development.

CFO Research Services (2003). *Human Capital Management: The CFO's Perspective*. CFO Publishing Corp. in collaboration with Mercer Human Resource Consulting.

Hackett Group (2005). *Optimizing a Return on Business Complexity: Performance Metrics and Practices of World-Class Companies*. The Hackett Group.

Kaplan, R.S. and Norton, D.P. (2004). 'Strategic management: An emerging profession', *Balanced Scorecard Report*, May–June.

Lawler, E.E. III (2003). *Treat People Right!* John Wiley & Sons, 144–152.

Lawler, E.E. III, (2005). 'From Human Resources Management to Organizational Effectiveness'. In *The Future of Human Resource Management: 64 Thought Leaders explore the critical HR issues of Today and Tomorrow* (Losey, M., Meisinger, S. and Ulrich, D., eds). Wiley.

Ulrich, D. and Beatty, D. (2001). 'From partners to players: Extending the HR playing field', *Human Resource Management.* **40**(4), 293–307.

Ulrich, D. and Brockbank, W. (2005). *The HR Value Proposition.* Harvard Business School Publishing.

Index